Conservation of Archaeological Ships and Boats

– personal experiences

Conservation of Archaeological Ships and Boats

– personal experiences

Per Hoffmann

with contributions by
Inger Bojesen-Koefoed, David Gregory,
Poul Jensen, James A. Spriggs,
Kristiane Strætkvern and Markus Wittköpper

In association with

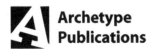

First published in 2013 by Archetype Publications in association with Deutsches
Schiffahrtsmuseum, Bremerhaven

Archetype Publications Ltd
c/o International Academic Projects
One Birdcage Walk
London SW1 H 9JJ
www.archetype.co.uk

ISBN 978-1-904982-82-1

British Library Cataloguing in Publication Data
A catalogue record for this book is available from the British Library.

Cover: Fine cleaning the *Bremen Cog* to remove residual polyethylene glycol (PEG) after
conservation.
Photograph: Per Hoffmann

Typeset by Newgen Knowledge Works Pvt Ltd

Printed and bound by Lightning Source Inc.

Table of contents

Foreword

Few can resist news about the discovery of an ancient shipwreck, conjuring up in the mind's eye the Jacques Cousteau-like exploration in the depths of the ocean, the horrors of the ship's final moments, and split hulls spilling forth their cargoes. Most of these wrecks have to remain where they are safest – on the sea-bed – normally protected by law and unavailable for public enjoyment. But there are a few surviving historic vessels that one can actually visit and go on board, an experience which further reinforces the sensation of voyaging to exotic lands, reminding one of hardships born by sailors or even evoking the stench of battle. Better still if you can combine the thrill of discovery of a new wreck site with the challenge of recovery and conservation, and finally present a spectacular and inspiring display in a well-designed museum on dry land. This fascination with maritime history is nothing new. In 1982 an estimated 60 million people watched the raising of the wreck of the famous warship *Mary Rose* on television. This single event made broadcasting history and the twists and turns of the project to conserve, research and display the ship and accompanying finds have made essential TV viewing ever since.

The *Mary Rose* is just one of a number of major ship-finds made in the latter half of the 20th century which led to major conservation projects, as several northern European nations sought to preserve something of their maritime past for public education and enjoyment. In 1961 the Swedish royal warship *Vasa* was raised virtually intact from the mud at the bottom of Stockholm harbour and finally, after many years of painstaking conservation, displayed in all her glory in a specially-built ship hall. Just a year later the recovery of five *Viking ships from Skuldelev* in Roskilde Fjord, Denmark, led eventually to their display in a beautiful specially-built museum overlooking the water at Roskilde. Germany has also been at the forefront of this effort with the recovery of the almost intact *Bremen Cog* trading ship, again in 1962, which was conserved by Per Hoffmann over a period of many years whilst on continuous public display in the Schiffahrtsmuseum in Bremerhaven. One should also mention the superb collection of Roman ships found in 1982, conserved and displayed in Mainz, which also feature in this book. Most recently Pisa in Italy, and Istanbul, Turkey, have acquired their own spectacular multiple ship finds deemed to be of international importance. Almost every other country in Europe will have celebrated their nautical history by facing up to the challenges that maritime archaeology and preservation present.

Behind each of these shipwreck recoveries lie teams of highly skilled specialists, often combining professionals with amateurs. Divers, archaeologists, engineers, scientists, conservators, curators, historians, designers and interpreters all contribute to the final success of the project, facing up to each new challenge with inventiveness and determination. Every boat find presents a unique combination of problems to be overcome, be they logistical, technical, financial, legal or political. Historically, the most challenging aspect of all these projects has been the conservation of the degraded wood, iron and other materials that make up a ship's hull and its contents. The materials and techniques used in this branch of conservation now are very different from those known about and used in the early 1960s when, it is probably fair to say, a truly scientific approach to conservation had yet to appear. However, coinciding with these discoveries a spirit of international collaboration sprang up, with conservation centres and laboratories around the world sharing their experiences and publishing the results of their research. Much of this collaboration was under the umbrella of the ICOM-CC specialist working group for Wet Organic Archaeological Materials (WOAM), led over the years by senior practitioners based in conservation research centres in Canada, USA, Western Australia, UK, France, Germany, Sweden and Denmark, but with major contributions from specialists in many other countries. This collaboration produced a continuous flow of new ideas and the technology of waterlogged wood preservation has advanced enormously over the past five decades. New chemical polymers have become available, plus the methodology to deploy them effectively: freeze-drying in huge vacuum chambers is now the preferred quick and safe way to remove excess water, and much more is now known about wood degradation processes on the sea-bed, and how to stop wood deteriorating further once on display. Whilst shipwreck conservation is still not an exact science, we are getting there.

Through his lifetime's experience working directly on ship and boat conservation projects, and advising on many more, Per Hoffmann is uniquely qualified to write this book. He has invited colleagues eminent in specific fields to provide chapters on areas of wood conservation which he feels (with characteristic modesty) they are better equipped to write about. The result is, I think, an excellent 'state of the art' exposition and essential reading for any archaeologist, conservator or museum curator tempted to take on the responsibility of preserving marine material. Waterlogged wood conservation, let alone the preservation of a whole boat or ship, is not work for the faint-hearted but the results are both rewarding and spectacular. So let Per Hoffmann, through the pages of this book, lead you through the intricacies and complexities of archaeological boat conservation!

James A. Spriggs

Acknowledgements

Most of my work with waterlogged wood, ships and boats described in this book could only be performed with the dedicated assistance of my colleagues, Silvia Weidner in the laboratory and Ulrich Finke as a versatile technician and conservator. Jörg Geier and his technical staff at the Deutsches Schiffahrtsmuseum provided support of all kinds. They moved ships and built tanks, scaffolding and installations.

Special thanks go to Egbert Laska for the processing of images for this book, and to Reinhold Breden for patiently producing the line drawings.

The suggestion that I compile my experiences with archaeological ships in a book came from Gabriele Hoffmann, journalist, author and editor. She followed my work with great interest and I thank her for much good advice. My thanks go to my co-authors, colleagues and friends of many years for agreeing to contribute to this book with their specialised knowledge: Poul Jensen, Kristiane Straetkvern, Inger Bojesen-Koefoed and David Gregory on freeze-drying, and Markus Wittköpper on the advanced use of Kauramin resin. Many colleagues and institutions have generously allowed me to reproduce illustrations, photographs and electron microscope images. Often these have resulted from joint investigation projects, and here is the place to thank my colleagues from outside the museum for sharing with me their interest in aspects of waterlogged wood. Their names can be found with the respective illustrations.

My old friend Oskar Faix, professor emeritus in wood chemistry, has checked the wood part of the manuscript for flaws, and Jim Spriggs, friend and experienced conservator of waterlogged wood himself, has – apart from writing a kind foreword and a welcome chapter on long-term care plans – undertaken to check for flaws in the conservation parts, and to weed out the most conspicuous linguistic faults. With essential suggestions they have both greatly helped to improve the clarity of the text, and I want to thank them both most cordially.

This book could not have been produced without substantial financial support or image processing by the Deutsches Schiffartsmuseum. I express my sincere thanks for their engagement.

Per Hoffmann, February 2013

List of authors

Inger Bojesen-Koefoed, Bachelor in Conservation has carried out conservation of several complex and very delicate waterlogged archaeological degraded structures such as fish traps, ropes and wickerwork. Working for more than 25 years at the National Museum of Denmark in the Conservation Department, she is experienced in the conservation of textiles and archaeological waterlogged organic materials. She has been author and co-author of several articles on conservation history, field conservation and conservation case studies.
E-mail: inger.bojesen-koefoed@natmus.dk

David Gregory, PhD., MPhil., BSc. Hons has worked on numerous maritime archaeological projects as a diver both in archaeological and conservation capacities. Currently a senior scientist at the Conservation Department of the National Museum of Denmark, he is investigating the deterioration of waterlogged archaeological wood, and methods of in situ preservation of archaeological materials in underwater environments. He is author and co-author of over 50 scientific articles and book chapters on this research.
E-mail: david.john.gregory@natmus.dk

Per Hoffmann, Dr.rer.nat., Dipl.-Holzwirt was the founding head of the Department and Research Laboratory for Wet Archaeological Wood Conservation at the Deutsches Schiffahrtsmuseum in Bremerhaven. Being responsible for the conservation of a dozen ships and boats, he developed treatment schemes for several more ship finds. Before retiring, he was a consultant for wet wood conservation projects in Germany and abroad, and a lecturer on properties of wood and the analysis and conservation of wet archaeological wood at universities in several countries. He has published more than 120 papers and book chapters on wood analysis, archaeological wood, and conservation science. Having been coordinator of the International Council of Museums (ICOM) group on Wet Organic Archaeological Materials (WOAM) for 17 years, and a member of the directory board of the ICOM Committee for Conservation (ICOM-CC) for 12 years, he is at present a member of advisory boards for the *Vasa*, the Mary Rose Trust, and the Newport Medieval Ship.
E-mail: per.hoffmann.bremen@gmx.de

Poul Jensen, Senior Researcher, PhD, MAgrSci was head of Conservation of Waterlogged Materials at the National Museum of Denmark and is now working at the museum as a senior researcher. He is experienced in the conservation and assessment of waterlogged organic archaeological materials with special emphasis on impregnation, freeze-drying and long term stability of wood. He has been a supervisor to PhD and Master's students, and is author and co-author of numerous scientific articles and book chapters on the assessment and conservation of waterlogged archaeological wood.
E-mail: poul.jensen@natmus.dk

James A. Spriggs Dip Cons, ACR, FIIC, MIFA, FSA is an archaeological conservation consultant specialising in waterlogged organic materials. He was for many years Head of Conservation at the York Archaeological Trust, UK, where he set up the York Archaeological Wood Centre which continues to be one of the foremost facilities for the conservation of waterlogged wood, from both marine and land sites, in the UK. He has been involved in many boat and shipwreck conservation projects in the UK and overseas, and was responsible for conserving the timbers from Viking-period houses and workshops, displayed at the Jorvik Viking Centre, York. He has published numerous articles and book chapters on many aspects of artefact conservation.
E-mail: spriggs.conserve@hotmail.co.uk

Kristiane Strætkvern, Cand. Scient. Cons. is coordinator (head) of Conservation of Waterlogged Materials at the National Museum of Denmark. She has been involved in the conservation of several boats and ships, and her special interest is freeze-drying of large objects. From 2004 to 2011 she was coordinator of the ICOM-CC working group on Wet Organic Archaeological Materials. She has been author and co-author of several articles on field conservation and archaeological wood conservation case studies, and of scientific articles in waterlogged wood conservation.
E-mail: kristiane.straetkvern@natmus.dk

Markus Wittköpper has been head of Conservation of Waterlogged Wood at the Museum für Antike Schifffahrt at the Römisch-Germanisches Zentralmuseum (RGZM) in Mainz since 1991. Originally a stonemason and sculptor in stone, he was educated as a conservator/restorer for archaeological materials at the RGZM. He has been in charge of conservation projects for several Roman ship finds, preferring to use the Kauramin method which he has developed to its present form.
E-mail: wittkoepper@rgzm.de

List of boxes

List of acronyms

ATR-FTIR	attenuated total reflectance Fourier transform infrared
DSM	Deutsches Schiffahrtsmuseum
DTPA	diethylene triamine pentaacetic acid
EDDHMA	ethylenediamine (O-hydroxy-P-methylphenylacetic) acid
FSP	fibre saturation point
HPLC	high-performance liquid chromatography
ICOM	International Council of Museums
ICOM-CC	International Council of Museums committee for conservation
LM	light microscope
MALDI-TOF	matrix assisted laser desorption/ionisation time of flight
NMR	nuclear magnetic resonance
PEG	polyethylene glycol
RGZM	Roman Germanic Central Museum
RH	relative humidity
SEM	scanning electron microscope
TEM	transmission electron microscope
TLC	thin-layer chromatography
WOAM	Waterlogged Organic Archaeological Materials
	Wet Organic Archaeological Materials

Display locations of the archaeological ships and boats

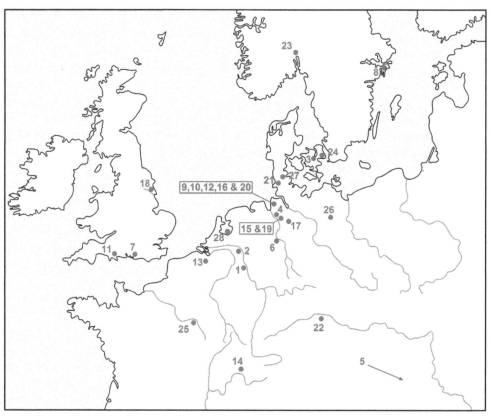

Copyright: D. Saunders

1 *Barge from Niedermörmter* – Rheinisches Landesmuseum, Bonn, Germany
2 *Roman barge from Xanten Wardt* – Römer Museum, Xanten, Germany
3 *Skuldelev Viking ships* – Vikingeskibshallen, Roskilde, Denmark
4 *Ship from the Teufelsmoor* – Kreismuseum, Osterholz-Scharmbeck, Germany
5 *Kinneret boat* – Yigal Allon Museum on Lake Kinneret (the Sea of Galilee), Israel
6 *Barges from Rohrsen* – Weser Renaissance Museum, Lemgo, Germany
7 *Mary Rose* – Naval Docks, Portsmouth, UK
8 *Vasa* – Vasamuseet, Stockholm, Sweden

9 *Karl* – Deutsches Schiffahrtsmuseum, Bremerhaven, Germany

10 *Bremen Cog* – Deutsches Schiffahrtsmuseum, Bremerhaven, Germany

11 *Poole logboat* – Poole Museum, Poole, UK

12 *Logboat from the Leine* – Deutsches Schiffahrtsmuseum, Bremerhaven, Germany

13 *Boats from Pommeroeul* – Gallo-Roman Museum, Ath, Belgium

14 *Barge II from Yverdon-les-Bains* – Museé Cantonal d'Archaeologie et d'Histoire, Lausanne, Switzerland

15 A partial hull – from the *Teerhof* – 'Beluga' Office Building on the Teerhof, Bremen, Germany

16 *Oberländer* – Deutsches Schiffahrtsmuseum, Bremerhaven, Germany

17 *Helstorf logboat* – Heimatmuseum, Helstorf, Germany

18 *Hasholme logboat* – Hull Museum, Hull, UK

19 *Beck's ship* – Bremer Landesmuseum, Bremen, Germany

20 *Schlachte ship* – Deutsches Schiffahrtsmuseum, Bremerhaven, Germany

21 *Ship from Friesland* – Schifffahrtsmuseum, Husum, Germany

22 *Roman ships from Oberstimm* – Kelten Römer Museum, Manching, Germany

23 *Bingen logboat* – Norsk Sjøfartsmuseum, Oslo, Norway

24 *Ejsbøl logboat* – Nationalmuseet, Copenhagen, Denmark

25 *Barge from Noyen-sur-Seine* – Musée de Préhistoire de l'Ile de France, Nemours, France

26 *Kaffenkahn* – Deutsches Technikmuseum, Berlin, Germany

27 *Nydam boat* – Archäologisches Landesmuseum Schloss Gottorf, Schleswig, Germany

28 *Boat from Meinerswijk* – Bataviawerf, Lelystad, Netherlands (still in conservation)

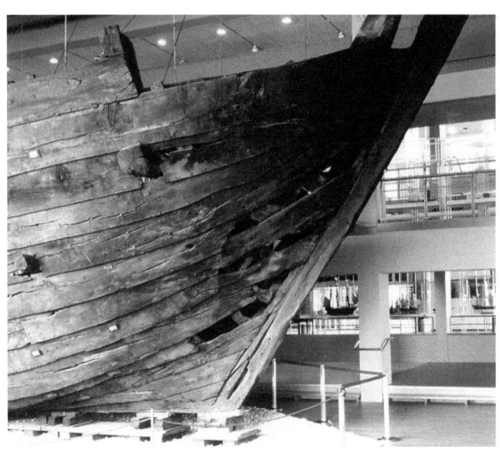

After conservation the *Bremen Cog* stands in the Deutsches Schiffahrtsmuseum in Bremerhaven. Photograph: Per Hoffmann

Introduction – A very special task

The task of the conservator confronted with an archaeological ship or boat of waterlogged wood is to transform the wet, delicate, and unstable object into a dry, robust, and stable object, without alteration or damage occurring during the process. This is not a simple task. What makes the conservation of a ship so special is both the strange material known as 'waterlogged wood', and the size of the ship or boat. Often the processes involved grow to a considerable scale and require great technical effort and financial expenditure far in excess of routine archaeological budgets. Because of this, the archaeologist in charge needs to have an overall view of the procedures, necessities, and implications of the conservation project, and of the scientific background and basis for such work. The archaeologist will in most cases represent the owner of the archaeological find, and be responsible for all major decisions including the raising of funds and for finding the means, and perhaps even the conservator, for the conservation project.

In writing this book I wanted to offer conservators, who normally work with many different materials, a chance to inform themselves about wood and waterlogged wood without having to study comprehensive textbooks and a vast literature.

Waterlogged wood is a complicated material with properties which can differ very much from those of fresh wood. Depending on its state of degradation, waterlogged wood can be more flexible than fresh wood, or it may be brittle and easily broken. Its surface is always soft and vulnerable. Waterlogged wood can be up to twice as heavy as air-dried wood. The most dangerous difference, however, is its reactions on drying: waterlogged wood shrinks enormously, warps, splits, and develops cracks and fissures across the grain. Such damage cannot be corrected. Drying threatens the integrity of a waterlogged wooden object. Waterlogged wood requires a lot of attention and forethought as it undergoes excavation, transportation and the conservation process.

A ship or boat can pose great difficulties during salvage and conservation. A ship, and even a boat or dug-out canoe, is large, much larger than most retrievable archaeological objects. It is not easy to handle, and can be moved only with great effort. The wet wood is heavy, and even larger timbers or a log boat cannot be lifted by hand. Cranes and heavy gear must be brought to the excavation site. At the same time the wood surfaces are soft and sensitive to impression, ropes and belts cut into them, corners and edges break off easily. With the heavy weight of the wood, the brittleness and low bending strength are a problem when handling. This problem is exaggerated by the proportions of ships timbers: they are long and slender and prone to breaking.

The idea of a ship is to enclose a large volume with as little material as possible. The result is a rather frail object, compared to its size. Before a ship find can be lifted, it often needs to be braced against the mechanical forces arising during lifting and transportation: compression, bending, and tensile forces, vibration and shock, all of which strain the timbers and joints. Originally, a ship was built to withstand the pressure from the surrounding water and waves, and to carry the weight of the cargo. In a ship on land the mechanical stresses are greatly inverted – more so if the ship is no longer in one piece, when additional precautions have to be taken to stabilise and secure the ship's remaining structure.

The size of a ship becomes very evident at the point where it needs to be transported. Very soon the loading platforms of normal trucks become too short and narrow, and the passage of such a large load through small towns and villages will require a fair amount of logistics.

The conservation process also has its own requirements with regard to organisation and finance. A large workshop, or even a warehouse is needed to house the ship and the conservation installations, and the space must be available for several years. Normally, an empty warehouse is not easy to find and hire. All conservation methods for ships rely on the impregnation of the wood with a stabilising agent dissolved in water which prevents the wood from shrinkage during the subsequent drying process. In most cases the impregnation has to take place in a tank; however, in some cases, depending on the state of the wood, a spray treatment can be used. The size of tank required for a ship will obviously vary according to the size of the ship. It will swallow a large amount of stabilising chemical at considerable cost. The *Friesland ship*, a small cargo sailing vessel of 12 m length, needed a tank with a volume of 100 m^3, and about 100,000 litres of impregnation solution. The tank itself can be a costly piece of equipment.

Several methods have been developed for the conservation of large waterlogged wooden objects. They differ in their technical and financial requirements, and in the demands of the qualified personnel performing them. They also differ in the quality of the possible stabilisation results, and in the probability of achieving the results. Good results cost money. However, is the best result always indispensible, or could a second class result be tolerated? In workshop scale conservation one would always opt for the best possible, but with the

effort, money and time involved, this question has to be discussed and decided before the conservation of a ship is planned. How can one find the appropriate method adequate for the ship? It has to be a method which can be handled and performed safely on a large scale, which is not dangerous nor involves toxic chemicals, using a process which is stable over a long time, and which will produce the expected result with appreciable probability.

The conservation of a ship or boat is an extensive and many-sided enterprise. It begins in the excavation pit and ends in the museum. It takes years and is expensive. Therefore the design of a coherent project is necessary and requires careful planning of the individual steps: salvage and transport; conservation; restoration and presentation. These steps need to be coordinated at an early stage of the project so that demands and processes of later work can be foreseen and taken into consideration while there is enough time to arrange for a smooth and efficient sequence of operations. The conservation of a ship calls for collaboration with specialists exhibiting staying power and tenacity in various fields. It is a rare and rewarding adventure.

When I was asked by the Deutsches Schiffahrtsmuseum thirty years ago to take over the conservation of the *Bremen Cog*, I read B. Brorson Christensen's book *The Conservation of Waterlogged Wood in the National Museum of Denmark*. He was a biologist and had to develop a conservation method for the *Skuldelev Viking ships* from Roskilde fjord, one of the first major ship conservation projects. His book is an account of his extensive laboratory experiments, and of his experiences made during the practical work, especially with the method finally adopted for the treatment of the *Viking ships*. I was a wood scientist from the University of Hamburg and had studied all sorts of aspects of wood, but had no idea what archaeological waterlogged wood was, and what one should and could do with it. Brorson Christensen told me. With the present book I want to pass on my experiences gained in conservation projects of about twenty ships and boats – in the Deutsches Schiffahrtsmuseum, and in joint projects with colleagues, archaeologists, engineers, and laymen – and in numerous discussions with colleagues about their ship projects.

There are no general recipes on how to conserve a ship. But after the evaluation of many projects I feel able to give at least some suggestions about how to approach and tackle the very special task.

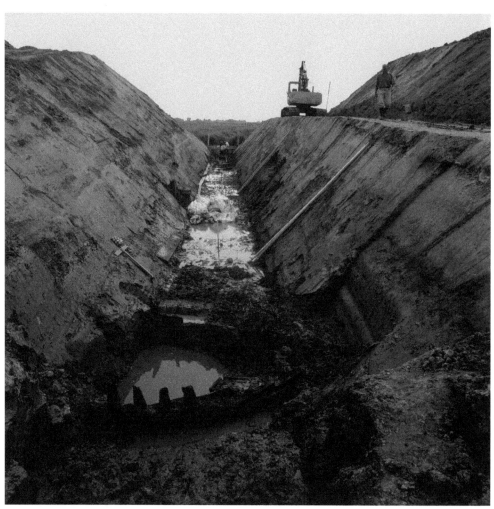

Ships are often found unexpectedly, and archaeologists and conservators must act quickly. In North Friesland, the work in the dyke had to be finished before the winter came and the dyke was closed. Photograph: Linda Hermannsen, Archäologisches Landesamt Schleswig-Holstein

1   From excavation to conservation

1.1   Where will the ship end up?

The first question when considering salvaging a ship find and embarking on a conservation project is the one about the end of the project: where will the ship end up? If this question is not answered in a satisfactory and definite way it is advisable not to start the project at all. If the end is not clear a lot of effort, money, time, and goodwill from many parts are at risk. The whole project may end in frustration and collapse. There are enough sad stories of this kind to learn from.

To know where the ship or boat will end up – in an existing museum, in a new museum, yet to be built specifically for this purpose, or just in storage – will influence many sorts of decisions right from the planning of the project and at each step along the way of its implementation. For example, should the ship be lifted from the excavation as a whole or in segments, or should it be dismantled and lifted timber by timber? How important is the integrity of the surface, or is it sufficient to rescue the structure? With the final destination in mind the location for the conservation treatment can be chosen so that the transport required and risks of damage are minimised. Perhaps the conservation can be organised at the place where it will be exhibited, and the conservation method may then be chosen according to the anticipated exhibition conditions of temperature, relative humidity, UV light, and expected fluctuations of these conditions. A formally agreed decision about the future of the ship, where it will

stay and how it will be accessible to the public sets the imagination of those involved in the project working, and their motivation will grow. As the project is going to cost more than the ordinary budgets of archaeologists and museums can provide for, it will be necessary to acquire help from many sides, in money and in kind. Only with a realistic plan and a vision will it be possible to convince sponsors to join the project.

Most important, however, is to find out right from the beginning of the project, who has an interest in it – and to put this down on paper. Who wants the archaeological find to be salvaged and transformed into a permanent exhibit, who is responsible for the project, for its financing and its continuity? Who is the one to make and answer for the vital decisions? As tempting as it may seem, this person cannot be the conservator. The conservator is not the owner of the ship, he or she only offers a service. He will not have the right to freely dispose of the ship and take responsibility for action on his own. The archaeological find will legally belong to someone, and it can only be this person or organisation, or a representative thereof – the archaeologist perhaps – who can take the final responsibility for any decisions concerning the archaeological object. Without clarity in this respect the initial enthusiasm and high motivation of those engaged in action will soon fade, and the project might slowly die as soon as obstacles turn up. Without motivation the work team will find it increasingly difficult to muster the necessary perseverance. A formal

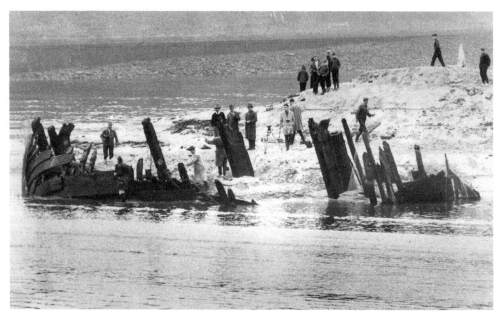

A strange wreck emerged in the river Weser. At rising tide it disappeared again. Photograph: Deutsches Schiffahrtsmuseum (DSM)

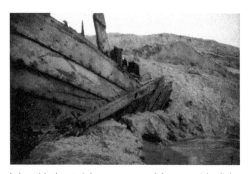

At low tide the straight stempost and the very wide clinker planks indicated that this was a medieval cog. The historian in charge decided to salvage the ship, not knowing where it would end up. Photograph: DSM

agreement about who wants the project done and who is taking the responsibility for it, and a clear definition of what the project is aiming at, is absolutely necessary. Otherwise the conservator should not get involved.

Once I was urged to take over a waterlogged forest – stumps, roots, logs, branches with leaves. 10,000 years ago the whole forest had been covered with 10 m of volcanic ash. The pumice – the former ashes – had been completely exploited as a valuable mineral,

the forest had reappeared. The historian in charge had no intention to do anything with it, but felt it a pity to let go of this perfect ice-age forest ensemble. 'Perhaps you could...?' I could not. It would have been the archaeologist's responsibility to find a place to finally put the objects, and to find the means and funds to get them there – if he had really wanted to.

Once a project has been formally set up, it is nevertheless highly advisable that the conservator makes notes of oral agreements, disagreements, and decisions made with the archaeologist in charge. Over the years words are forgotten, personnel retire or move to other jobs, and when things do not run smoothly the apportioning of blame can too easily poison the atmosphere.

When looking for a suitable room or building to finally house the conserved ship there is a tendency to be content with a space that will just accommodate the ship, perhaps restored to its original size. This is a mistake. It is true, the object might be rather large, and it is tempting to argue that you only need space for the ship and for visitors to go round it.

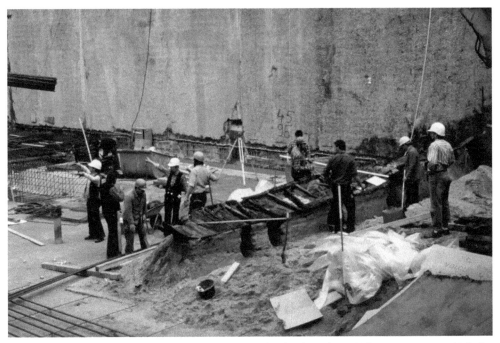

The Carolingian river barge *Karl* from AD 800 had to be removed within three days as 50 lorries were expected, bringing concrete to pour the base plate for the future hotel. Photograph: Per Hoffmann

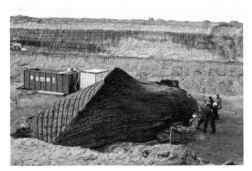

The *Doelse Cog* appeared during the excavation of a new dock basin in Antwerp in 2000. Archaeologists dismantled the ship, and stored the timbers in water-filled tanks. Even now the final resting place for the ship has not been decided. Photograph: Per Hoffmann

However, this is not enough. A ship or a boat has an enormous potential as the big central object in an exhibition dealing with all sorts of aspects connected to the ship and its use: who built it and how, who used it, for what purpose, what cargo did it carry, when and where, etc. There are endless possibilities to make the ship speak, to make it interesting, to connect it to people. This is what museums' visitors want to learn about – people. But that needs enough space around the central object to arrange a comprehensive exhibition. The argument that space is too expensive must be countered with the question of whether it is worth embarking on a ship conservation project and then not taking advantage of its potential as the focus of a cultural, sociological, technical, and economical context. And if one really wants to attract visitors, one must provide enough space for them to step back from the ship so that they can take a photograph of the whole of it.

In real life, finding answers to all these initial questions will take some time from the moment the archaeological find is exposed until it is fully understood. During this time the excavation has to go on and probably the ship or boat has to be lifted and taken away from the site. To keep the option to conserve it, precautions have to be taken immediately to prevent irreversible damage caused by handling and by exposure to air, wind, and sun.

9

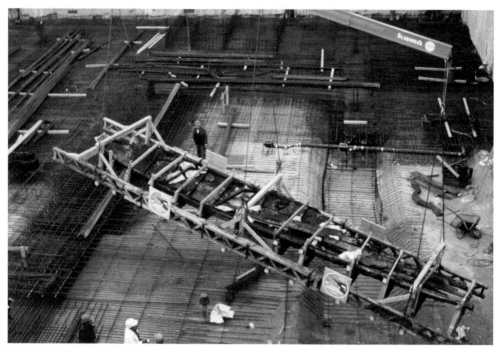

Finding a ship in a building site has its advantages: craftsmen, tools and equipment, and a crane are all available and helpful. Photograph: Egbert Laska (DSM)

Ship finds can create a great deal of public interest and the public relations aspects of the project are important in reaching a political decision to have the ship preserved. This will, in turn, help to secure resources to make the work possible. However, political will is fickle and decisions made may only be good for up to three or four years, the political cycle. This needs to be factored into any project planning.

1.2   Reducing damage during salvage and transport

As soon as waterlogged wood is exposed to the environment it starts to dry, even on a foggy day. There is always a difference in water vapour pressure between the wood and the air, except when it is raining and a layer of water forms on the surface of the wood. When the wood dries it will soon begin to shrink and develop splits and cross-grain cracks. Such damage becomes more and more serious as the drying proceeds, ending in irreversibly disfigured, distorted, and even

self-destroyed timbers. From the moment of exposure the wood must be kept wet, dripping wet. How this can be achieved depends on the situation. A garden watering hose 'fan' is excellent; its reach can be adjusted to allow work in some areas while others are kept wet. Hand-held pump sprayers will do too, but have to be applied very frequently. Absorbent cloth or babies' nappies can be laid out or wrapped tightly around protruding ends of planks, ribs, and the like. When soaked, these materials will hold the moisture much longer than foam sheeting. In addition, it is advisable to cover the ship with a tarpaulin or a layer of polythene sheet.

The way a ship or boat is removed from an excavation site will depend on the results of assessments of several aspects. An assessment of the wood condition needs to be made swiftly after discovery by an experienced conservator or wood scientist to identify options for lifting and storing. If it is anticipated that the ship will eventually be exhibited, it is preferable to lift a ship in one piece, leaving the original joints – treenails, dowels, iron bolts

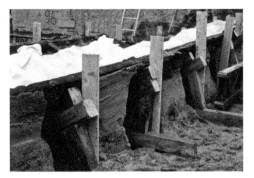

Conservators and carpenters created a wooden support cradle under the ship while it was still resting on the sand as found. We named it *Karl* for Charlemagne, who reigned when it was built. Photograph: Per Hoffmann

and nails, rivets, etc. – untouched. The alternative, to dismantle the ship on site, has severe consequences: iron fastenings will most probably have rusted and oxidation products will have permeated the wood around the nails, bolts, or rivets, making it brittle and fragile. Trying to extract them will leave large holes of broken-out wood. Drilling the fastenings out with a core drill also leaves big holes. Suitable techniques will have to be developed in each case. The brittleness of archaeological wood will cause the sharp edges and ends of timbers to break off or become 'rounded' during handling. Planks may break, and a lot of debris will disappear. Dismantling and re-assembling a ship needs capable craftsmen, and they need a good amount of time for the job. Even after successful conservation and re-assemblage the ship will not look like it did – it will have lost part of its integrity and smoothness.

However, part of a sturdy *Roman barge*, 7.0 × 2.6 × 0.6 m, was found upside down near *Xanten-Wardt* during gravel extraction in an old bed of the river Rhine. The archaeologist saw no way to turn the barge back over again: she feared the structure would collapse the moment it passed through the vertical position. She decided to carefully dismantle the ship, salvage and conserve the timbers, and reconstruct the barge. The result is quite acceptable and can be seen in the museum in Xanten. During the process she learnt about

several construction details which she would not have seen without taking the two layers of planking of the ship apart.

Detailed documentation of the ship's structure in situ, and of its elements if it is taken to pieces, is very important. It helps to understand how the ship is constructed, and it may be vital for putting together the elements when reconstructing the ship for display. The *Viking ships from Roskilde* had been crushed under the weight of their original cargoes of stones. Documentation and lifting, fragment by fragment, could only be done in a conventional archaeological excavation after a cofferdam had been constructed around the ships and the seawater pumped out. An advanced device for the exact documentation of ships' timbers is the FaroArm system: the tip of a flexible mechanical 'arm' is passed along edges and other features of the timber and the movements of the tip are directly transferred to a computer. Drawings and three-dimensional images can then be produced as required, and the data can be fed to a computer-aided milling machine to cut models of the documented timber.

It seems, at least to me, more problematic to cut a ship or boat into manageable sections, confidently expecting that after conservation the sections can be exactly reconnected. But they will never fit perfectly. There is always some slight residual shrinkage in the timbers, even after the best stabilisation. The cuts will most probably always remain visible and annoyingly obvious. The typical feature of a ship or boat to me is the smooth outer surface of the hull, composed of planks running the length of the ship, or of one uninterrupted surface in the case of a dug-out canoe. A vertical cut destroys this characteristic of a ship; it should be avoided. When it is not possible to avoid this then a very oblique cut is less obtrusive, or a cut along the seams and overlapping ends of planks.

On the other hand, lifting a ship as a whole can be a major engineering task. It is one thing to lift a dug-out of 5 m length, but quite another task to lift a barge of 30 m length and 6 m width. Only when lifting will you find

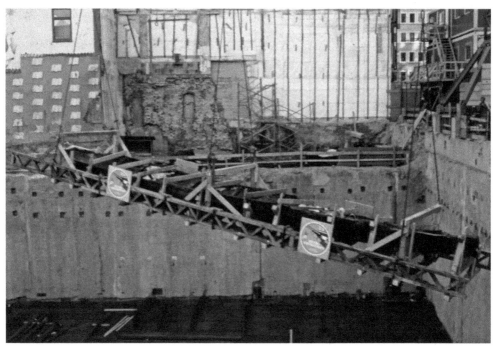

A cradle lifted at three points will not bend even if it is long and slender. Photograph: Gabriele Hoffmann

out how huge it really is. If heavy cranes and low-loader vehicles cannot come to the excavation site there may be other ways.

For a 19th century barge found in a wet meadow near Bremen, a canal was dug from the ship to the nearby river, leaks in the ship were sealed, a tarpaulin closed the hole made by the ripped-off bow, and with a happy party, beer, and music on board, *the ship from the Teufelsmoor* was floated (see photograph by Erwin Duve) and drawn by tug to the nearest small harbour where there was a strong enough wharf for a mobile crane to stand on. Sometime later the 20 m vessel was lifted onto a long vehicle for the last 12 kilometres to the premises of the local museum in Osterholz-Scharmbeck where it was to be treated (see photograph by Anna Suchodolski). A similar case was the salvage of the *Kinneret boat* in Israel. Found at the shore of Lake Kinneret – the Sea of Galilee – the very fragile boat from about the time of Jesus was encapsulated in polyurethane foam and floated across the lake to a conservation facility. Regrettably, the eager excavators

forgot to insert cutting wires inside the foam – without them it was extremely tedious to remove the foam later on without damaging the soft wood surface. A less extravagant way to transport a ship found in or near a river is to let a floating crane lift it onto a barge or pontoon and tug it to a convenient place. Two 18th century *barges* found in the river Weser at *Rohrsen* with their cargo of hewn sandstone blocks still in the hold were taken 80 km upstream on a pontoon before they were lifted onto low-load vehicles and driven to the Renaissance Museum in Lemgo. The barges' cargo was transported separately. The transport by road of two ships, both 20 × 5m, was a major affair; police escorted the trucks and stopped all traffic; the route had been checked for narrow passages, bridges, tunnels, sharp turns; low-hanging traffic lights were removed, and in the end the transport was only allowed to take place at night.

The biggest floating crane in the world had to be brought in to lift the *Mary Rose*, King Henry VIII's battleship, from a depth of 17 m in the Solent, off Portsmouth, UK.

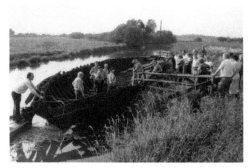

The *ship from the Teufelsmoor* took a party of local enthusiasts on board for its voyage from excavation to conservation. Photograph: Erwin Duve

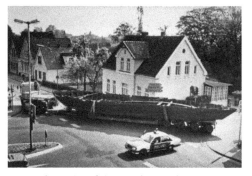

The last few miles of the *ship from Teufelsmoor*, on dry land, required careful manoeuvring. Photograph: Anna Suchodolski

Perhaps the most famous salvage is the lifting of the *Vasa*, King Gustavus II Adolphus' magnificent battleship, in the harbour of Stockholm. At a depth of 35 m, a gang of Navy helmet divers dug six tunnels under the ship using water jets and suction hoses, and passed steel wires through them. The men from the salvage party then exchanged the steel wires for six-inch lifting cables, and fastened the cables to two pontoons, one on each side of the *Vasa*. The cables ran under the *Vasa* and around the pontoons. This salvage technique is old. Olaus Magnus, archbishop of Uppsala, described it in 1555:

> The pontoons are flooded until their decks are at water level. The men tighten the cables. They then pump out the pontoons. The pontoons rise and lift the sunken ship. The men sail them to

shallower water till the wreck touches ground, flood the pontoons and repeat the process.

In 18 lifting stages, the *Vasa* was brought to rest in 16 m of water. During the following 18 months the hull was made watertight, and preparations for the next steps of the salvage were made. Then, in an excited festival atmosphere, huge winches mounted on pontoons lifted the ship until it broke the surface. Strong pumps drained it, and the old hull came afloat. On its own keel *Vasa* sailed into a historical dry dock and, after archaeologists had excavated much of the mud and sediments that had filled the hull, came to rest on a pontoon. This pontoon became the base of the future conservation hall which was later erected around the ship.

Whenever lifting a ship, or even a dug-out, the soft surfaces and the reduced breaking strength and brittleness of waterlogged wood must be kept in mind. Broad belts are safer to use than ropes. There is an old rumour about the ship that was cut into slices by the cables which were meant to lift it. Protective boards or cushioning on the outside are obligatory, as are cross-beams inserted into the hull to stabilise the structure against lateral compressive forces which might occur during lifting. The way a ship is to be lifted is the decision of the archaeologist in charge, but if it is meant to be conserved it is wise to ask the conservator for his or her opinion and advice. In the end it is the conservator who must work with the ship, and he or she might have demands other than those of the archaeologist.

Often it is necessary to build a support or cradle of some kind around the ship on site, and then lift and transport the whole. Once the support is in place it does make sense to leave the ship resting on it throughout the conservation process. This is only possible with some foresight. Wood is a pleasant and cheap material, and easy to work with. However, a cradle built from seasoned wood will not only float when lowered into a tank with water or conservation solution, it will show a strong buoyancy. A single spruce wood beam of 10 × 10 cm and a length of 1 m will develop a buoyancy of about 5 kp; in other words, it is nearly impossible to keep a wooden cradle of some size underwater. A support structure should be built of steel right from the beginning if the ship is to go into a conservation tank. A steel support must of course be coated against corrosion, so a corrosion inhibitor must be added to the impregnation solution.

The wood of a ship find may be so soft, degraded, and broken into small pieces, that the ship cannot be lifted in one piece, nor be dismantled and the individual timbers salvaged. However it may be possible to lift the wreck on a block of sediment and conserve it still resting on the sediment. A treatment with a high molecular weight polyethylene glycol (PEG) will stabilise the degraded wood and most types of sediment. Only clay is impermeable to water and PEG. When clay dries it crumbles into small cubes. But then the wood will be consolidated, and the clay can be substituted by another support. To carry out conservation treatment on a sediment bed the sides of the block must be secured with planks or boards to prevent the sediment trickling out and floating away during the conservation process. The wood must be secured against floating off the sediment bed; even if it is heavily degraded it might still have some buoyancy, and the slightest turbulence in the conservation tank will set small pieces moving. If the sediment block is lifted and one steel plate pushed underneath it, this plate can then be used as the base of a steel conservation tank built on it.

During the preparations for lifting, and also during transport, the ship must be kept wet and protected against accelerated drying from exposure to wind and sun. It should be sprayed and wrapped up again several times an hour.

The greatest dangers to an archaeological ship during transport are bumps and vibrations. Heavily degraded wood is extremely brittle. It may break without warning quite differently from fresh wood, which breaks slowly with a fibrous rupture. Good shock-absorbing cushioning is imperative. Several layers of stiff and soft mineral fibre sheets laid out on the low-loader, fitted to support the ship or its cradle evenly over its entire length, have been used successfully. A bed of old tyres is also a good shock-absorber. The conservator should accompany the driver of the truck to persuade and remind him when necessary to drive only very slowly so that no vibrations will build up.

In an ideal situation the ship can be transported from the excavation directly to the conservation facility. Sometimes, however, it has to be put into interim storage until the questions of conservation, financing, and final destination have been answered. One option is to place the ship somewhere where a spraying system can be set up which can work continuously. Such a system must also be able to reach the undersides of all timbers and cover them with a film of water. A spray system needs a certain amount of maintenance. Spray nozzles will clog, hoses disconnect, pumps fail. If the water is taken from the public water supply the costs will become substantial over time. It is worth looking for a river, a lake, or pond for water. Parking a ship under a spraying system is not really safe in the long run. A Carolingian river barge which we called *Karl* had to be lifted in three days from a building site in Bremen in a frosty early April, and was placed in an archaeological excavation tent. A garden sprinkler system kept it wet, and planning the conservation began. The town archaeologist had given the ship to the Deutsches Schiffahrtsmuseum and into my hands; representatives of the Bremen administration had promised funds to follow – with loud words, and in a fit of enthusiasm – but nothing of the like happened. We started the search for funds and for a place to house a conservation tank. Summer came early and was very hot, *Karl* suffered in his tent. It took more than a year before *Karl* could be submerged in a purpose-built concrete tank, and in this time shrinkage had occurred in the ribs, and in the broad and heavy bow plate, deep splits opened

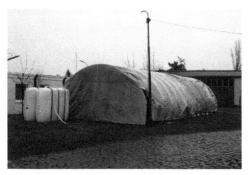
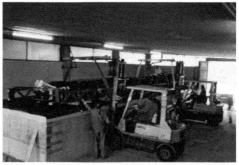
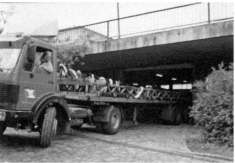
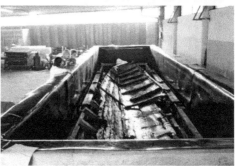

After waiting for months in a tent with improvised water spraying, *Karl* could be placed in a concrete tank lined with heat resistant heavy-duty foil for conservation with polyethylene glycol. Photographs: Per Hoffmann

and some fragments broke off. This happened while the sprinkling was in action. We saw it happen but could do nothing. Over the years I have learnt that an interim solution can take a very long time to come to an end.

During the extended excavation of a series of ships in a former Roman harbour in Pisa, conservators from Grenoble developed a technique to help provide a new interim solution. The technique was to cast a jacket of fibreglass around each exposed ship, and to establish a top-pressure of water between the wood and the jacket with garden hose equipment to keep it wet while it waited to be lifted from the site.

A much simpler option is to re-immerse the ship in water. A pool, a lake, a hole dug in the ground and lined with plastic sheeting and filled with water will do. Best of all is a harbour basin with a strong wharf. An archaeological ship will normally still have a buoyancy which should not be underestimated. Even water-logged wood will contain a certain amount of air. Before re-immersing the ship some work has to be done. Any loose parts have to

be secured to prevent them floating off. In a plank-built vessel the original fastenings may not be as strong as they might appear. All parts of the structure should be secured against lifting forces, either by weighing them down with sandbags or netting, or by some other arrangement. If the ship is sitting in a support or cradle, it needs to be braced against floating within the support or even leaving it. Again, one has to consider the potential buoyancy of the materials used to stabilise the ship.

Once the ship or boat is submerged, archaeologists and conservators can relax; now there is no imminent threat to the object. Plans and decisions for the next stage of the project can be developed and discussed. Preparations for conservation can now be made.

1.3 Preparing the ship for conservation

A thoroughly cleaned ship is a prerequisite for successful conservation. All wood surfaces must be exposed so that the conservation

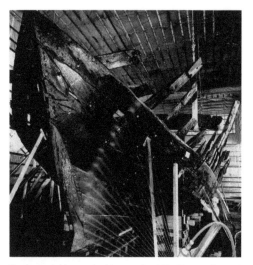

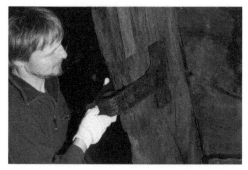

Metal attachments, like this gudgeon on the stern post of the cog, should be removed from the wood before conservation with polyethylene glycol. Photograph: Per Hoffmann

Garden sprinklers and mist sprays kept the *Bremen Cog* wet during the years of reconstruction, to prevent the timbers from drying and shrinking. Photograph: Meyerdierks, DSM

reagent applied in an impregnation bath or spray can diffuse unhindered into the wood. Silt and sediment must be removed and washed out of seams and joints, from holes, corners, and hidden pockets. The spaces along ribs and futtocks in between inner and outer planking, and under bottom planks, are common reservoirs for sediments which will seep out endlessly during conservation if they are not rinsed out completely beforehand.

Clay is a very sticky sediment and difficult to remove, and many ship finds have been sitting in clay. Spatulae and brushes of varied hardness, patience and lots of water are required to clean the wood and rinse the pores and splits in the timbers. A steam-jet, handled very cautiously so as not to remove the wood surface as well as the sediment, can be very useful.

Apart from making impregnation difficult, there is also the aesthetic of residual sediment. It will always show after conservation – grey or whitish – and at that stage it is really difficult to remove as it has been consolidated into the wood. It will look like dirt, and it is dirt.

For a conservation en bloc, i.e. the ship is still sitting on the sediment, the visible surfaces of the wood must be rinsed and cleaned as thoroughly as possible. This may be difficult without washing away too much of the supporting soil, but with the suction from a wet-vacuum cleaner the wash-water and dissolved dirt can be removed directly from the wood.

Sediment may be strongly attached to the wood as sand–rust concretions. Such concretions may contain items such as iron, heads of nails and bolts, sintels holding down caulking material, fittings of all sorts, pieces of chains, gudgeons for a rudder, or other objects associated with the ship. If this is the case, it is a task for a metals conservator to advise on how to remove the concretions and lay open their iron cores. If not, then all concretions must be removed mechanically. Iron fittings and iron objects of all sorts should be detached from the wood before conservation to minimise the formation of new corrosion during treatment. Corrosion products may settle onto and diffuse into the wood, where the iron can catalyse or take part in various chemical reactions which may lead to degradation of wood components, and of the substances used for stabilising the archaeological wood.

Iron stains on the wood surface should be removed as far as possible if they are not interpreted as being part of the ships history when it was still in service. Solutions of strong complexing chemicals can be applied by dabbing with swabs, or in bandages. Diethylene triamine pentaacetic acid (DTPA) and

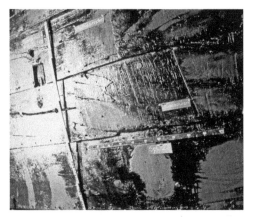

Fine surface details, like these marks from the big saw which cut the plank, must be documented before conservation. They may not survive a stabilisation treatment: even a slight shrinkage of the wood will make them disappear. Photograph: Egbert Laska, DSM

ethylenediamine (O-hydroxy-P-methylpheny lacetic) acid (EDDHMA) have been found to be most effective agents for iron removal from wood surfaces. EDDHMA is a commercial product used in agriculture to keep iron dissolved and available to plants in alkaline soils. DTPA is a registered product mainly used in the pulp and paper industry to bind noxious metal ions. The extraction of iron from deep within the wood, however, has not yet been possible.

Whichever way the ship is cleaned, one has to keep in mind that it is the soft and delicate surface layer which contains the most interesting information: tool marks from the shipwrights, tar and paint from surface treatment and decoration, signs and marks from wear and from typical techniques and procedures carried out on board such as rowing or rigging, towing, fishing with nets or lines, keeping open fires, etc. Surface traces are easily washed away.

During the cleaning process the conservators get to know the ship thoroughly – the dimensions of its timbers, the wood species, the strong and weak points of the construction.

The proportions of heavily degraded and lesser degraded wood within the ship and within the individual timbers are assessed. The state of degradation is important information for the design of an appropriate conservation treatment. A basic knowledge of the structure and properties of archaeological wood is necessary.

Notes to §1.2 Reducing damage during salvage and transport

– The salvage and conservation of the *Roman barge from Xanten-Wardt* is described by J. Obladen-Kauder, 2008.
– The story of the *Viking ships from Roskilde* is presented in O. Crumlin-Pedersen, 2002.
– The recovery, transport, and conservation plan of the *Kinneret boat* – also called the *Jesus boat* – is described by O. Cohen, 1990.
– The conservation of the *Teufelsmoor ship* is dealt with in Section 4.4.
– The salvage of the *barges from Rohrsen* is described in Lüpkes, 2001, and their conservation is discussed in Section 4.4.
– The spectacular lifting of the *Mary Rose* and the pioneering recovery of the *Vasa* are comprehensively described by G. Hoffmann, 2001.
– Experiments on the stabilisation of sediments with PEG, see P. Hoffmann and J. Pätzold, 2002.
– For the recovery and conservation of the Carolingian barge *Karl*, see P. Hoffmann, 2005.
– Olaus Magnus describes the lifting of a ship with pontoons in his book 'Historia de gentibus septentrionalibus', Romae 1555. Text here is cited from Hoffmann, G., 2001.

Notes to §1.3 Preparing the ship for conservation

– Extensive studies into the effects of iron in archaeological wood have been initiated within the 'Preserve the *Vasa*' research project, 2003–2006: G. Almkvist and I. Persson, 2009, T. Iversen *et al.*, 2009.
– For the extraction of iron with new complexing agents, see G. Almkvist and I. Persson, 2006.

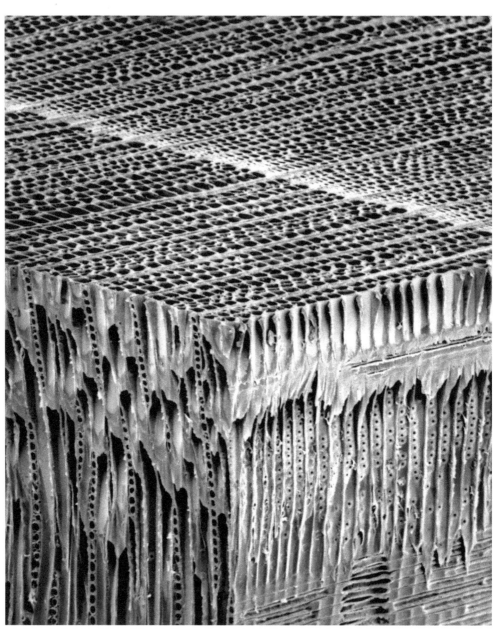

Looking at the corner of a cube of a softwood with a scanning electron microscope (SEM) reveals the fine structure of the wood, consisting of cell walls and empty cell lumina. Micrograph: Tanja Pötsch, Federal Research Centre for Wood and Wood Technology, Hamburg

2   Wood in its archaeological context

2.1   Sound wood

Only with a clear picture in his/her mind of the internal state of the wood to be stabilised, and its actual fine and ultrafine structure, can the conservator select an effective stabilising agent and design the appropriate treatment scheme. And only with a basic knowledge of the structure of sound wood can the degradation of waterlogged wood and the consequences for various conservation possibilities be understood. In this chapter the structure of sound wood is described, from the macroscopic level down to the microscopic, electron microscopic, and molecular levels.

The living tree

A living tree generates wood according to the following process. Just beneath the bark, the tree – stem, branches, twigs, and roots – is totally enveloped in a very thin coat of living and expanding cells capable of cell division, known as the cambium. The cambium cells have walls which enclose the cell plasma with the cell nucleus and the cell organelles. The cells divide into daughter cells towards both the stem and the bark. The cell plasma of the daughter cells extrudes cellulose fibrils onto the cell walls until the new layer has grown to a considerable thickness. The plasma then secretes various phenolic substances which diffuse into the cell wall where they polymerise to form lignin – i.e. the cell walls lignify. After the lignification of its walls, the cell dies and the plasma and nucleus dissolve. The

framework of dead cell walls and now empty cell lumina which they enclose is what we call wood. The cells which were formed towards the outside of the cambium become bark.

The transport of water from the roots to the leaves, the organs of assimilation, takes place in the dead wood cells just inside the cambium. The transport of assimilates – sugars – from the leaves to the living and growing cells of the cambium, and to specialised storage cells in the wood takes place in the inner bark. In the living tree the wooden stem and branches support the top of the tree and spread the leaves out so that they can catch as much light as possible. The roots hold the tree upright. The wood has to withstand compression, bending, and tension forces. Compared to other materials of the same specific weight, wood has remarkable strength properties. Its strength has its origin in the fine structure of the material. It is a composite of wood substance, water, and air. It may also contain small amounts of so-called extractives like resin, fats and waxes, sugars and starch, colouring substances, minerals, and chemicals that make the wood more resistant to fungal, microbial, and insect attack. The structure of wood is complex, from the macroscopic level down to the ultrastructural and molecular levels. At all these levels the structure can be characterised by its high porosity. Pores and capillaries pass through the substance and form a coherent and continuous system of voids in the wood. This void system occupies about two thirds of the wood volume in most tree species from temperate zones. In extremely light wood

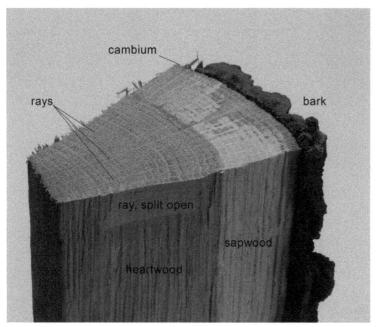

A piece of air-dried oak wood displaying some structural features. Photograph: Egbert Laska, DSM

species, such as balsa (*Ochroma lagopus*) or ceiba (*Ceiba pentandra*), it can occupy up to 90%; in extremely heavy wood species, for example ebony (*Diospyros crassiflora*) or guaiacum wood (*Guaiacum officinale*), the figure is down to 40%.

Wood structure at close inspection

With the naked eye or a magnifying glass, structural features of wood well known to everybody are visible. Wood has a fibrous consistency with an axial – or longitudinal – orientation. On a clear-cut cross-section, concentric growth zones – annual rings or increments – are apparent in woods from temperate zones where distinct growth and rest seasons alternate. Tropical woods may or may not have growth zones due to their more or less constant growth conditions. Wood from some hardwoods – i.e. deciduous or broad-leaved trees – show visible pores along the borders of the annual rings: oak, ash, elm, chestnut, to name a few. The inner part of the stem – the heartwood – can often be distinguished from the surrounding sapwood by a darker colour or a drier appearance.

Rays going outwards – radially from the centre – are discernible with a magnifying glass in most species. On an exactly cut, or split, radial surface – a surface cut in a radial plane – rays are visible as slightly glossy bands. In softwoods and in some hardwoods the rays are very fine and difficult to see. On a tangential surface – a longitudinal plane cut parallel to the tangent of an annual ring – cross-cut rays can be seen resembling fine to coarse longitudinal lines, from less than one millimetre to several centimetres long.

Microscopic views

Under a transmitting light microscope, or better even, a scanning electron microscope (SEM), the porous structure of wood becomes evident (see micrograph with the caption: *Looking at a corner of a cube of oak wood ...*). A cross-section reveals most

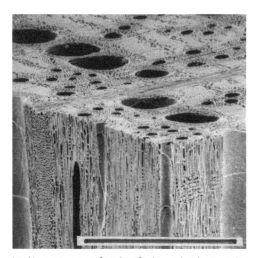

Looking at a corner of a cube of oak wood with a scanning electron microscope (SEM) shows it is composed of different sorts of cells: ones with large diameters – vessels; ones with small diameters and thin cell walls – tracheids; and ones with thick cell walls – fibre cells. Micrograph: Tanja Pötsch, Federal Research Centre for Wood and Wood Technology, Hamburg. Scale bar=1 mm

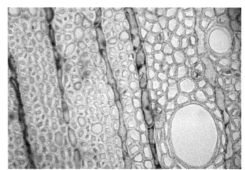

A cross-section of oak wood viewed under the optical microscope: the blue stained rows of cells are rays. Micrograph: Per Hoffmann

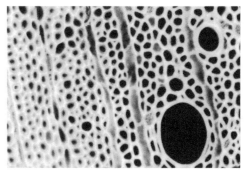

The same cross-section as in the micrograph above, viewed under UV light: the cell wall substance exhibits yellow to light green fluorescence. Micrograph: Per Hoffmann

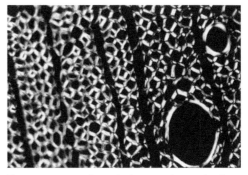

The same cross-section as in the two micrographs above, viewed in polarised light: the crystalline cellulose in the cell walls appears white, it shows birefringence. Micrograph: Per Hoffmann

information. There are thin-walled cells with large lumina (tracheids), and thick-walled fibre cells with only narrow lumina. There are thin-walled cells with large to very large diameters – so-called vessels. There may be resin ducts lined with living, resin-producing parenchyma cells. On a cross-section, rays appear as single rows of oblong cells, or as bundles of rows running in the radial direction. A radial or tangential section shows the reason for the fibrous character of wood: the bulk of the wood cells are very long thin tubes closed at the ends and arranged in the axial direction of the stem, branch, or root. Most tracheids and fibre cells are 30 to 150 times longer than they are wide. Vessel cells are short and cylindrical, and stacked on top of each other in long axial rows. The cell walls at their ends have large openings, or may even have dissolved completely so that tubes of considerable lengths are formed. The vessels are effective water ducts, but they are in service for only a few years. In some wood species they are then filled and clogged with tyloses, membrane bubbles growing into the vessels from adjacent still-living parenchyma cells. Tyloses are typical in, among others, European oaks; they make the wood impermeable to water, and this is one of the reasons

Box 1

Fibrils, voids, and water – the complicated structure of wood cell walls

The figure is to be read from right to left.

Very long cellulose chain molecules comprising up to 15,000 glucose units combine to form strands with a largely crystalline structure. Enveloped by shorter carbohydrate chain molecules (hemicelluloses) and lignin (an amorphous high-molecular weight polymer of aromatic compounds), cellulose strands form fibrils. The hemicelluloses bind the lignin to the cellulose strands. In the growing cell, fibrils are laid down onto the middle lamella, which separates the newly formed cell walls into discernible layers (primary wall (p); S_1, S_2, S_3, outer, inner, and terminal secondary or tertiary walls, respectively). This principle is the same for all cells, but the thickness of the individual cell wall layers may differ among cell species. Within and between fibrils, void spaces and capillaries in the cell walls contain water and air. During heartwood formation, these can be partly filled with secondary extractives including tannins, colouring matter and toxic substances which make the wood resistant to fungi and insects. Illustration: Per Hoffmann

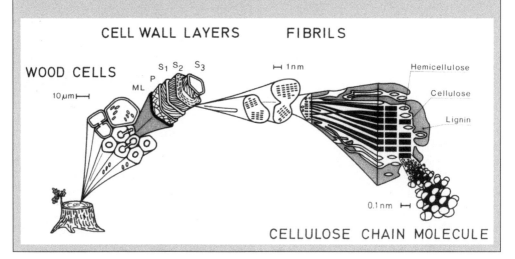

why oak is a favourite material of ship builders. American red oak on the other hand has no tyloses, the wood is not watertight and therefore of no use for shipbuilding.

At higher magnification in a light microscope or SEM, small channels through the walls of adjacent cells become visible, especially in the overlapping tapering ends of cells which sit on top of each other in the tree. These channels – called pit channels – are passages from one cell lumen to the lumen of the neighbouring cell. At the border between the cells, as part of the middle lamellae gluing together the neighbouring cells, a membrane is stretched across the pit channel. However, there are minute pores in the pit membrane, so the passage is only restricted, not closed. Every cell lumen in the wood is connected to the cell lumina of all cells in contact via dozens of pits. Tangential sections can reveal intercellular capillaries in and along the rays, the long empty channels between the lines of ray cells. From the lumina of the ray cells, and from the lumina of the axial tracheids and vessel cells, pit channels lead to these intercellular capillaries. The three-dimensional continuous system of lumina, capillaries, and pores, penetrates the wood in all directions.

A transmission electron microscope (TEM) resolves the fine structure – the ultrastructure – of the cell walls. Cell walls are

---

Box 2

Diameters of capillaries and fibrils in wood

30–500µm lumina of vessels in hardwoods

10–20µm lumina of tracheids in softwoods and hardwoods

2–5µm lumina of fibre cells in hardwoods

~1µm pit channels

0.1–1µm pores in pit membranes of softwoods

0.05–0.15µm (= 50–150 nm) pores in pit membranes of hardwoods

10–80nm capillaries between fibrils (interfibrillar capillaries)

Up to 2nm

Capillaries within fibrils (intrafibrillar capillaries)

4 × 4 nm fibrils

Volume of the capillary system in wood: 40–90% of the wood volume, with the average at 65%

The amount of capillaries results in an enormous internal surface in moist wood: 20–100 m^2/g.

---

built from very fine filaments – microfibrils – laid down onto the middle lamellae when the cell was still alive. Microfibrils aggregate to form fibrils, and these fibrils are arranged in layers, well aligned in a helical structure around the cell lumen. A normal cell wall consists of four layers. A very thin primary wall is attached inseparably to the middle lamella. The secondary cell wall has a thin outer layer (abbreviated S$_1$), a central layer of greater and variable thickness (S$_2$), and a thin final layer towards the cell lumen (S$_3$).

The microfibrils are built from three groups of macromolecular biopolymers – cellulose, hemicelluloses, and lignin. Cellulose and hemicelluloses are very long linear carbohydrate chain molecules which aggregate to long strands, the microfibrils. Lignin is an amorphous three-dimensional aromatic macromolecular substance which has polymerised around and in between the strands of cellulose and hemicellulose chains. The hemicelluloses bind the lignin to the bundles

of crystalline cellulose chains. The result is microfibrils which combine the flexibility and tensile strength of the carbohydrate chains with the stiffness and compression strength of the three-dimensional network of the lignin.

Between the fibrils, and also within the fibrils, there are voids and capillaries – interfibrilar and intrafibrillar capillaries. The pore system in the wood extends from the lumina into the cell walls, and even penetrates the cell walls from one lumen to the next. Diameters in the pore system span a wide range, from about 2 nm to 300–500 µm. The very high porosity of wood results in an enormous internal surface of up to 100 m^2/g. The internal surface in the cell wall is the place for physical and chemical interaction of the wood substance with water and other chemicals.

Water in wood

There is always water present in wood – except in extreme laboratory conditions – and it can exist in four forms: as chemically bound water; as water adsorbed in a monomolecular layer on the wood substance; as free capillary water; and as water vapour. The water has an influence on most physical properties of the wood – strength and rigidity, swelling and shrinking, thermal, acoustic and electrical conductivity. With waterlogged wood the determination of the water content is a simple way to obtain information about the state of the wood and its degree of degradation. The water content of wood (symbolised as 'u') is calculated and expressed as a percentage of water present compared to the absolute dry wood substance. The water content is in equilibrium with the water vapour pressure of the surrounding ambient air, expressed as the relative humidity of the air, or % RH. Lowering the relative humidity of the ambient air makes water evaporate from the wood, so that its water content decreases, and vice versa. Seasoned wood sheltered from rain will have a water content – or moisture content – of about 12 to 17% by weight.

When the system of lumina and cell wall capillaries is totally filled with water the wood

---

Box 3

Diameters and molecular weights of some molecules relevant in wood conservation

		Diameter	Molecular weight
Water		0.3 nm	18
Sucrose		0.4 nm	342
Lactitol		0.4 nm	344
Trehalose		0.4 nm	342
Kauramin prepolymer	~	0.5 nm	400–700
PEG 200, short hydrated chain molecules	~	0.5 nm	200
PEG 400, short hydrated chain molecules	~	0.5 nm	400
PEG 3000, hydrated random coil molecules	~	90 nm	3,000
PEG 4000, hydrated random coil molecules	~	100 nm	4,000

Histological stains used to differentiate lignified from non-lignified cell walls

Astra blue – stains only non-lignified cell walls in fresh wood, and swollen lignified cell walls in archaeological wood	~	1,000
Chrysoidine – stains lignified cell walls in fresh wood		249
Acridine red – stains lignified cell walls in fresh wood		465

---

contains its maximum water content of u_{max}. The maximal possible water content depends on the void volume in the wood. This again is inversely proportional to the amount of wood substance per unit volume, called the 'conventional density' R (g/cm³) of the wood in question. The relation is expressed by the equation:

$$u_{max} (\%) = (1.5 - R) \times 100/1.5 \times R \, (\%)$$

where 1.5 is the density of the wood substance.

The equation can be transformed to

$$R \, (g/cm^3) = 100/(66.7 + u_{max}) \, (g/cm^3).$$

As the density of wood substance (the specific weight) is about 1.5 g/cm³, waterlogged wood will not float when the amount of air in it has decreased below a certain value. This is true for many archaeological woods. Their actual weight will often be about 1.0 g/cm³, so that they are nearly weightless and easy to lift under water. But when they break surface they become twice as heavy as dry wood.

The interaction of wood with water or water vapour results in swelling and shrinking of the wood. The hydrophilic nature of cellulose and hemicelluloses in the cell wall and the easy access for the small water molecules into the inter- and intrafibrillar capillaries make available water press into the ultrastructure of the cell wall, expanding the fibrils and the whole cell wall, resulting in a swelling of the wood. The process is reversed when the RH of the surroundings decreases. As water evaporates from the ultrastructure, the microfibrils and fibrils become slimmer and can aggregate together. The cell walls shrink, and with them the whole wood structure.

With its axial orientation of the bulk of the cells, the helical structure of the cell walls, the radial orientation of rays, and the circular growth rings, the anatomical wood structure is not the same in all directions – it is anisotropic. As swelling and shrinking are a result of the structure of wood, these phenomena are anisotropic, too. Wood swells and shrinks – the maximum is in the tangential direction,

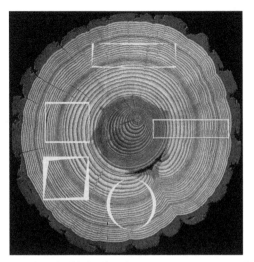

Distortions (highlighted) on drying seen in cross-sections of timbers cut from green or wet wood. Illustration: Reinhold Breden, DSM

and the minimum in the longitudinal direction. A rough rule of thumb says

$$\alpha, \beta \text{ (tan)} : \alpha,\beta \text{ (rad)} : \alpha,\beta \text{ (long)} = 1.7 : 1 : 0.1$$

where α = swelling and β = shrinkage.

The extent of the shrinkage from the wet to the dry state varies with wood species. It is roughly correlated to the specific density, or gravity, of the wood; the more cell wall substance it has per volume the greater is the shrinkage. In the majority of wood species, the tangential shrinkage from wet to dry is 5–12%, the radial shrinkage 3–7%, and the longitudinal shrinkage is ~0.3–0.7%.

The anisotropic reaction of wood to changes in water content has consequences for the dimensions and the shape of a worked piece of wood. Cross-sections will not only shrink or swell but will also become distorted; flats will dish and warp. The type of distortion is characteristic for the position within the tree trunk from where the timber has been cut. This knowledge can help to reconstruct the original dry shapes and dimensions of waterlogged finds.

The anatomy of wood – its quantitative composition of the different cell types, the spatial arrangement of these cells, the diameters of the water-conducting cells, the presence or absence of clogging substances in them – differs between wood species. The anatomy of the wood influences its permeability to aqueous solutions, and hence also to conservation treatment solutions. Even if the wood in archaeological finds has been modified over time its specific features and properties will still be present to some extent. Therefore, it is useful to know the wood species to be treated when choosing an appropriate conservation method. Luckily, wood species can easily be determined by their macroscopic anatomical features, with the help of a magnifying glass or microscope.

2.2 Waterlogged wood

Wood found in an archaeological context is usually wet and more or less filled with water, and is termed 'waterlogged'. A considerably increased shrinkage on drying, and an extremely anisotropic kind of shrinkage, are the most important and dangerous characteristics of archaeological wood compared to fresh wood. There have been alterations of cell wall features at the ultrastructural level. To understand how waterlogged wood differs from fresh wood, and to be able to take the right measures to neutralise the detrimental properties and reactions of archaeological wood, one must know what has happened to the wood during the long period of waterlogging, and how its structure and ultrastructure have been affected. The degradation patterns found in the wood govern the choice of a stabilisation method.

Degradation of waterlogged wood

As a part of the biological recycling of organic matter, wood is attacked, degraded, and consumed by many different organisms, sometimes already in the growing tree, but as soon as the tree has died, insects, larvae, and molluscs bore into and digest the wood. Termites and shipworms (*Teredo* species) are especially effective. The most efficient wood degraders,

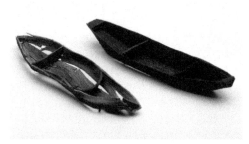

Model boats built from waterlogged archaeological wood: one was left to dry without conservation, the other dried after an impregnation with polyethylene glycol. Photograph: Egbert Laska, DSM

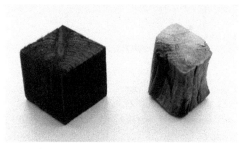

A cube from waterlogged spruce wood, before and after air drying. Photograph: Per Hoffmann

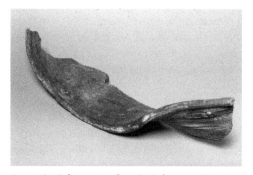

An air-dried fragment of a plank from a clinker-built archaeological boat find demonstrates the need for stabilising such objects prior to drying. Photograph: Per Hoffmann

Wood-destroying fungi are generally grouped according to the gross structural changes in wood caused by the organisms into brown rot fungi, white rot fungi, and soft rot fungi, belonging to the classes basidiomycetes, ascomycetes, and fungi imperfecti, respectively. Brown rot and white rot fungi are basidiomycetes. They need oxygen for their metabolism. They can only grow in well aerated wood. The cell walls should be wet, but the system of cell lumina must be void to provide sufficient ventilation. Basidiomycetes will attack wood above the groundwater table. In such environments they are the leading competitors in wood degradation. Soft rot fungi – ascomycete fungi and fungi imperfecti – can live with less oxygen present. They can grow in largely waterlogged wood, even underwater and in sediments not completely deprived of oxygen. Some species have adapted to a saline seawater environment. Soft rot fungi can grow where basidiomycetes cannot.

One variety of bacteria is capable of metabolising wood under anaerobic or near anaerobic conditions where even soft rot fungi cannot grow. Such conditions develop on lake bottoms and in slow-moving rivers, and in waterlogged sediments where the degradation of organic matter by other microorganisms has consumed the available oxygen. Archaeologists find most wooden objects in such environments: anaerobic sites at or below groundwater level. In nearly oxygen-free sediments sunken wooden ships and boats survive for long periods of time, because the degradation by soft rot fungi and bacteria is slow.

Whatever organisms attack and degrade the wood, one of the results relevant when considering the conservation is the degree of increased porosity and permeability of the wood.

Degradation patterns

Soft rot fungi colonise the cell walls. Most common is a form of attack where the fungal hyphae grow in the cell wall layer S_2 following the helical arrangement of the fibrils.

however, are fungi from a great number of species. Bacteria on the other hand are the slowest degraders of wood, but given enough time – centuries and millennia – they, too, can completely digest and degrade wood.

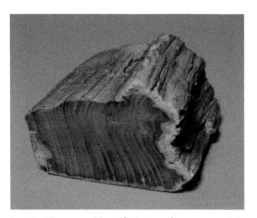

In a 20 million year old petrified piece of cypress wood the heavily degraded outer layer is clearly visible, now being lighter in colour. Photograph: Per Hoffmann

With their enzymes they dissolve the surrounding cell wall material to a certain distance and thus produce tube-like cavities, or chains of shorter cavities within the cell wall. On microscopic cross-sections these cavities appear as empty holes of varying diameters. As the fungal attack progresses, more and more hyphae grow in the cell wall, and in the final stages of degradation only the middle lamella and sometimes the S_1 layer survives. When the degradation takes place underwater the removed cell wall material is replaced by water. The water stabilises the frail and brittle residual structure, and the piece of wood retains its original shape and dimensions. To the touch, however, the black-looking wood feels soft – hence the name soft rot – and the surface layer is easily crushed and rubbed off. A soft rot attack starts on the wood surface, and progresses from cell to cell into the wood. As a result, the piece of wood will consist of an inner core of non-degraded wood tissue enveloped by a layer of degraded tissue. The borderline between the two wood qualities is quite visible, as the soft-rot degraded tissue has in almost all cases become dark brown or black. Probing with the point of a knife or a needle will reveal the pronounced loss in hardness of the degraded tissue.

Softwoods stored underwater, or under sporadic wetting – as is often the case after a storm has blown down large amounts of trees – are often colonised by bacteria which attack and degrade pit membranes in tracheids and ray cells. The bacteria may also degrade the thin walls of ray parenchyma cells. The porosity of the wood is increased, and the passages for liquids and dissolved substances are widened. However, the actual cell walls are not degraded by this group of bacteria.

The true degradation of waterlogged wood by other groups of bacteria results in three types of degradation patterns, depending on which group of bacteria has successfully colonised the wood: (i) erosion bacteria attack the cell wall from the lumen and degrade it completely – erode it – towards the middle lamella. The cell wall becomes thinner and thinner, and in the end only the three-dimensional system of middle lamellae is left. For a while the cell lumina may contain leftovers of the cell wall, mostly lignin, and a succession of other microbes which live on the debris; (ii) tunnelling bacteria preferentially colonise the S_2 layer of the cell wall. Each bacterium produces a tunnel as it moves forward in the cell wall, dissolving and digesting the wood substance just in front of it. Starting with a few bacteria and tunnels in the cell wall, the bacteria multiply and so do the tunnels until only the middle lamella and S_3 layer are left. In the end they, too, are attacked, perforated and broken down completely; (iii) cavitation bacteria penetrate the cell wall and produce cavities in the S_2 layer. The cavities will enlarge until finally the entire S_2 layer has been consumed. The degradation of wood by bacteria progresses from the wood surface towards the inner parts of the timber. The bacteria move from cell to cell, and along the rays. They may attack clusters of cells and leave neighbouring cells unaffected. But on the whole, in an infected timber there is a visible degradation front between degraded and non-degraded wood tissue.

The degradation patterns produced by soft rot fungi and by the different groups of bacteria have two characteristics in common, which are important with regard to the conservation of the wood. First, the degradation

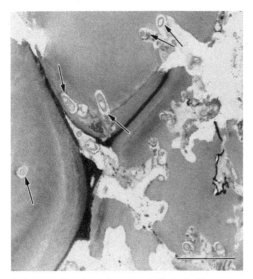

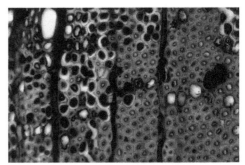

Degradation front in a cross-section of oak wood: in degraded cells the secondary cell walls have been reduced to amorphous, light-absorbing residues, detached from the middle lamellae. Micrograph: Per Hoffmann. Magnification about 200×

Active tunnelling bacteria – some indicated with arrows – in a medieval foundation pole of oak: tunnelling bacteria can penetrate the middle lamellae between cells and thus destroy the whole wood structure. Transmission electron microscopic micrograph of a cross-section: Robert A. Blanchette, University of Minnesota, St.Paul. Magnification about 3500×

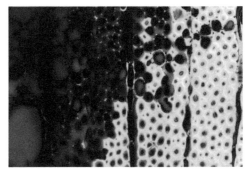

The same section of oak wood, viewed in UV light: degraded cell walls show no fluorescence. Micrograph: Per Hoffmann. Magnification about 200×

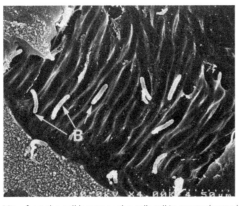

View from the cell lumen to the cell wall in a waterlogged medieval construction timber: active rod-shaped erosion bacteria dissolve the cell wall, each moving in its own furrow. Scanning electron microscopic micrograph: Charlotte Björdal, Swedish Agricultural University, Uppsala. Magnification about 7000×

However, several variables have an influence on the velocity of the degradation. The burial conditions, the amounts of available oxygen, the chemistry of the groundwater, the prevalent degrading organisms and changes of these conditions over time, make it impossible to judge the age of wood by its state of degradation. While the archaeological stratigraphic evidence and cultural characteristics of the object may give an indication, only dendrochronological or radiocarbon dating of the wood can actually date the wood. Second, bacteria and soft rot fungi dissolve all cell wall components simultaneously and in one step. However, the enzymatic action is restricted to the immediate vicinity of the microbe. The cell wall substance beyond this zone seems to be largely unaffected. As long as

progresses from the outside inwards, and in most cases with a narrow front-zone in which the bulk of degradation takes place. The progress of anaerobic degradation is slow. Soft rot fungi may degrade several millimetres per year, but bacteria only about 0.1 mm.

there are parts of cell walls left, these maintain their original structure and density. The piece of archaeological wood thus contains only two characteristics of wood – intact cell walls, and degraded cell walls within a residual system of more or less intact middle lamellae. Debris of the degraded cell walls may be present as an amorphous mass which will dissolve with time leaving the former cell empty. The fact that light microscopy and/or electron microscopy show only two of the characteristics of degraded wood is of great importance to the conservator. When considering the choice of a conservation treatment, he or she can concentrate on dealing only with degraded and non-degraded cell wall material, with degraded and intact wood.

Degradation by non-biological processes in waterlogged wood can seldom be proved, as environments that completely exclude microorganisms are rare. On microscopic cross-sections, however, sometimes evidence for a loosening of the fibrillar structure of cell walls may be observed, without traces of microorganisms, and without changes in the chemical composition of the wood. The cell walls will take up histological stain, which in sound wood does not stain lignified cell walls because the stain molecules are too large to enter the cell wall structure. The stained cell walls often have a swollen appearance, bulging into the cell lumen. What causes this swelling, and why it does not occur in the moist wood of centuries-old standing trees, are questions that are still unanswered. An acidic environment, on the other hand, may cause a slow hydrolytic degradation of hemicelluloses within buried wood, and high concentrations of various salts can attack and dissolve the middle lamellae and thus lead to a disintegration of wood tissue.

Characterisation of degraded waterlogged wood

The degree to which a piece of wood has been degraded is best seen by microscopic examination. But this is time-consuming, and the

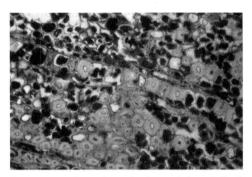

Cross-section of waterlogged oak wood: degraded cells (black) and non-degraded cells (light blue) are present in a mosaic-like pattern. Micrograph: Per Hoffmann. Magnification about 200×

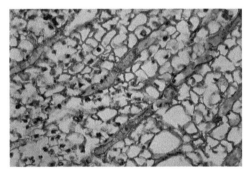

Cross-section of a heavily degraded oak wood: only the frail system of middle lamellae is left, ruptured in many places and only held by the water which fills it completely. Micrograph: Per Hoffmann. Magnification about 200×

very detailed information it provides is not always needed to establish a conservation concept. A simpler method is the determination of the conventional density R of the wet degraded wood, or of its maximum water content, u_{max}. Both values are easy to determine, and a comparison with the values for sound wood shows the decrease in density due to the loss of cell wall material. The loss of substance is reflected by a corresponding increase of the maximum water content. A series of measurements taken across the diameter of a timber will reveal the distribution of heavily degraded and less degraded or non-degraded tissue. A 5 mm core taken with an increment borer extracts enough material for these measurements. This method of describing the degree

Box 4

Under the microscope

Wood can be investigated using the light microscope (LM), the transmission electron microscope (TEM) or the scanning electron microscope (SEM). For each technique the wood samples have to be prepared and treated in a different way, and this preparation modifies their appearance. Thus the images from the same wood look slightly different: details are pronounced, obscured, or modified.

Cross-sections from three degraded oak woods are shown:

Top: as seen in a light microscope; middle: as seen in a transmission electron microscope; bottom: as seen in a scanning electron microscope.

Each technique has its advantages. In the light microscope, differences in the chemical composition of cells and cell walls can be made visible by histological staining, and large areas can be viewed. The transmission electron microscope can produce the highest magnification and the best resolution of finest structures, but only of an extremely thin section through the object, and only of a very small area at a time. The scanning electron microscope produces three-dimensional images of the surface of the object. The accuracy and clarity of details, however, are inferior to TEM images, and fine and soft structures may appear coagulated and distorted.

How does the wood look, and which images are closest to the truth? The answer requires a lot of work, and is expensive: all three images of a sample are required in order to provide the best possible visualisation of the wood in question – to discover the closest approach to the truth. Micrographs: Per Hoffmann, Mark A. Jones, Narayam Paramesvaran

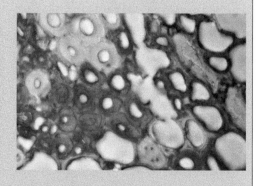
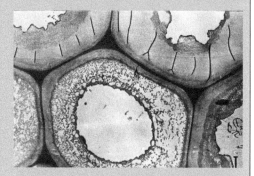
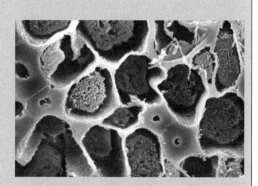

Box 4 (cont.)

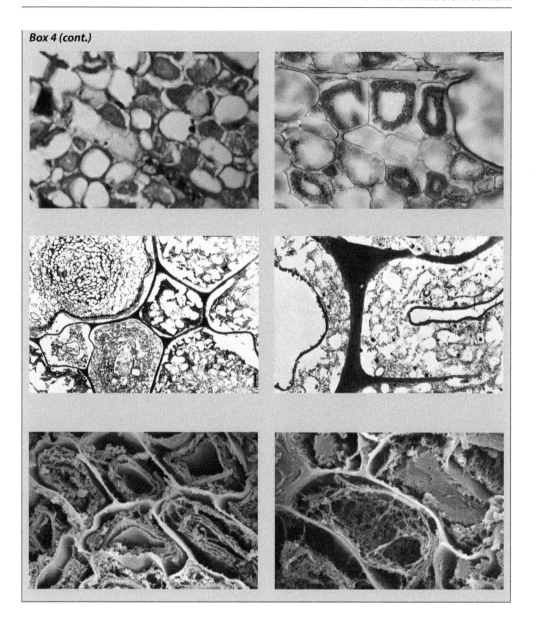

and distribution of degradation in a timber will also produce intermediate values between heavy degradation and no degradation, due to the fact that, in the area near the degradation front, clusters of degraded cells will exist in an otherwise non-degraded tissue, and vice versa. Within single cells, too, the volumes of intact cell wall and of degraded cell wall vary with the progress of the degradation process.

The gradual degradation of the wood tissue is a different process from the one-step degradation of the cell wall material within a single cell. It is the cumulative effect of what happens in the individual cells.

For the conservator it is important to get a clear picture of the degree and distribution of degradation in the timbers of an object. The most simple but very effective way to get an

Box 5

How useful is a chemical analysis of archaeological wood?

Freshly cut cross-sections of archaeological waterlogged wood in most cases display two or more zones distinguished by differences in colour and hardness – checked by pricking with a needle. When cut with a saw, the harder portion of the cross-section often has a woolly appearance due to protruding fibres and fibre bundles. The softer areas tend to look very clean-cut, indicating that the fibrous structure of the tissue has undergone a thorough modification.

The analysis of the wood for its chemical constituents – holocellulose (cellulose + hemicelluloses), lignin, extractives, and ashes – reveals that the modification of the wood is mainly due to the degradation and removal of the carbohydrates. The original amount of lignin remains in the degraded tissue. This is all that chemical analysis can tell us. It is microscopy that reveals where the lignin is: in the middle lamellae, in secondary cell walls if still present, and in the amorphous, granular, or cloudy mass seen in the cell lumina, the remnants of secondary cell walls.

Chemical analysis is not very useful as a means of characterising archaeological wood. It gives an average chemical composition of the wood, but says nothing about the occurrence of degraded and non-degraded cells, and of their distribution. It does not give information on the fine structure, the porosity, and the probable permeability of the wood, i.e. all those parameters that are decisive in the planning of an appropriate stabilisation treatment. Examination using light microscopy, and the combination of electron microscopic images, produced with different techniques, are much more helpful in understanding the character of the wood in question, its properties and probable reactions to a treatment.

idea of the situation is to systematically thrust the point of a small knife or mounted needle into the wood surface along the timbers and observe, and map on a sketch, how deep it penetrates, i.e. how thick the soft heavily degraded outer part of the timbers is. This is a rather subjective approach. It can become more unbiased using a device where a calibrated spring drives a standardised needle into the wood surface, e.g. the Pilodyne tester. A more sophisticated device is the resistometer, e.g. the Siebert drill. It applies a fine drill bit with standardised drilling force and measures the resistance which the wood offers to the drill. Using a long flexible bit, and with a digital output, the resistometer is useful for swiftly detecting and recording degradation in the heart of timbers which may be concealed by a shell of non-degraded wood.

X-ray and nuclear magnetic resonance (NMR) tomography, too, can show density or water distribution in pieces of wood. These sophisticated and expensive methods may be valuable for small and precious objects, but they are not easily applied to a ship, and they do not provide any more practical information than the methods described above.

Physical properties

The physical properties of archaeological waterlogged wood can be very different from those of sound wood. The extent to which the properties have been modified depends on the degree of degradation of the original wood structure. The following comments apply to all species of wood.

The strength properties of the wood – impact bending, bending strength, tensile and compression strength – decline as soon as degradation has affected and broken down cellulose fibrils in cell walls. In advanced stages of degradation the frail system of water-filled middle lamellae bubbles creates a foam which can easily be compressed and rubbed off with bare fingers. The very low bending strength makes degraded wood brittle. Under load it may snap with a non-fibrous fracture, and

Box 6

The maximum water content (u_{max}) – a good measure of the porosity in wood

The determination of u_{max} gives the weight proportion of wood substance to water in a sample of wood completely filled with water. u_{max} is expressed as the weight of the water as a percentage of the weight of the dry wood substance.

Taking the density of the wood substance proper into account, about 1.5 g/cm³, the void volume in the wood can be calculated as a percentage based on the volume of the wood: void volume = u_{max} / (u_{max} + 66.6) (% of the volume of the wood). The proportion of the volume of substance to the empty space gives a description of the porosity of the wood. A comparison of the values obtained for a given archaeological wood with the values for fresh wood of the same species, indicates the degree of material loss, in other words, the degradation in the archaeological wood.

The maximum water content and the normal density of a given wood are complementary expressions for the situation in the wood. The following equations convert u_{max} into the normal density R, and vice versa: R = 100 / (66.6 + u_{max}) (g/cm³) and u_{max} = 100 (1.5 – R) / 1.5R (%). Whether one prefers to work with u_{max} or with R, is a question of personal preference. The relations between density and volume proportions of wood substance and voids can be visualised in a simple diagram:

The determination of u_{max} depends on weighing only, it is not necessary to measure the volume of a wood sample. This facilitates working with small samples, like increments of a wood core. The procedure is simple:

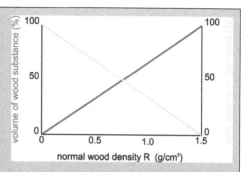

the water-filled sample is weighed, dried at 105°C until all the water has evaporated, and weighed again. The weight difference is the evaporated water, and this weight is expressed as a percentage of the weight of the dry sample. The calculation assumes that the wood is completely filled with water at the beginning, which is not the case with many archaeological woods. Residual air in wood can be removed and exchanged for water in two ways: (i) the sample is submersed and weighted down underwater in a vessel which is placed in a vacuum chamber, and a water jet vacuum is applied until air bubbles cease to emerge from the wood, after about 20 to 30 minutes. The vacuum is released, and the normal air pressure will force water into the wood, for another 30 minutes. This cycle is repeated three times. Finally, it may take several hours for water to fill the capillary system of the cell walls completely; (ii) the wood samples, submersed and weighted down, are boiled for 10 minutes, and allowed to cool down underwater. On boiling, water vapour forming in the wood will drive out any air, and on condensing on cooling will 'pull' water into the wood. Again, several hours must be allowed for the ultrastructure of the wood to be totally filled with water.

without warning. This explains why so many small and delicate objects break in the hands of fast-working archaeological excavators. The objects consist of nearly nothing held in shape by water. Much damage can be avoided if there is a conservator on the excavation team to secure and lift wooden finds. The reduced strength

of waterlogged wood combined with its heavy weight calls for good planning and careful handling and transport of large timbers.

Shrinking on drying, swelling on wetting, and warping of sawn timbers on swelling and drying are characteristics of wood. Every woodworker develops a knowledge

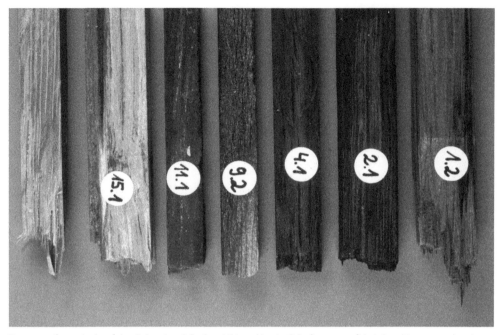

Staves cut from planks of the *Gokstad* and *Oseberg* Viking ships in Oslo for a test of their breaking strength: whereas sound wood breaks with a typical warning noise, degraded archaeological wood just snaps with non-fibrous fractures. Photograph: Federal Research Centre for Wood and Wood Technology, Hamburg

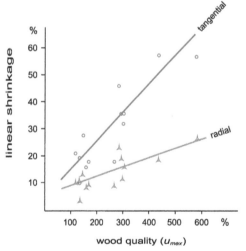

Tangential and radial shrinkage on drying of waterlogged archaeological oak wood of increasing degradation: even at low u_{max}, the shrinkages are about twice as high as for sound wood. Illustration: Reinhold Breden, DSM

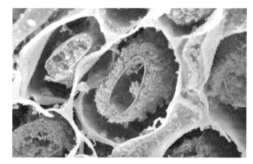

The wood with heavily degraded cell walls is held in shape by the water which fills it completely. SEM micrograph: Mark A. Jones, The Mary Rose Trust, Portsmouth

by experience for this behaviour of wood. However, waterlogged and degraded wood is different. Its modified structure and ultra-structure have a bearing on the nature and magnitude of dimensional response to changes in moisture content. In degraded wood, shrinkage on drying increases with degradation. This is contrary to the behaviour of sound wood, where the shrinkage decreases with decreasing wood density. For six water-logged oak woods from various ship finds, we found a linear relation between the volume shrinkage from wet to dry and the degree of degradation expressed as maximum water

Box 7

Cell collapse in degraded wood

The collapse of cells and cell walls in heavily degraded wood follows the evaporation of the water in the wood, starting at the wood surface and proceeding deeper and deeper into the wood. Fissures and cross-grain cracks may open in the wood surface, and then become deeper and wider; tangentially-cut surfaces may 'dish', or develop surface depressions, radial surfaces take on 'wash-board patterns'. Hollows may open up in the interior of the wood. Drawing: Per Hoffmann

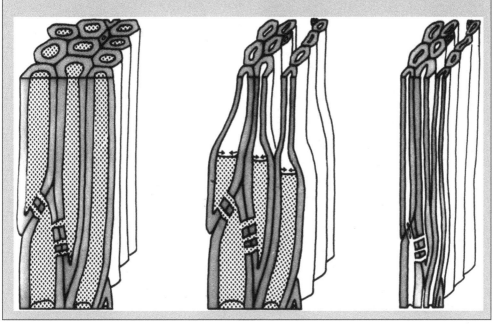

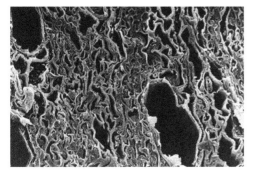

These degraded cells have collapsed during the drying of the wood, resulting in heavy shrinkage of the timber. SEM micrograph: R. James Barbour and L. Leney

content u_{max}. It is remarkable that with a slight degradation the shrinkage was twice as high as that of sound oak. Volume shrinkages from 35 to 75% were measured in this investigation.

The greatest part of the shrinkage occurs even at very high relative humidities of the surrounding air. While water evaporates from cell lumina and larger cell wall capillaries, many small water surfaces are generated within them. The surface tensions of all these minute surfaces pull at the surrounding cell wall material. Degraded cell walls cannot withstand these contractive forces, and the whole cellular structure collapses. With increasing proportions of degraded tissue in a piece of waterlogged wood, the proportion of collapse in relation to the normal shrinkage of the non-degraded part increases. The average contraction upon drying – the overall shrinkage – becomes much greater than the values known for sound wood. Collapsed wood cannot swell back to the original shape

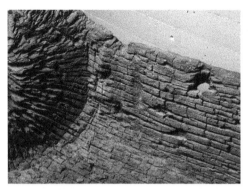

Collapse in the more degraded outer layer of the wood of this dug-out canoe has resulted in a bark-like pattern of longitudinal and cross-grain cracks. Photograph: Egbert Laska, DSM

and dimensions; the crushed cellular structure cannot be restored. Experiments to swell and restore collapsed wood with alkali, hydrofluoric acid, or lactic acid have given promising results on thin cross-section wafers; however, there are no reports of any successful applications to larger pieces of collapsed wood.

Collapse is the greatest threat to waterlogged wood, as it may start while the timber still feels damp and moist. I have seen oak planks develop collapse – visible as longitudinal fissures and cross-grain cracks – on their undersides while they were sprinkled on the top and side surfaces. Where the sprinkling did not reach, the relative humidity was only about 96%, and evaporation persisted. The high shrinkage and the collapse of heavily degraded wood – normally in the outer parts of a timber – and the lesser shrinkage of the lesser degraded interior portions, result in heavy stresses in the

timber. Warping, cracking, surface fissures, and even disintegration of timbers on drying are the consequences. In this way a boat or ship can be completely destroyed if it is allowed to dry even a little. This justifies the advice to keep an archaeological ship find dripping wet from the moment it is exposed until it sits safely in a conservation tank or spraying installation.

Notes to §2.1 Sound wood

– Further information on the structure, ultrastructure, and chemical composition of wood, its genesis and degradation, its physical and chemical properties, etc., can be found in textbooks on botany, wood anatomy, wood chemistry, wood physics, in publications and conference proceedings. The literature is extremely vast, as wood is still the number one basic working material.
– The data on capillaries in wood are compiled from various sources; still very valuable in this respect is the standard book by F. Kollmann and Côté, 1968.
– The data on molecule dimensions are compiled from chemistry textbooks, Wikipedia, and data sheets from Clariant Ltd., formerly Hoechst AG.

Notes to §2.2 Waterlogged wood

– Literature on the biodegradation of wood and of waterlogged wood is mostly found in conference papers and articles in various journals dealing with wood science, microbiology, geochemistry, and related subjects.
– A recent study on the restitution of the shape of collapsed wood has been published by L. R. Jensen et al., 2009.

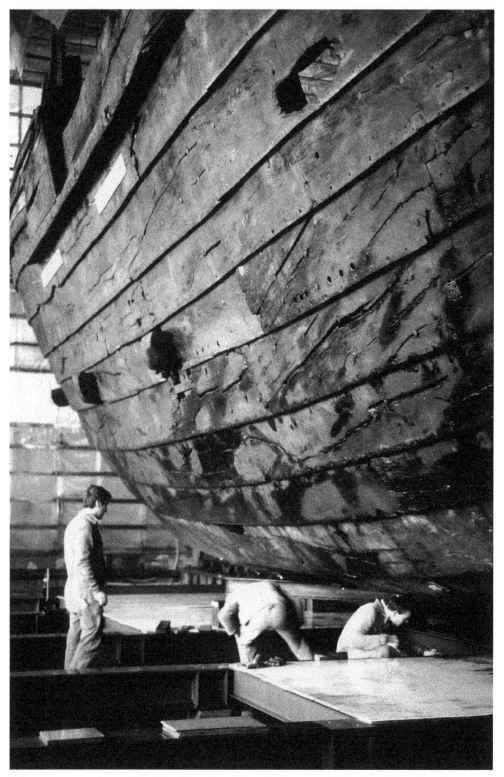

Bulking treatment or freeze-drying? The choice depends on the dimensions of the ship and whether a freeze-drying vacuum chamber is available. Here, steel workers push the bottom of the impregnation tank under the *Bremen Cog*. Photograph: Per Hoffmann

3   Two approaches to the conservation of a ship or boat

The aim of any conservation treatment is to reduce or eliminate shrinkage of the wood during drying, and thus to conserve its original shape and dimensions. Two different approaches are possible to prevent excessive shrinkage and collapse in waterlogged wood. One is to fill the degraded wood with material which will solidify and block the tissue against any contraction. This treatment is known as a bulking method. The other approach is to avoid the development of contractive tensions in the wood during the drying process.

Bulking treatments are the traditional methods for stabilising waterlogged wood. The bulking material, dissolved in water, is introduced into the wet wood and it solidifies there before or during the drying process. Several different chemicals have been suggested as bulking agents, starting with alum around 1859: wax or wax mixtures, rosin, various polyethylene glycols (PEGs), *in situ* polymerised resins, sucrose, sugar alcohol (Lactitol), polyurethane resin (Kauramin), and quite recently lignophenols. The use of waxes, rosin, cured resins and fatty acids requires that the water in the wood be exchanged for an organic solvent before the bulking chemical can be introduced. However, nowadays only a few reagents are used in the conservation of ships, all of them water soluble: various PEGs, Kauramin resin, sucrose and Lactitol.

There are two methods to avoid contractive surface tensions during drying: freeze-drying and supercritical drying. In freeze-drying the water in the wood is frozen to ice, and the ice then sublimes under reduced atmospheric pressure in a vacuum chamber. As liquids have a surface tension, and solids do not, no capillary contractive forces develop in this process, and no collapse occurs. Freeze-drying is the preferred treatment for smaller wooden archaeological objects. The stabilisation is good in most cases, the wood looks beautiful and natural, and no further cleaning of the surface is necessary.

For ships, however, the method has its limitations: large vacuum chambers are extremely expensive, and less than a handful of workshops in the world can treat objects the length of a medium-sized dug-out canoe. But if a boat has been dismantled or cut into sections during the excavation, then freeze-drying of the parts is an option.

Supercritical drying of waterlogged wood is, at the moment, still being investigated in laboratory experiments. The idea is to exchange

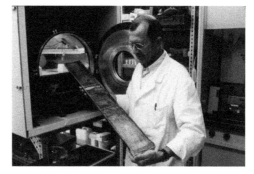

Freeze-drying is an elegant method not only for wood, but also for deep-sea sediment cores. Photograph: Gabriele Hoffmann

the water in the wood for methanol and then extract the methanol with liquid carbon dioxide under supercritical conditions, that is, under elevated temperature and pressure where the liquid changes to the physical state of a 'fluid', a state between a liquid and a gas. A 'fluid' has no surface; its molecules are separated from each other as in the gaseous state, and since no surface tension can build up, no contractive tensions will arise in the wood. The process seems to work well with some woods, but not so well with others. Time will show if this method can be developed into a reliable routine treatment for smaller objects. Its advantage would be short drying times and no surface cleaning, its drawback the need for sophisticated and expensive equipment which can be run only in explosion-proof workshops.

In choosing a conservation method for the dimensional stabilisation of a ship, certain criteria must be considered. The method must be practicable on a large scale. The chemicals used must be neither dangerous nor poisonous, either to the people working with them or to visitors to the workshop or museum in the case where the conservation tank is part of the display. It must not be harmful to the biological breakdown process in sewage plants, where the waste treatment solutions will end up one day.

The bulking chemical must be cheap because large quantities will be required, especially if a tank treatment is planned. The method must work with water – a ship cannot be encapsulated in a closed vessel for treatment in organic solvents. The necessary technical installations must be simple, so that the methods can be applied in a workshop and do not require a sophisticated laboratory, and they must work reliably over a long time. Several methods fulfil these demands, and variations of the basic methods have been developed. Today a sufficient variety exists to find a suitable treatment for any large object and its specific conditions. In the following chapters these methods and their application to a range of archaeological ship finds will be described and discussed.

Notes to Chapter 3

- A vivid description of the procedure of the legendary, now outdated alum treatment is given by B. Brorson Christensen, 1970.
- The first information on the use of some bulking agents not discussed in this book can be found in the following publications: wax mixtures – B. Brorson Christensen, 1970; rosin – L. Fox, 1989; cured resins – A. Ginier-Gillet et al., 1984 and R. Schaudy et al., 1988; lignophenols – T. Kataoka et al., 2009.

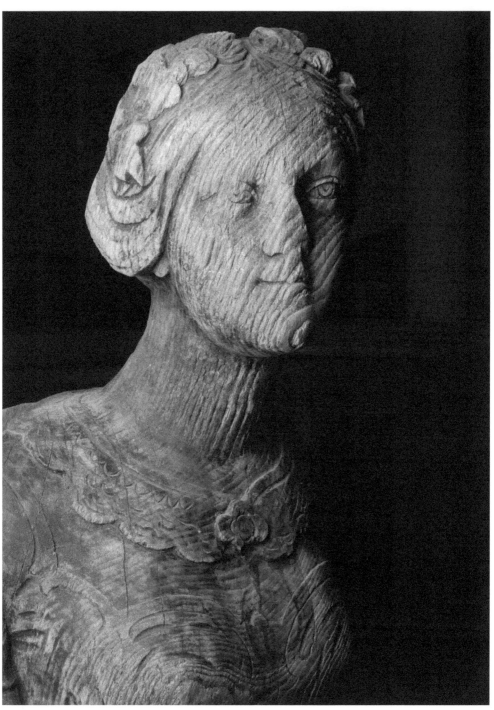

Softwood is easier to stabilise than oak wood. This figurehead lay in the North Sea for 150 years and rolled onto the beach in a storm before fishermen brought the lady to the museum and we named her *Martha*. She is carved from Weymouth pine (*Pinus strobus*) from North America. Photograph: Egbert Laska, DSM

4   Methods of application of polyethylene glycol

4.1   Some surprising laboratory experiments on wood

Three large ship finds were salvaged during 1961 and 1962: the *Vasa* from the harbour in Stockholm, Sweden; the *Skuldelev Viking Ships* in Denmark, and the *Bremen Cog* in northern Germany. At that time, the conservation of archaeological wood was still in its infancy, and the scientists from the three countries who had to develop conservation projects for the ships discussed what could be done.

A few years before, in 1955, the Swedish chemists Bertil Centerwall and Rolf Morén had published a paper on the use of polyethylene glycol (PEG) for the stabilisation of waterlogged archaeological wood. PEG had been used since the 1930s to stabilise fresh wood – veneers and gunstocks, for example – against shrinkage and warping, and now its great potential for the treatment of archaeological wood was demonstrated – but for small items only.

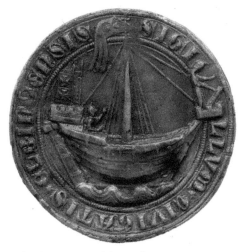

Medieval cogs were only known from engravings on town seals and from references in customs files until the wreck in the Weser was found. This is the seal of Elbing near Gdansk from about 1350 AD. Reproduction: Klaus Stiedenrod

PEG for ships – in one way or another

The scientists associated with the three ships agreed that PEG was the obvious choice of stabilising agent for the waterlogged ships. However, the question was: which PEG and which molecular weight would be best? The heavy *Vasa* timbers were very thick and only slightly degraded, and the whole ship was very large – 61 m long, 12 m wide, and 20 m high to the top of the stern castle. It was

totally unthinkable to construct a tank for the 1,200 tonnes intact hull. Lars Barkman, head of the *Vasa* conservation project, decided on a spraying treatment using an aqueous solution of PEG 1500. With this molecular weight a sprayable solution could be made with a higher concentration than with PEG 4000 – which was recommended by Centerwall and Morén – and it would penetrate better into the wood. The planks and timbers of the *Skuldelev Viking ships* were thin, heavily degraded, and very soft and brittle. They needed mechanical strengthening in addition to dimensional stabilisation. B. Brorson Christensen chose a treatment of impregnation of PEG 4000 in a

Box 8

Hygroscopicity visualised in sorption isotherms

The potential of a body or substance to take up or give off water from the atmosphere at varying relative humidities (RH) is best demonstrated with sorption isotherms. These curves show which moisture content (u) is in equilibrium with a respective RH. In the diagrams presented here the moisture contents of treated woods are based on the weight of wood + PEG, since the water which is bound to wood components and the water bound to PEG cannot be distinguished.

Figure (a) compares the sorption curves for a moderately degraded oak wood, for pure PEG 200, and for the PEG-treated wood. The impregnated wood consists of about equal parts of wood and of PEG; its sorption characteristics, however, are very much like hose of pure PEG 200. If the same wood is impregnated with PEG 3000 (b), then its sorption behaviour is more like that of PEG 3000 itself; the compound body in this case consists of two parts of PEG and only one part of wood. The sorption curve for the wood treated in two steps is almost identical (c). The high hygroscopicity of the wood after the first impregnation has disappeared; after the second impregnation the wood does not take up any more moisture from the air, as if it had only been treated with PEG 3000. The PEG 3000 seems to have shielded the hydrophilic sites on the PEG 200 molecules.

Sorption curves, however, do not indicate at what RH the treated wood becomes wet. For conservators, this is the crucial question in the discussion of the hygroscopicity and deciding on a suitable museum climate, and when it must be gauged empirically in laboratory tests.

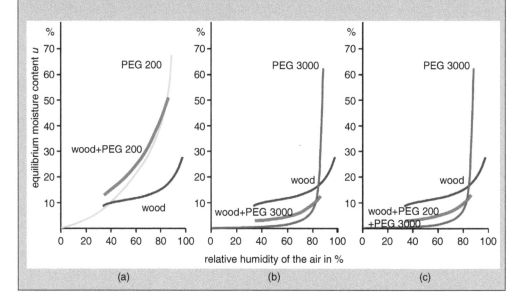

(a)   (b)   (c)

hot tank. This PEG becomes solid and hard on cooling. The dimensions and the state of degradation of the timbers of the *Bremen Cog* were in between those of the other two ships.

The group of wood scientists from the Federal Research Centre for Forestry and Forest Products in Hamburg, who had been asked by the excavators of the *Bremen Cog* to suggest a conservation concept, carried out a series of experiments and recommended a tank treatment with a 60% solution of PEG 1000. This molecular weight was meant to be a compromise between small molecules which would penetrate more easily into the wood but would not strengthen the degraded wood portions – they were liquids – and

Box 9

PEG – some physical and chemical properties relevant to wood conservation

Polyethylene glycols (PEGs) are a family of synthetic oils and waxes. They consist of chain molecules of different lengths, built from ethylene glycol units according to the general formula $HO(-CH_2-CH_2-O)_nH$. PEGs are synthesised with chain lengths of up to 6,000 units and more. The commercial products are narrow fractions of homologues, and they are described by their mean molecular weight added to the abbreviation PEG.

PEGs 200–800 are viscous liquids with densities of 1.12 g/cm^3, PEGs 1000 and higher are solids at room temperature with densities of 1.22 g/cm^3. Their hardness and brittleness increase with their molecular weight from soft to hard wax consistency. Melting points lie from 35°C to about 60°C. At ambient temperature, solid PEGs are soluble in water up to about 50%. For higher concentrations, heating to 40–60°C is necessary to dissolve the PEG, and to keep the solution liquid. Solid PEGs are soluble in most organic solvents, especially at raised temperatures, but not in benzene. Solid PEGs are not soluble in liquid PEGs. However, all PEGs have solvent properties for a wide range of substances, paints, lacquers, glues, and they can act as plasticizers in wood and other polymer formulations.

Several popular polymers are resistant to PEG, for example polyethylene, polypropylene, products from natural rubber, polytetrafluoroethylene, polyoxymethylene,

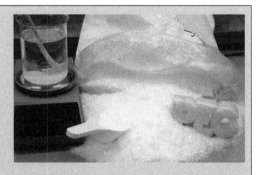

silicones, and unsaturated polyester resins. Those which are not resistant to PEG include soft polyvinyl chloride, polymethyl methacrylate, cellulose acetate, celluloid, and polyurethane elastomers. Polymers which are not resistant at higher temperatures are phenol-formaldehyde resins, urea-formaldehyde, and melamine-formaldehyde resins.

Solutions of low molecular weight PEGs are slightly acidic, and will cause corrosion on iron and mild steel, but not on stainless steel, brass, titanium, tin, and zinc.

PEGs are not very hygroscopic at low and medium relative humidities, but from about 75–85% RH they take up so much moisture from the air – 10 to 35% of their own weight – that they liquefy; low molecular weight PEGs are more hygroscopic even at low RH.

PEGs are used in many fields, especially in the chemical and pharmaceutical industries. There is a vast literature dealing with scientific and applied aspects. Detailed data sheets and compilations of physical and chemical properties of PEGs may be obtained from the manufacturers or from Wikipedia for example.

large molecules which would form a solid in the wood, but would not easily penetrate into it. Low molecular weight PEG is more hygroscopic than high molecular weight PEG. It would perhaps attract too much water from the air and render the impregnated wood damp or even wet after treatment. The conservation plan estimated that it would require 30 years with the treatment solution maintained at 60°C in order to achieve sufficient impregnation.

The wood scientists recommended that the big medieval sailing vessel, the *Bremen Cog* – 23 m long, 7 m wide, and 7 m from the keel to the capstan on the castle deck – 40 tonnes of oak wood salvaged in 2,000 pieces, be rebuilt from its waterlogged timbers before conservation. They feared that the planks might lose their flexibility when the PEG solidified in them. They also feared that the planks sawn from trees with heavy branches, resulting in a very irregular grain, might have growth stresses which would be released in the hot bath and the planks would warp and split. In both cases it would become difficult, or impossible, to rebuild the ship from the conserved timbers. So the *Cog* was rebuilt in an atmosphere of constant spray mist, being incessantly sprayed with water. When I joined the project the reconstruction of the *Cog* was still going on. With a novel approach to displaying a ship in a museum in mind, shipwrights reassembled the *Cog* and suspended it from the ceiling, with steel rods fastened to many points of the hull, to take its weight, but allowing the keel to rest on the floor. No outer supports would interfere with the view of the magnificent hull.

More experiments with waterlogged wood

While waiting for the ship to be finished and a conservation tank to be constructed around it, I set up a pilot scale conservation experiment with wooden objects of three different species, a small figurehead from elm wood, a thick wooden buoy from pine, and a floor timber from a small ship of oak. I wanted to see how fast the impregnation would be, and whether there would be any differences between the wood species. My main attention was on oak, as nearly all of the *Cog*'s timbers were made of oak.

The tank for the *Cog* was ready, the ship sat in it submerged in water, and we had funds to add 40 tonnes of PEG a year. I changed the scheme from the suggested PEG 1000 to PEG 1500 on the advice of Kirsten Jespersen, who was now head of the waterlogged wood conservation unit in Copenhagen. She said from her vast experience that PEG 1000 was too hygroscopic and that wood treated with it would never dry. I was told that PEG 1500 was a brand which had often been used by conservators, with satisfying results.

The pilot scale conservation treatment with the three woods – elm, pine, and oak – lasted for five years. I had allowed a long time in order to get meaningful results. To track the impregnation of the woods with PEG, core samples were extracted from the timbers with a 5 mm

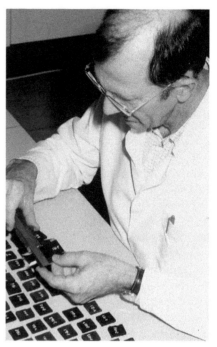

Test series for the stabilisation of waterlogged wood. Photograph: Gabriele Hoffmann

incremental drill, and analysed for PEG with a simple print-off method. The wood cores were pressed onto a moist filter paper, and removed again. The filter paper was then sprayed with a reagent solution, and a colour reaction indicated where PEG had been transferred from the wood core onto the filter paper, i.e. where the wood core contained PEG. In the elm wood figurehead, PEG was found throughout. Similarly the 30 cm diameter pine wood buoy also showed that PEG had impregnated the entire object. But in the oak wood floor timber PEG had only impregnated a few millimetres in five years. So, the evaluation of the pilot scale experiment was therefore most revealing. Even after 30 years the wood could not be fully impregnated. I had to draw up a new conservation plan for the *Cog*.

Systematic laboratory experiments into the relationships between molecular weights i.e. molecular sizes, stabilisation potential, hygroscopicity of treated wood, and the state of degradation of waterlogged wood yielded new and helpful facts.

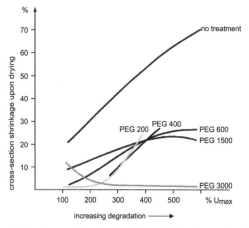

Stabilisations achieved with different PEGs in woods of increasing degradation. Illustration: Reinhold Breden, DSM

The obvious idea of treating a degraded wooden structure with larger molecules, and less degraded wood with smaller molecules which would penetrate the wood structure more easily was verified. Stabilisation experiments on eleven waterlogged oak woods of different degrees of degradation with PEGs of molecular weights 200, 400, 600, 1500, and 3000 gave clear results: slightly degraded woods were only well stabilised with low molecular weight PEG 200 or 400. Heavily degraded wood was best stabilised with high molecular weight PEG 3000. Surprisingly, the PEGs with medium molecular weights, PEGs 600 and 1500, did not stabilise any wood very well. No one PEG could stabilise both the slightly degraded and the heavily degraded oak wood. The efficiency of low molecular weight PEG ceases when the degradation of the oak wood has reached a level where the maximum water content u_{max} is about 240% of the dry weight. At the same time this is the state of degradation where the stabilising effect of high molecular weight PEG begins.

With the degradation patterns of waterlogged wood in mind, as described in Section 2.2, the experimental results are easily explained. In only slightly degraded wood most cell walls are intact, and only small PEG molecules can penetrate into them, replacing some of the water in the fibrillar structure. When the wood dries, the PEG remains and thus keeps the cell wall, and the whole wooden object, in a permanently swollen state. The dimensions and the shape of the wet timber are therefore stabilised. From a certain state in the degradation process onwards, degraded and dissolved cell walls begin to predominate in the wood. Here only high molecular weight PEG is efficient, which settles to form a solid interior skeleton in the delicate structure of middle lamellae and cell wall debris. The solid PEG fills and consolidates the tissue and stabilises the degraded wood against collapse on drying. From the experimental results, it is obvious that in the pilot scale experiment the oak wood timber, which was very little degraded throughout, could only have been impregnated with a low molecular weight PEG, PEG 200 or 400.

Low and high molecular weight PEGs not only stabilise different structures in degraded wood, they also do it in different ways.

A two-step treatment for two-quality timbers

The fact that waterlogged archaeological wood in most cases consists of two distinct qualities – parts with degraded cell walls and other parts with non-degraded cell walls, be it in separate areas or in a mosaic-like distribution within a timber – calls for such timbers to be stabilised with two PEG qualities for a good result. Numerous series of experiments with two-quality woods – oak and four different softwoods – helped to establish the optimal treatment parameters for stabilisation using two PEGs, and to see what results could be obtained. At the same time the hygroscopicity of the PEG-treated wood was investigated: impregnated with the different PEGs, how would it respond to fluctuations in the humidity of the air? Is it safe to use low molecular weight PEG? This was thought to take up too much moisture and make the wood wet. Conservators were sceptical about a successful outcome.

In attempting to find the smallest PEG molecule which could be used to infiltrate non-degraded cell walls, stabilisation experiments were made with the oligomers of the PEG homologues, mono-, di-, tri-, and tetra-ethylene glycol, the shortest chain molecules of the PEG family. The stabilisation was excellent, as expected, but it does not last where the mono-, di-, and trimers have been used: these oligomers evaporate with time, and the cell walls shrink accordingly. The tetramer, which is the main component of the commercial product PEG 200, is the lowest homologue to permanently remain in impregnated cell walls. It is the best option for the treatment of only slightly degraded wood. PEG 3000 is the lowest homologue which is solid and has excellent stabilising properties for degraded wood, while still having a low hygroscopicity. PEG 2000 is too close to PEG 1500 with its sub-optimal stabilisation properties. With PEGs 200 and 3000, either using one alone or the two in combination, woods of all qualities and in all states of degradation can be stabilised. Where the one PEG does not work, the other will.

A disappointment was that the two PEGs cannot be applied to the wood in one mixed solution. Impregnated wood will be excellently stabilised, but it never dries. It stays damp and sticky. Any mixture of low and high molecular weight PEGs forms a hygroscopic paste. It does not solidify, and transfers its stickiness to the wood which has been filled with it. Two-quality wood has to be stabilised in two consecutive impregnation treatments.

In a first bath PEG 200 diffuses into the cell walls of the non-degraded interior parts of the wood. In a second bath PEG 3000 diffuses into the degraded and more permeable outer parts of the wood. At the same time, in this second bath excess PEG 200 diffuses out of the degraded parts of the wood and from cell lumina in the interior parts. It remains in the cell walls of the non-degraded interior, held back by physical forces. This theoretical assumption, backed up by the very good stabilisation results obtained with the two-step method, was verified by a quantitative and locally differentiating simultaneous analysis of both PEGs.

The stabilisation end result of a treatment depends on the amount of PEG incorporated into the wood. This amount is regulated by the PEG concentration of the treatment solution, provided the wood is kept in the impregnation bath until the water in the wood has attained the same PEG concentration as the impregnation solution. Repeated series of experiments established the optimal conditions for a two-step treatment. For best dimensional stabilisation the concentration of PEG 200 in the first bath has to be about 50% for oak wood, and only about 20% for softwoods. In the second bath with PEG 3000 the optimal concentration is about 70% for oak, and about 50% for softwoods. Both PEGs applied in optimal concentrations stabilise the respective wood qualities to the same high degree. In the experiments, the shrinkage on drying was reduced to less than 2% on a cross-section. Without a treatment the same slightly degraded oak wood shrank about 20%, and the heavily degraded oak wood about 66%. Several waterlogged softwoods were also stabilised to the low level of only 2% or less residual shrinkage of a cross-section. The fact that both wood qualities are stabilised to the same degree means that treated timbers which contain both degraded and non-degraded parts will not warp and crack on drying.

The low optimal concentration values for PEG 3000 were a pleasant surprise. Evidently, it is not necessary to carry on the impregnation to a final bath concentration of 100%, that is, to a hot melt of PEG 3000, as was the traditional practice with smaller objects. The treatment with a solution of 70 or 50% PEG leads to a final equilibrium where the water in the wood also contains about 70 or 50% PEG. The void system in the wood still contains 30 or 50% water. When the wood dries, this water evaporates and is replaced by air. The PEG-treated wood is then full of minute air bubbles, and incident light is reflected at the air–PEG and air–wood substance interfaces.

This gives a natural and dry look to the wood, although it contains a lot of PEG. It does not look like a dark piece of wax with a wood structure, as is the case with 100% PEG-filled archaeological wood.

A second advantage of the low optimal concentrations of PEG 3000 is that these solutions need not be heated to a very high temperature to stay liquid enough for an efficient diffusion of PEG into the wood. 40–60°C is sufficient, compared to 70–80°C needed to keep PEG 3000 molten. The PEG suffers no thermal degradation at these temperatures and can be re-used for another treatment. Reduced heating over a long time negates the need for an expensive high performance heating system, and saves on energy costs.

Hygroscopicity

Low molecular weight PEG 200 is more hygroscopic – absorbs more water from the atmosphere – than PEG 3000, and it transfers the hygroscopicity to wood impregnated with it. The sorption characteristics of wood impregnated with a 50% PEG 200 solution are very similar to those of pure PEG 200. The wood is more hygroscopic than before the treatment, and will take up water even at slightly increased RH. It will become damp and wet at relative humidities above 75–80% RH. The same wood impregnated with 70% PEG 3000 solution has become less hygroscopic than the wood itself, according to the low hygroscopicity of PEG 3000. When the wood has passed a two-step impregnation with PEG 200 followed by PEG 3000, its hygroscopicity is very much like that of the wood which has only been treated with PEG 3000. The surplus PEG 200 has obviously completely diffused out of the degraded wood tissue, which is now filled with PEG 3000 alone. The wood has attained a stable state, and its hygroscopicity is quite low at an RH below 80–85%. It does not differ in appearance or touch from wood treated only with PEG 3000. These findings from laboratory investigations have since been confirmed on a large scale. None of the ships I have treated in a two-step impregnation has shown hygroscopicity problems as long as they have remained in a normal museum climate.

A novel conservation plan for the Bremen Cog

Based on the results of the laboratory experiments, a new conservation plan for the *Bremen Cog* was developed. As all timbers of the *Cog* – keel, ribs, bow and sternpost, planks – contained both degraded and non-degraded wood, a two-step method would be the only way to a achieve a satisfactory stabilisation of the ship's timbers. A plan was drawn up: in a first tank, PEG 200 would be used, and then a second immersion would follow in a solution of PEG 3000. The concentrations would be 50 and 70% respectively; the first tank would not be heated, the second would need to be heated to between 40 and 60°C. The duration of the process was unknown, but would be determined by monitoring the progress of the impregnation with each PEG, with a method yet to be developed. The process was expected to be completed in much less than 30 years. In 1985 the directors and the board of the Deutsches Schiffahrtsmuseum invited world-leading conservators of waterlogged wood to a symposium in Bremerhaven: Kirsten Jespersen from the National Museum of Denmark; Lars Barkman, chief conservator of the *Vasa* project in Stockholm; David Grattan from the Canadian Conservation

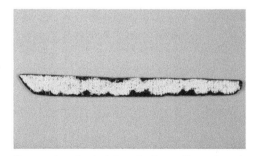

Cross-section of a plank from the *Bremen Cog*: an irregular layer of heavily degraded wood (dark) envelops the lesser degraded interior wood (painted white). Photograph: Egbert Laska, DSM

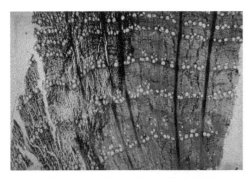

Cross-section of a plank from a *Roman ship* from Mainz on the Rhine: degraded surface wood on the lefthand side, non-degraded interior on the righthand side. Micrograph: Per Hoffmann

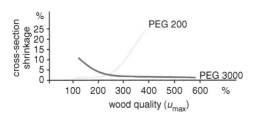

The basis for the two-step PEG-treatment: low shrinkage with PEG 200 in woods with u_{max} up to about 240%; low shrinkage with PEG 3000 in woods with higher u_{max}. Illustration: Reinhold Breden, DSM

Institute in Ottawa; Detlef Noack, my professor from the Federal Research Centre in Hamburg, who had suggested the treatment with PEG 1000; and Kurt Schietzel, director of the Archaeological Museum and Workshops of Schleswig-Holstein and excavator of the Viking ship from Haithabu. The experts examined the experimental results, the concept of the novel two-step stabilisation for two-quality wood, and the new conservation plan. They agreed, and recommended that we change to the new plan.

4.2 Scaling up – ships in tanks

Scaling up from the conservation of small objects to the conservation of a ship or boat changes the process from a small and conveniently manageable occupation to a technical and engineering *tour de force*. Many practical aspects of the procedures gain in importance and need to be considered well in advance.

The workshop

The workshop must not only be able to accommodate the impregnation tank or tanks, but there must also be enough space either for a crane or fork lift truck to lift the ship into the tank, or to build the tank around the ship, as was the case with the *Bremen Cog*. The tank must be accessible from all sides, and the staff must be able to go round it freely. Besides a water supply there should be a spillage gully in the floor –this is often not the case in spaces available to conservation projects. A high-voltage electricity supply will be needed for heavy-duty pumps and heating. Central heating would be an asset, as the system can be used for a simple and effective heating of the tank.

If the workshop has to be rented, the option must be for a period exceeding the estimated duration of the project by several years. This agreement has to be written down. The success of the project will be at risk if the impregnation has to be aborted prematurely.

The tank

The impregnation tank should be tailored to neatly accommodate the ship and, where applicable, the cradle holding the ship. Any dead volume will have to be filled with costly treatment solution. To reduce the dead volume, displacement objects can be placed in the tank: bricks, or containers filled with gravel and water or with gravel and brine – as items filled with water alone will float in concentrated PEG solutions. There are many possibilities. But displacement bodies, too, cost money, and it is advisable to do a calculation in order to find the most economical solution. If it is going to be a huge tank it may be wise to check if the floor of the building is strong enough for the weight of the tank and contents.

Care must be taken to have the tank outlet valve mounted absolutely flush with the

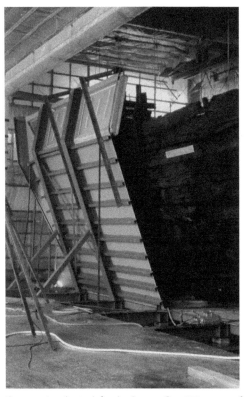

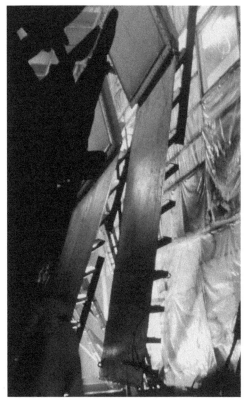

Constructing the tank for the *Bremen Cog*: 110 tonnes of steel, 37 tonnes of stainless steel – a volume of 800 m³. Photograph: Egbert Laska, DSM

Pre-fabricated elements were assembled on site. Photograph: Egbert Laska, DSM

bottom of the tank, or even better, in the base itself. The tank will probably have to be emptied completely several times during the project.

Various materials can be used for fabricating an impregnation tank: mild steel painted with a PEG-resistant polyester or epoxy resin, stainless steel, wood lined with polythene sheeting or laminated with polyester resin, brick or concrete or adobe bricks combined with a heavy-duty lining. Even a hole in the ground lined with a plastic liner as used for garden ponds can do as a tank. The large *Poole logboat* in England was impregnated with a sucrose solution in the tank from a petrol road tanker.

In a steel tank it is a good idea to have eyes welded to the inner walls in different places, which can be used when it becomes necessary

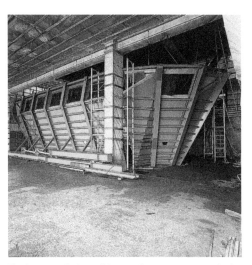

The laminated glass of the windows was 11.5 cm thick to withstand the hydrostatic pressure of the PEG solution. Photograph: Per Hoffmann

to tie down the ship, or parts of it, to stop it floating. An arrangement inside the tank will not interfere with a tight-fitting cover or lid on the tank. Working in the tank is greatly facilitated if the inside of the tank is lined or painted in a light colour. This enables operators to see if fastening straps or constructions to hold down timbers have loosened and started to float, to find and recover tools dropped into the tank, etc., and to pass belts under the ship to lift it.

Where the conservation process includes an impregnation with high molecular PEG at an elevated temperature, the tank needs to have very efficient insulation. Heating a considerable volume of liquid over months and years is really expensive, and any effort to reduce heat losses will save more money than it costs. It is easily forgotten to insulate the bottom of the tank and to make the lids on the tank close tightly. Even if it produces more possibilities for heat leaks, it is important that the lids are made in segments small enough to be lifted off by two people. Conservators in Yverdon, Switzerland insulated the surface of their tank, where the top of the cradle stuck out from the solution, by using two layers of polypropylene balls 40–50 mm in diameter. When pushed aside, they allowed the evaporation of water in a controlled manner.

Heating

Direct heating of a PEG solution with electric elements is not the best choice. The temperature of the elements must be quite high to have an effect on the big volume, and the PEG in contact with them is overheated and can degrade with time. More effective, and safer, is external heating of water, which is then circulated through pipes or heat-resistant tubes – for example polyurethane tubes or hoses – laid out on the bottom of the tank. An elegant solution is to connect a circuit of tubes to an existing central heating system. The boiler of such a system will in many cases be strong enough to deliver the additional heat. The temperature of the bath is easily regulated

with a valve in the circuit to accommodate the water flow, and the temperature of the circulating water can be set at the boiler. No pump is needed in the bath; if ample heating tubes are laid out, convection will produce an even temperature distribution, with differences in the range of 5°C at the most. The tubes can be led into the tank over the rim and penetrations of the tank walls, possible sources of leaks, are thus avoided and any maintenance or replacement is easy. The most important decision, in my eyes, is to be sure to overestimate the size of the heating system. An external water heating system, heated with gas, oil, or electricity, is often calculated to perform under ideal conditions and to come on and off periodically. However in reality the insulation of the tank is often less efficient, the flow velocity of heated water through the tubes is lower than expected, and the water heater itself becomes less efficient with time, or breaks down if it is permanently run at full capacity. If this happens, then the temperature in the bath cannot be kept high enough, and a concentrated solution of PEG 3000 becomes too viscous and may even solidify. It takes a long time to melt the solution again, and that will require more heating. It is much safer to run an oversized system at half power.

Filling the tank

When the ship is well secured and all its parts and timbers are prevented from floating, the tank can be filled. The sequence is important: first put in the wood, secure it against floating, then fill with water. If heavy timbers, or a whole boat or ship, start to float it is all but impossible to press them down under the water again. Also, before the tank is flooded, it is the last chance to position a series of markers – pins and target points – and take measurements across them so that shrinkage or swelling during the treatment and drying processes can be observed. These markers must be fixed firmly so they will not be worn off, displaced, or removed by chance or carelessness. They must also be PEG and heat resistant, and remain visible even after several years. The conservator needs to be able to document the success of the treatment exactly through these measurements.

Should the ship, for some reason, remain in pure water for a while, then a biocide must be added right from the beginning to prevent the growth of algae, moulds, yeasts, fungi and bacteria, all brought in with the wood. Otherwise, after some time dead microorganisms will cover the wood surfaces with a greyish layer, and impede the impregnation. Quaternary ammonium salt biocides are suitable as they effectively react with the organisms which are thereby destroyed. With time the biocides disappear from the water, which then can be dumped as waste water without a problem. The infection of the solution with microbes from the air can be reduced by a floating plastic lid which is drawn up over the rim of the tank. The plastic should be black as the absence of light reduces or inhibits the growth of algae in the water. Other conservators reported good results using ultraviolet cells or copper/silver ion technology to control biological activity in treatment tanks.

The danger of osmotic shock

The concentration of PEG in the treatment solution has to start at a low value, and then be increased in several steps over time to reach the final optimal value. The reason for working this way is to avoid the danger of a damaging osmotic pressure building up in the wood, known as osmotic shock.

The substitution of PEG for water in the wood can only take place by gradual diffusion. The waterlogged wood is already filled with water, and no flow of solution into the wood is possible. PEG molecules must diffuse from the solution into the water in the wood. Compared to water, the PEG molecules are very large and their diffusion very slow. PEG diffuses into the wood at the same time as water molecules diffuse out. Due to their small size the water molecules move out much faster than the PEG molecules move in. The

result is an osmotic effect, a reduced pressure inside the wood, which leads to shrinkage and even collapse in the wood while it is still submerged. To avoid excessive osmotic forces developing during impregnation, the concentration gradient of PEG from the bath to the interior of the wood must be kept gradual. The idea is to increase the bath concentration only at the same rate as PEG diffuses into the wood. As a consequence, impregnation treatments must be planned to take many months or even years.

Preparing PEG solutions

An impregnation with PEG 200 can start with a solution of 20% concentration. As PEG 200 is a liquid, it is easy to prepare the solution. The PEG 200, usually supplied in drums, can be pumped directly into the calculated amount of water in the treatment tank. The specific gravity of PEG 200 is 1.12 g/cm^3 at 25°C, and all concentrations are usually given as percentage by weight. All calculations are made in masses, and not in volumes.

Pure PEG because of its specific gravity will settle at the bottom of the solution, and it must therefore be mixed into the water, for example by pumping the solution from the bottom to the surface for a while. Once an even concentration is established in the tank, no further stirring is necessary to maintain it. The concentration of the solution can be determined with a refractometer and a calibration curve prepared beforehand. Hand-held refractometers are practical and accurate enough for this purpose (see the two photographs overleaf).

The preparation of large amounts of a solution of high molecular weight PEG needs more effort, and takes some time. Solid PEG can be in the form of flakes or powder, and it has to be dissolved in a vat or container outside the tank. The dissolution is slow and needs thorough stirring. The process consumes energy: if the solution cools down, the dissolution slows down. Heating the container enhances the dissolution and hot water should be used. Always add PEG to the hot water – if the water

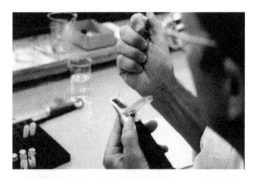

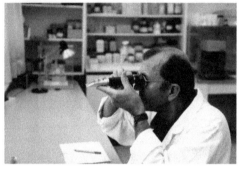

The concentration of one-component PEG solutions is easily measured with a hand-held refractometer. Photographs: Gabriele Hoffmann

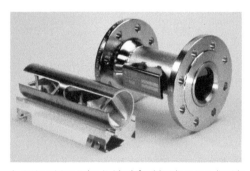

A static mixing tube is ideal for blending two liquids. Photograph: Sulzer Chemtech

is poured onto a pile of PEG, the surface layer will hydrate and form a gel which seals off the rest of the PEG. Stirring will then produce lumps of gel-encapsulated PEG which take a very long time to dissolve.

An elegant method to prepare a solution of high molecular weight PEG is to arrange with the supplier to have it delivered in the desired concentration, or as a hot melt at about 100°C

directly from the production line. In a heated road tanker the temperature of the melt will still be 80–90°C after 12 hours driving. The hot melt and water can be fed simultaneously through a so-called static mixer, a short tube with a series of interior whirl-producing obstacles, and a perfectly uniform solution can be pumped into the treatment tank. The size of batches to be delivered must be negotiated with the producers. In my experience this is the easiest way to prepare larger quantities of solutions of high molecular weight PEG.

The impregnation of heavily degraded wood, or wood that is predominantly heavily degraded, with only high molecular weight PEG 3000, can begin with a 20% concentration. The degraded wood tissue will be so highly permeable that the large PEG molecules can move quite easily through it, and no dangerous osmotic pressure will build up at this concentration gradient.

Monitoring the impregnation

It is not easy to predict the time necessary to impregnate archaeological wood of more than a few centimetres in thickness. The wood species, the state of degradation, possible sediment matter in the wood pores, and other factors play a role. In timbers thicker than about 3 cm the only safe way is to monitor the impregnation process – to determine at regular intervals the quantitative distribution of PEG in the wood.

Two methods have been successfully used which require only very small wood samples, and both build on the analysis of extracts from small wood samples taken at increasing distances from the timber surface. With an incremental drill, as used in forestry, a thin 5 mm diameter wood core going through the timber from surface to surface is taken and divided into 1 cm increments. Specimens, from which cores can be taken, could include loose timbers from the ship, or broken-off pieces from timbers, if they have the thickness and state of degradation representative of the ships timbers. A set of three to four specimens is ideal. For repeated sampling over time, the specimens must be placed in the tank in a net, or

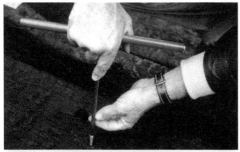

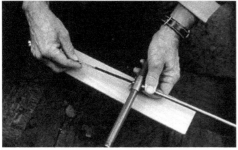

Extracting a wood core with an increment borer used in forestry. Photographs: Gabriele Hoffmann

bound to a line so that they can be taken out when needed.

Trying to take a core from a submerged timber cannot produce a useful sample. Alternatively, a part of the solution can be pumped off into a separate tank or vat until the top of the ship breaks surface and can be sampled before refilling the tank. The cores are subdivided into incremental sub-samples, each of which is cut to shavings and extracted with a minimum of water. The extracts are then analysed either semi-quantitatively with thin-layer chromatography (TLC), or more exactly with high-performance liquid chromatography (HPLC). The values obtained from the consecutive increments set in a line will give a PEG profile through the wood. The PEG in the increments can be calculated as mass per increment, as a percentage based on dry wood, or as a percentage based on the PEG–water solution in the increment. The latter expression allows a direct comparison of the PEG concentration in the water in the wood with the PEG concentration in the treatment bath.

Monitoring the impregnation twice a year will be appropriate. Each time the core samples must be taken from the same set of timbers. The bore holes should be closed with wooden plugs before the timbers are re-immersed, so that the impregnation process is not biased by the opening of new entrances for the treatment solution. The PEG analysis using HPLC is best arranged in cooperation with a chemical laboratory. The equipment is expensive, to operate it requires practice, and experience is indispensable for the interpretation of chromatograms. Only in big conservation projects is it advisable to install this facility within the project, where a larger number of samples need to be taken and analysed regularly.

New methods for the analysis of PEG in wood have recently appeared – namely attenuated total reflectance Fourier transform infrared (ATR-FTIR) spectroscopy for quantification, and matrix assisted laser desorption/ionisation time of flight (MALDI-TOF) mass spectroscopy for the determination of the relative amounts of different PEGs in the wood. It remains to be seen if this method has the potential to become a routine method in the conservation of waterlogged timbers.

When the water in the wood has reached the same PEG concentration as the impregnation solution, it is time for an upgrading of the treatment bath.

Raising the PEG concentration

The concentration of a PEG solution in a treatment tank can be raised in several ways. Some of the old solution can be pumped off and be replaced by pure PEG. This results in some PEG being lost in the removed solution. Another way is to evaporate water from the tank and add PEG to the old solution. No PEG is wasted, and a minimum of new PEG is required. Evaporation, however, has its costs. A cold solution of PEG 200 has to be passed through some sort of evaporation unit. The principle of saltworks can be applied: the solution is trickled over stacks of brushwood, gratings, or screens, while a stream of air is passed through. Manufacturers of climate control

Box 10

Quantitative determination of the impregnation of PEGs in wood

My approach to monitoring the progress of an impregnation is to repeatedly compare the PEG concentration in the water in the wood to the PEG concentration in the impregnation solution. Once or twice a year concentration profiles through some of the thickest representative timbers are established. When the water in the wood has obtained the same PEG concentration as the treatment solution throughout the timber, the impregnation has come to an end.

The procedure is as follows:

1　**Extract a wood core of 5–10 mm diameter, and divide it into a series of increments 10–15 mm long. Immediate weighing gives the *wet weight* of each increment.**
2　**Cut each increment into fine shavings, place them in a small vial, cover them with an exactly measured minimal amount of water, and extract the PEG over 5 days at 60°C. Weighing the extracted and oven-dried shavings gives the *dry weight* of the increment.**
3　**The *dry weight* subtracted from the *wet weight* gives the amount of *water in the increment*.**
4　**The determination of the amount of PEG in the extract, or of each PEG if two are present, gives the amount of PEG in the increment. Chromatographic methods are well suited for this determination. The extract is the amount of water added to the shavings plus the *water in the increment*.**
5　**Calculate the concentration of the PEG in the *water in the increment*, that is, all PEG dissolved in the *water in the increment* only.**
6　**Compile the results for all increments in a concentration profile through the timber, and compare it to the concentration of the impregnation solution.**

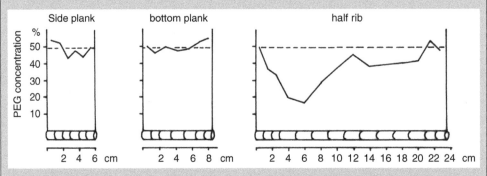

Concentration profiles for PEG 200 in the water in three timbers of the *ship from the Teufelsmoor* at the end of the spraying treatment. Illustration: Reinhold Breden, DSM

equipment produce these types of evaporating units, known as air humidifiers. Water will evaporate directly from the hot solution in the tank, and the evaporation rate can be increased with a fan blowing air over the surface. In this case the process is very simple, but the heating system has to provide the additional evaporation energy.

Pure PEG 200 can be added directly to the tank, and the new solution is then mixed thoroughly by being pumped through a circuit. Solid PEG 3000 flakes or powder have to be dissolved in the old solution in an external tank or container. Intensive stirring is necessary, but nevertheless it is a slow process, especially at higher concentrations. Again, it is an option to get molten PEG delivered and to mix it into the old solution as described above. Colleagues at the Archaeological Conservation Workshop in Schleswig, Germany, float sacks of PEG flakes, perforated by ample stabbing with a knife, on the hot solution in the tank. With time the flakes melt and dissolve and the concentrated solution seeps out of the sacks and disperses into the old solution.

An ideal PEG impregnation would be a process in which the optimal concentration gradient from bath to wood is maintained as the driver of the diffusion. This would mean starting with as high as possible a bath concentration without risking a collapse in the wood due to osmotic pressure, and then raising the bath concentration continuously at the same rate as the PEG concentration in the water in the wood rises. For practical reasons such a process is often difficult to establish. Continuous monitoring of the increase in PEG content in the wood is time consuming, as is the continuous adjustment of the bath concentration. A stepwise increase of concentration is more feasible.

A treatment solution of PEG 200 can be increased in 20% concentration steps without the danger of too much shrinkage of non-degraded cell walls by osmosis. Treatment solutions of PEG 3000 can also be increased in 15–20% steps. If the degraded wood is thick, more than 4 cm perhaps, the lower value is recommended. When the PEG 3000 treatment is following a first impregnation with PEG 200, then the initial concentration of the solution should be at least the same as the final PEG 200 concentration. However, it can easily be 10–15% higher to keep the diffusion of the different substances going. Water and PEG 200 will diffuse out of degraded tissue, and PEG 3000 will diffuse into it. In non-degraded cells and tissue, PEG 200 and water will remain in the cell walls, held back by physical and chemical forces. A further increase of the bath concentration can take place following the results of the monitoring analyses of PEG in the wood.

Box 11

Mixing a treatment solution to a target concentration

A simple way to calculate how to mix a solution to a given target concentration is to use the Rule of Mixtures. The Rule of Mixtures is a method to find the amounts – from two solutions of known concentration – necessary to mix a new solution of a certain target concentration.

The Rule of Mixtures only functions with masses. If volumes are required, then the masses must be converted to volumes with the help of the density:

volume (ml) = mass (g) / density (g/cm³).

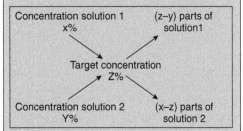

Rule of mixtures

Mixing liquids

Solutions of known concentrations are written on the lefthand side of the cross (see figure), the one with the higher concentration being on top (X%). The target concentration is written in the middle of the cross. The difference between the values at the top left (X%) and middle (Z%) is given at the bottom right. The difference between the values of concentration Y% shown at the bottom left and that of the target solution Z% in the middle is given at top right. Negative signs are omitted. The resulting values on the right are the parts by weight of solution 1 (top) and solution 2 (bottom) that are necessary to mix a solution of the target concentration.

The end of the PEG treatment has arrived when the concentration of PEG in the water in the wood has reached equilibrium with the final bath concentration, or when no further impregnation can be detected in consecutive analyses.

Disposal of spent PEG solutions

The disposal of spent PEG solutions must be planned years in advance. PEG is neither toxic nor noxious in the waste water system or in the sewage treatment plant – it completely biodegrades into harmless substances. However, the authorities do not believe it; they have ethylene glycol in their list of substances not allowed in effluent. In most cases, the administration responsible for giving a permit to dump industrial effluents does not believe that polyethylene glycols are different from ethylene glycol, and that they have different properties. It may be a long process to provide expert opinions and certificates about the harmless nature of PEG solutions, but this procedure can be worth following through. I tried it successfully during the course of the *Bremen Cog* project – it took five years. The alternative was to have 800 tonnes of spent solution disposed of as hazardous waste, and that would have been really expensive.

Ships from oak wood and ships from softwoods

Shipwrights and boat builders in northern and western Europe have for thousands of years preferred oak wood (European white oak, *Quercus robur* L.). The trees grow to large dimensions; some develop curved heavy branches good for ribs and knees, straight stems can be cleft to thin planks, the wood is hard and strong, it is extremely impermeable to water – timbers submerged for centuries may still be dry inside – and it is relatively resistant to biological degradation. Most archaeological ship finds in northern Europe are of oak, and quite naturally most research into waterlogged wood and its conservation deals with oak wood.

However, in other parts of the world there are also ships built from softwoods, from pine species (*Pinus* sp.), fir (*Abies* sp.), spruce (*Picea* sp.), cedar (*Cedrus* sp.), and American and Asian softwoods. Research done on four Chinese and Korean softwoods has shown that waterlogged softwoods need less PEG for optimal stabilisation than oak wood. A 20% PEG 200 solution is sufficient to treat little degraded softwood, and a 50% PEG 3000 solution sufficient for highly degraded softwood. For the conservator this has pleasant consequences. The expenses for PEG are reduced. A 50% solution of high molecular weight PEG need not be heated, it is liquid at ambient temperature. This not only saves money on heating a treatment tank over long periods of time, but also the tank itself can be much cheaper. No heating installation and no insulation is necessary. The solution can even be sprayed. It also takes less time for the wood to reach equilibrium with a solution of 20% PEG 200 than with one of 50%. Similarly a 50% solution of PEG 3000 also takes less time for the wood to reach equilibrium than a 70% solution. A conservation project for a ship built of softwood timbers is simpler, cheaper, and takes less time than a comparable project for an oak-built ship.

4.3 One-step or two-step – the range of tank treatments

With PEG as a stabilising agent treatment schemes can be designed for any ship find. The state of degradation of the wood, i.e. minor degradation, heavy degradation, or somewhere in between, dictates whether a one-step or two-step treatment will produce the desired stabilisation. If the wood is predominantly only slightly degraded, or hardly degraded at all, then an impregnation with low molecular PEG alone is adequate. A thin layer a few millimetres thick of degraded wood surface can be tolerated, it will come out looking natural, dry, and velvet-like to the touch. Longitudinal surface cracks may open, but they will not be deeper than the thickness of the degraded layer. If the wood is predominantly heavily degraded and more than 60–70% of the cross-section of the timbers consist of degraded tissue, then a treatment with high molecular weight PEG will stabilise the main body of the timbers sufficiently to counteract any collapse or warping tendencies in the areas of less degraded interior tissue. For all multi-quality timbers a two-step treatment is a safe way to an optimal stabilisation. A series of case studies detailed in the following pages demonstrates the range of PEG tank treatments which have been applied to ships, how the treatments were performed, and their results.

One-step low molecular weight PEG impregnation

A tank treatment with PEG 200 is a relatively simple affair. Its advantage is that it needs very little attention. Once installed, the boat or ship can be left alone for long periods of time. For a large and very heavy *logboat from the river Leine*, Germany, dated to the 10th century, a tank treatment was convenient. The hull of the boat was not very degraded and up to 15 cm thick. There was only a thin layer of degraded wood on the surface. Our museum had enough space in a workshop for a tank to be built to fit the boat of length 6.50 m and diameter 1.50 m, and our technical staff built a tank of wooden planking held by a steel framework and lined with white fibreglass–polyester laminate. The only control and maintenance necessary during the impregnation was to replace evaporated water twice a year to maintain the volume. The very small staff at the Deutsches Schiffahrtsmuseum could concentrate on the *Bremen Cog* project and on the conservation of two other medieval ships taking place at the same time.

After six years, a PEG analysis of the wood showed that the impregnation was finished, and the boat was brought to the museum to dry. It has attained a light brown colour, and the surface feels smooth and soft. After years of drying, no cracks or splits have developed. Markers to monitor possible shrinkage on drying got lost due to the frequent moving of

the heavy hull within the museum. So, regrettably, nothing can be said about a residual tangential shrinkage of the hull. The appearance of the huge heavy-duty log boat, however, is very agreeable.

One-step high molecular weight PEG impregnation

The *boats from Pommeroeul* in Belgium are perhaps the most prominent examples of total impregnation with high molecular weight PEG. The two boats come from the Gallo-Roman period; one is a log boat of 9.70 m preserved length, and the other a part of a broad barge of 12.70 m preserved length. The boats consisted of quite degraded oak wood with a water content between 380 and 480%. Conservator Alfred Terfve treated them with PEG 4000. The impregnation started with a 10% solution in an epoxy-painted mild steel tank heated to 60°C, and the concentration was increased continuously to 95% over 24 months. This final concentration was kept for a further 4 months. The increase in concentration was achieved by adding a commercial standard solution of 55% and evaporating water from the bath surface. After a thorough and laborious cleaning, the impregnated wood looks medium brown and dry. The stabilisation of the heavily degraded wood is good, and today the boats are on exhibition in the purpose-built museum at Ath in Belgium.

The Gallo-Roman *Barge II from Yverdon-les-Bains* in Switzerland (see photograph overleaf) dated to about AD 400, is the first ship conserved with PEG 4000 in a non-total impregnation. The barge is about 10 m long and 1.50 m wide. The thin oak planks – only 2 to 3 cm thick – were heavily degraded, their water content was about 380%. Based on a discussion of the new conservation plan for the *Bremen Cog*, the archaeologist Gilbert Kaenel, director of the Musée Cantonal d'Archéologie et d'Histoire in Lausanne, and his colleagues decided on a treatment with PEG 4000 in a solution of only 80% maximum, at 60°C. The concentration

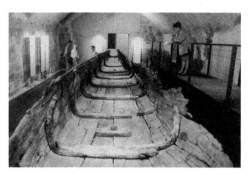

The *Barge II from Yverdon-les-Bains* in Switzerland was only treated with PEG 3000. Photograph: Musée Cantonal d'Archéologie et d'Histoire, Lausanne

was increased continuously over 21 months, and kept at 80% for another two months. After patient cleaning with sponge and scalpel, the wood attained a natural brown colour, instead of dark or even black, as feared. Residual shrinkages after drying, measured in separate specimens, were 2% in the radial and 4.5% in the tangential direction, compared to 13% and 48% respectively for untreated wood. In the boat itself no shrinkage could be detected.

A part of a medieval hull, found in the *Teerhof* construction site in Bremen, was conserved in the cheapest possible way, accepting a probable second-rate result. The state archaeologist Dieter Bischop was not able to keep the 3 × 6 m part of a clinker-built ship's side in the state museum, and offered it to the owner of the site, a ship owner who was erecting a new office building, to hang on the wall as a decoration. In this way the ship find could be saved. He also offered to conserve the ship's side if the ship owner would pay for it, and then asked me for a conservation plan and for practical advice and help. The calculated costs for a proper hot PEG 3000 treatment of the degraded timbers were too high, however, so the archaeologist asked for a cheaper solution. I suggested an unheated impregnation with PEG 2000. But as this product was not available, I accepted a batch of PEG 1500 for a special low price. The unheated solution would not contain enough PEG for a good stabilisation, and PEG 1500 was not optimal, but

an inferior result would not matter very much. The clinker-laid planks could be fastened onto a metal grid in a close arrangement any which way, as there were no ribs found which would dictate the correct original spacing of the planks. 20 months impregnation in a scrap lorry back followed: 6 months at 23% and 14 months at 55%. The planks were cleaned, dried for some months, and mounted in the lobby of the building – the shipping company's new headquarters. The sight of the somewhat strange object suspended over black leather sofas is satisfying – no transverse cracks and no warping in the thin planks have developed. Money was only spent on PEG and some other materials, and the polythene sheeting to line the tank.

Two steps for the Bremen Cog

The conservation treatment of the *Bremen Cog* is by far the largest tank impregnation ever performed. The tank treatment was planned in a time of economic prosperity, and the singularity of the ship find justified the best possible treatment to stabilise and conserve the ship. It was to become a unique exhibit in a purpose-built museum.

The tank was made of 10 mm stainless steel, and held a volume of 800 m³. It was built around the reconstructed waterlogged ship, and had a steel top against which the ship was braced to prevent it from floating. A row of windows allowed the public to view the ship during the years of conservation, and submerged lamps illuminated its interior. However, the *Cog* was not visible all the time. When we first filled the tank with water it only took a week before she disappeared in green clouds of algae. A dose of a quaternary ammonium salt killed them, and they settled in a thick grey layer on the ship. We had to pump off the 800,000 litres of water, scrub down the ship and fill the tank again, with the addition of a biocide. In time, resistant microbes evolved and the *Cog* disappeared again, some days before the President of the

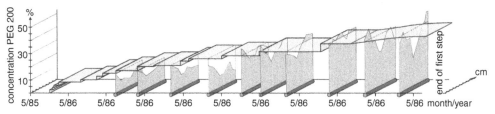

PEG concentration profiles from core samples taken through the same frame timber of the Bremen cog at time intervals during the first impregnation step. Blue: PEG 200 concentration in the water in the wood; yellow: PEG 200 concentration of the impregnation bath. Illustration: Reinhold Breden, DSM

Senate of Bremen was to come and inaugurate the project. It was not feasible to use large amounts of biocides in a museum, in case the tank should spring a leak and splash visitors with treatment solution. Therefore we decided to remove the microbes mechanically, pumping the solution continuously through gravel filters. Aluminium sulphate added before the filters acted as a cheap flocculant, coagulating the microbes into larger flakes, and thus increasing the efficiency of the filters. This technique worked well. We began to add PEG to the water, first PEG 1500 – modified from the suggestion of the Hamburg scientists (see page 44) and then PEG 200 when we changed to the new two-step treatment. Parallel to the development of the new scheme, I tested to see if the 12% PEG 1500 already in the tank at the time of the change would impede the stabilisation. This was not the case. We could save the cost of draining the tank and refilling it with water. Twice a year 20 tonnes of PEG 200 were pumped into the tank, an increase in concentration of 5%. In the months before the lorry with the PEG arrived, water was evaporated from the tank in an efficient evaporation unit, which had been installed in the basement, to make space for the new PEG. After a while beautiful silvery bubbles of hydrogen sulphide passed by the windows: the solution had turned anaerobic, and sulphate-reducing bacteria thrived on the sulphate from the flocculant. The bacteria also produced black patches on the wood. We had to change to a more expensive alkaline aluminium polychloride for a flocculant in the filters. It turned out

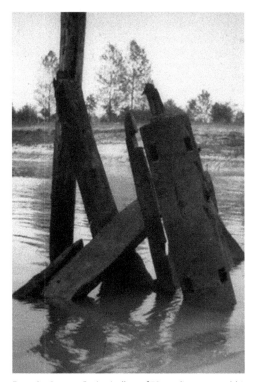

Even the *Bremen Cog*'s windlass of 53 cm diameter could, in several years, be impregnated with PEG 200. Photograph: DSM

to be very efficient and we used this system for the next seven years. Then the filters lost their efficiency. At about 30%, the PEG 200 seemed to interfere with the filtration. For the last years of the first bath, the *Cog* could no longer be seen.

Considering our limited budget, and the fact that much of the PEG 200 would diffuse out of the wood again in the second bath, I decided to take the bath concentration to just 40%. After 15 years the timbers had taken up the planned amounts of PEG 200. We had completed the first step.

The enormous size of the tank had forced us to find solutions for three major problems:

1 At the end of each treatment step, how do we dispose of the large amount of spent solution?
2 How can we prepare hundreds of tonnes of a 60% PEG 3000 solution and then increase its concentration to the final 70%? The evaporation unit would not work with a highly concentrated solution of PEG 3000.
3 How can we reduce the large dead volume in the tank?

Five years in advance, negotiations with the authorities started about the disposal of the spent PEG solution. After tests in the laboratories of the sewage plant, and listening to several experts' opinions, an investigation by a freshwater science laboratory proved that PEG 200 and PEG 3000 are both biodegradable. The microbes from the biological cleaning stage of the sewage plant degraded PEG 200 completely within one week; PEG 3000 took longer. We were eventually allowed to feed the conservation solutions from both treatment steps into the sewer, at a very low rate. It took 63 days to empty the tank of the first solution. A colleague in Antwerp had asked if he could have 5 m³ but nobody else had any use for the remaining 795 m³, and to store the solutions would have cost the same as to buy new PEG.

There was no danger of drying to the ship while it hung in the empty tank for several weeks before the second immersion solution was introduced. Because of the humid atmosphere in the drained tank the PEG-impregnated wood did not dry, its own hygroscopicity kept it wet. During this time – several weeks – we washed some fine sediments from the hull, and laid out four circuits of heat- and PEG-resistant tubes, 240 m in all, and connected them to the central heating of the museum.

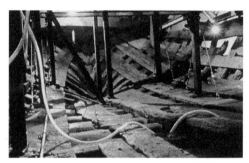

In the hold of the *Bremen Cog*: The first impregnation bath has been pumped off. Photograph: Per Hoffmann

Over a period of seven weeks, 13 road tankers brought 260 tonnes of 90°C hot melt of PEG 3000. The melt was pumped through a static mixing unit, together with 195 tonnes of water from a fire hydrant, and the resulting 60% solution, still hot, was pumped into the tank containing the *Cog*.

To reduce the dead space in the tank, while the solution was filling the tank, 160 elastomer-lined textile balloons of 2.5 m³ volume each were laid under the ship and in its hold, and then filled with brine. The concentration of the salt solution was adjusted to the density of the PEG solution so that the displacement balloons were able to float weightlessly in several layers, and not press on the ship or the lid of the tank. Two men worked to dissolve 80 tonnes of salt in a separate tank, and two men worked with the balloons. The balloons reduced the free volume in the tank to half the original volume. A year later, one layer of balloons was removed, and their volume filled up with 70 tonnes of PEG melt to raise the concentration to the final 70%. After two further years the PEG analysis of the wood gave the expected result: the solution of PEG 3000 had filled the degraded outer wood, and sufficient PEG 200 had remained in the non-degraded interior parts of the timbers.

A narrow zone contained both PEGs, this would be the degradation front where both degraded and non-degraded wood cells were present. The impregnation was terminated and the PEG solution could be pumped off

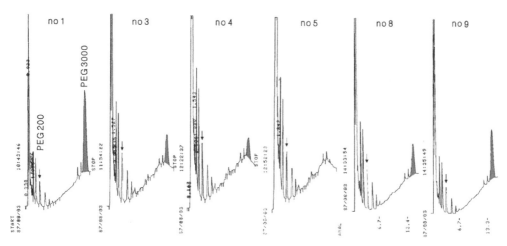

HPLC-chromatograms of extracts from the increments of a cut-up wood core from the *Bremen Cog*: the samples from the surfaces of the timber – nos. 1, 3, 4, 8, 9 – contain PEG 3000, sample no. 5 from the interior does not. All samples contain PEG 200. Chromatograms: Per Hoffmann

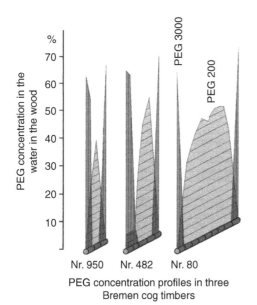

PEG concentration profiles in three Bremen cog timbers

At the end of the second impregnation step: PEG 3000 is present in both ends of the wood cores – the surface layers of the timbers; PEG 200 is still present in the interior. Illustration: Per Hoffmann

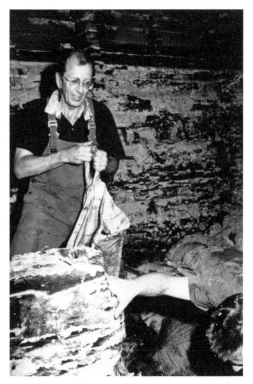

very slowly into the sewer. The brine from the displacement balloons, however, had to be pumped into the saltwater of the Bremerhaven docks, as it would have corroded the concrete tubes of the sewage lines.

While the second impregnation bath was pumped off, the displacement balloons were successively emptied and removed from the hold of the *Bremen Cog*. Photograph: Gabriele Hoffmann

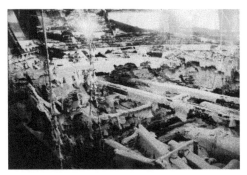

Solidifying PEG 3000 solution settling on the ship during pumping off made the *Bremen Cog* look like a ship in the Arctic. Photograph: Per Hoffmann

The conservation of the big ship in a huge tank took 19 years. A tank treatment was definitely the best possible treatment method for this complicated structure; the PEG had impregnated the degraded wood totally. The stabilisation effect is correspondingly high. After nearly six years of drying, 16 ships timbers showed residual shrinkages perpendicular to the grain between 0 and 5.4%, the average being 3.1%. No longitudinal shrinkage was detectable. Without stabilisation the shrinkage of representative specimens was from 6 to 29%. About 80% of the shrinkage of untreated timbers had been suppressed by the treatment. The novel two-step PEG impregnation led to very good dimensional stabilisation. We rate the treatment of the *Bremen Cog* a success.

The stainless steel tank stayed watertight for all these years; some minor leaks in welding seams could be sealed when the first bath was pumped out and the tank was temporarily empty.

Large tank treatments are expensive because huge amounts of PEG are needed to fill the tank. The wood of the ship only takes up a fraction of the tank volume; the *Cog* for instance took up 5% of the 800 m^3 tank. However, the reconstruction-first concept was the right path to follow with regard to possible warping of timbers during conservation.

After conservation and drying, the planks became hard and stiff. They would need to be warmed to 60°C to become pliable once more. It would have been very difficult to spend seven years reconstructing the *Cog* while warming up the timbers – and keeping them

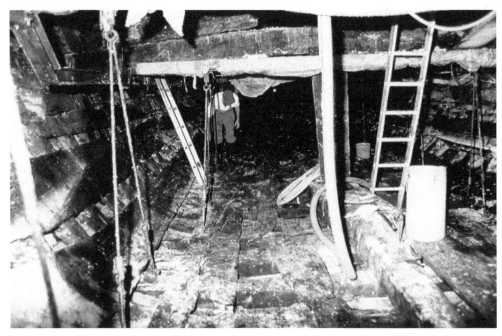

In the slippery hold of the *Bremen Cog* after the second treatment step. Photograph: Gabriele Hoffmann

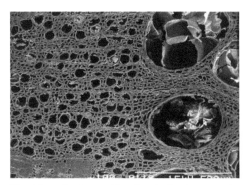

Wood from the *Bremen Cog* after the first impregnation: the cell lumina are empty, all PEG 200 has been absorbed by the cell walls. SEM photograph: Adya Singh, New Zealand Forest Research Institute, Rotorua. Magnification about 100×

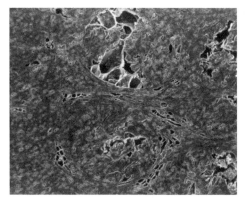

After the second impregnation: the lumina of nearly all cells are filled with PEG 3000. SEM micrograph: Adya Singh, New Zealand Forest Research Institute, Rotorua. Magnification about 100×

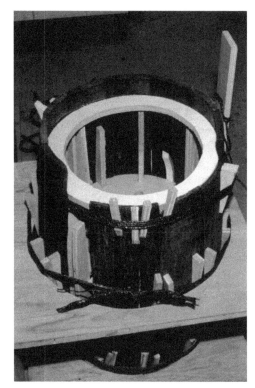

Reassembling the stabilised staves of a barrel from the *Bremen Cog* was a little tricky. Photograph: Per Hoffmann

warm while being reshaped. A temperature of 60°C is also too hot for them to be easily handled. Conversely, waterlogged wood before conservation is soft and pliable, and can be bent without heating. To keep it wet while working has not proven too difficult.

Twenty years for a conservation procedure, however, is much too long. It was 40 years between the salvage of the ship and its stabilisation. It is only due to luck that a succession of devoted archaeologists, ship builders, engineers, and a then young wood scientist and conservator, developed and pressed forward with the project, enabling

the ship to finally reach a stable state and survive. Looking back, I would say that for any ship the conservation must be planned to be completed within ten years at the very most. Otherwise the risk of the project dying is high: the personnel involved move to other jobs, retire or die; politicians and sponsors become interested in new projects and the funds are no longer provided; and the equipment wears out and breaks down. There are many such sad stories. However, even a big ship can be stabilised within ten years – using the two-step PEG treatment.

A case of emergency

The conservation of the Carolingian river barge *Karl* was an emergency project, and from its beginning it suffered from insufficient funding and adverse circumstances. When the quite well-preserved early medieval barge

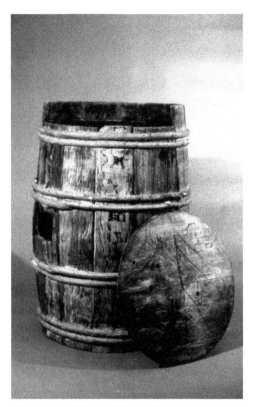

The two-step PEG-treated barrel. 600 years ago it carried tar from Poland to the shipbuilders in Bremen. Photograph: Per Hoffmann

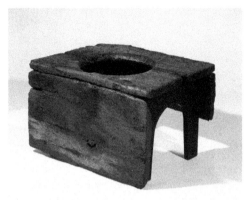

The captain's toilet from the *Bremen Cog* is the oldest of its kind worldwide. Photograph: Egbert Laska, DSM

was unearthed 10 m deep in a building site in Bremen, three days were allowed to remove it, after which fifty-two lorries would come and pour concrete for the base of the hotel which was to be built on the site. The state archaeologist gave the ship to our museum, which is an independent foundation, and the Landesminister promised to pay for the conservation. The ship came to Bremerhaven, but no funds came with it. I was forced to try to raise a considerable sum. I decided to keep the ship in a tent with water sprinklers surrounding it, the idea being that financial support might be easier to obtain if the object requiring the support was visible. This was a wrong decision. During a warm summer the ship suffered heavy shrinkage damages, in spite of being sprayed. We should have submerged it somewhere until a conservation tank was ready.

An empty working space was difficult to find. *Karl* finally ended up under a bridge in a concrete tank built and donated by a class of apprentices from the local vocational school. The town electricity supplier gave us an external electric hot water heating system which they said would be just fine; Hoechst AG offered a batch of PEG 3000 from fire-damaged stock at a special price. The state of the waterlogged wood called for a two-step treatment, and the first step – PEG 200 – went well. During the second treatment the heating system began to fail repeatedly. The donated heater elements were not strong enough for constantly working at full capacity. As a result, the bath cooled down during a long weekend, and the PEG solution solidified. It was weeks before new heaters could melt it again, and even then the temperature did not exceed 40 to 50°C. This was too low to enable a good diffusion of PEG into the wood, as we found out later. The drying planks warped, and literally all the wooden treenails holding together the clinker planking shrank and fell out of their holes. Even worse, the L-shaped half-ribs collapsed, lost their correct angles and most of them broke. When we reconstructed the ship from the assemblage of loose planks and ribs, we not only had to reshape and flatten most of the broad planks, as described in Chapter 10, we also had to deduce the correct angle between the bottom and the sides from the position the sides adopted with the least tension when the planks had been dowelled together again. The residual tangential shrinkage was 4–6% in the planks, but 10–15% in the ribs.

It took me nearly a year to collect the funds calculated necessary for the conservation – in small sums mostly, and this turned out not to be enough. With a more efficient heating system the impregnation and stabilisation would have been much better, and most importantly the half-ribs would have survived. The impressive bow plate would not have split, and tool marks from the shipwright's adze would possibly have remained visible on the planks. The lesson learnt from this project is bitter: one should not begin a project with insufficient money. Optimism alone is a dubious counsellor, although it is difficult not to start working with a ship you find interesting, important, or beautiful.

A case of extreme warping

The heavy timbers of a small barge of the *Oberländer* type from the Rhine had to be re-formed to their original shape after conservation but before the boat could be reconstructed. The 6 m boat had been constructed from a heavy log boat of 1 m diameter, split lengthwise in two halves. Two inserted bottom planks and a bow plate widened the boat to about 2 m. The original bulkhead which closed the end was not found during the salvage of the boat's timbers from a flooded sand extraction pit in an old river bed. The hull and bottom planks were 6 to 8 cm thick and, as expected, had varying zones of degradation – in the interior the water content was around 110%, but 300–500% in the outer parts. An excellent stabilisation was achieved in an impregnation over three years in a solution of PEG 200 with increasing concentration from 20–46%, followed by two years in a solution of PEG 3000 with increasing concentration from 45–85%. The high final concentration was due to unnoticed evaporation during several weeks towards the end of the treatment. PEG profiles confirmed an optimal uptake and a

distribution in the timbers of the two grades in agreement with what we had expected: a high content of PEG 200 where there was no, or very little PEG 3000, and vice versa. The residual shrinkage after several years of drying ranged from 0–5%, with an average of only 2.9%. Wooden treenails still fitted tightly, and the surface of the hull was smooth and without cracks and fissures. However, in the 60°C hot bath, the two hollow side shells of the boat had warped, probably due to the release of growth stresses in the sturdy oak trunk. High temperatures soften lignin in wood and render the wood pliable, and PEG 200 in the cell wall structure acts as a lubricant. Under stress the cell wall fibrils can glide a little along each other and thus release the stress. Distortions of up to 15 cm meant that reconstruction of the boat was not possible without prior re-shaping of the timbers. For the first time I tried the three-dimensional reshaping of extremely thick and heavy archaeological timbers, with success. The procedure is described in Chapter 10. This labour could have been spared, had we mechanically braced and stabilised the shape of the curved sides before the hot treatment.

A low budget project – the Helstorf logboat

The *Helstorf logboat* project is an example of a low budget two-step treatment for a simple object. A local history enthusiast from a small village in Lower Saxony asked us for help. Together with the local fire brigade, he wanted to rescue a logboat, 6.30 × 0.70 × 0.70 m, from the small river Leine. The archaeologist responsible for the find had attested that it could well have been the ferry boat from the old and well-known river crossing, and had handed it over to the enthusiast to conserve for his small local museum. A log boat in Lower Saxony was not my responsibility, but the man seemed determined, competent and careful, and I developed a simple plan for him. Before they could lift the boat from the river, he would have to dig a narrow hole in his back yard, cushion it with peat dust, line

Box 12

Excursus: stabilisation of fossilised wood

Fossilised, non-petrified wood, many dozens of millions of years old, is sometimes found in brown coal mines. Only rarely are large pieces found, as stumps or even as whole trunks of trees. Natural history museums, geological, and botanical institutes are keen to keep these rare objects for their collections. They look like wood, and they are still wood, maybe wet or even waterlogged. When they dry, they shrink heavily, split and crumble, and layer after layer exfoliates. It is quite natural that a conservator known to work with large objects of waterlogged wood is consulted.

The microscopic analysis of fossilised wood will most often reveal that the cellular structure is quite intact, although it is often compressed from having been buried deep under younger sediments. However, a chemical analysis will show that most of the cellulose, and all hemicelluloses have disappeared, probably having been very slowly hydrolysed and dissolved from the cell walls by the groundwater.

Several treatment schemes have been tested to stabilise fossil wood: low molecular weight PEG, high molecular weight PEG, and sucrose, combined with air-dying or freeze-drying. Regarding stabilisation, the integrity of test specimens, their colour and surface appearance, a tank treatment with 25% PEG 300 gave the best results in my experiments. The concentration of the PEG is calculated so that all PEG introduced into the wood with the treatment solution can be absorbed by the cell walls when the wood dries and the water evaporates from the cell lumina.

An impregnation with low molecular weight PEG does not disturb even ultrastructural details within cell walls, and it is fully reversible. The stabilised wood will remain a useful specimen for future studies: it can contain an exciting wealth of information about the history of the tree, the longevity of the organic material wood, and the process of fossilisation.

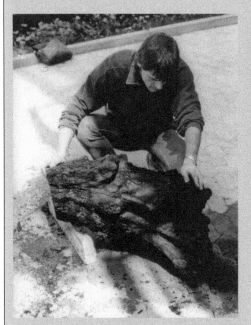

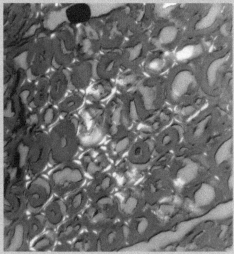

In polarised light, remnants of crystalline cellulose still appear white, they show birefringence. Micrograph: Per Hoffmann. Magnification about 500×

The non-petrified fossil trunk of a 23 million year old cypress is still waterlogged. Photograph: Per Hoffmann

Box 12 (cont.)

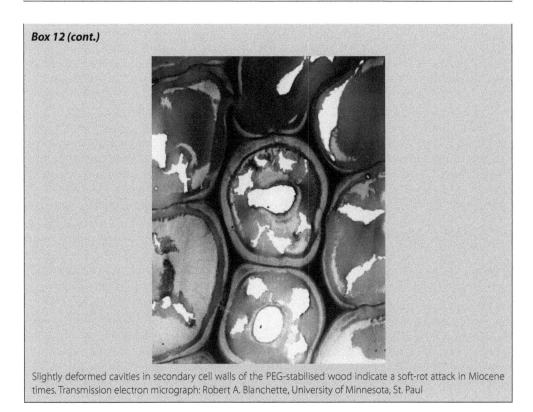

Slightly deformed cavities in secondary cell walls of the PEG-stabilised wood indicate a soft-rot attack in Miocene times. Transmission electron micrograph: Robert A. Blanchette, University of Minnesota, St. Paul

it with garden pond plastic liner, and position some railway sleepers on top of the liner. He could then place the boat on the sleepers, and weigh it down with some stones. Before filling the pit with water he would need to determine how deep he could stick the point of his knife into the inner and outer surfaces of the boat at about 1 m intervals. He marked these readings on a sketch of the boat. Penetrations of 4–15 mm – the thickness of the wood being 35–40 mm – indicated that a two-step treatment would be necessary. With a series of water-filled plastic drums in the boat he could reduce the effective volume of the pit, and then immediately cover the boat with water. He then purchased PEG 200 to prepare a 40% solution, and exchanged this solution for the water. A floating plastic sheet covered the pit and prevented evaporation. One year later, the second treatment step was started with 60% PEG 3350. I had suggested PEG 2000 at 60% because such a solution would stay liquid even without heating – at least most of the year. But

PEG 2000 was not available in small amounts, and so we decided to take the offer of a batch of PEG 3350. Limiting the concentration of the solution to 60% was a compromise to keep the project feasible, as the cost of heating was prohibitive.

The degree of impregnation achieved in the following 17 months was frustrating as the outer parts of the wood had not taken up as much PEG 3350 as expected. It turned out that the second solution had only contained about 35% PEG. The pins inserted at different places to measure distances before and after conservation had been removed by mistake before the end of the drying period. So, nothing precise can be said about the stabilisation result. However, the boat dried without warping. No cracks or splits developed, the surface became hard and smooth, and everybody was pleased. It seems that this compromise treatment could be a low-budget method for simple wet archaeological objects – log boats, pontoons, water pipes, tree trunk coffins, wells made from hollowed-out trunks – where the stabilisation of the shape against warping in the first treatment step is more important than the first-class collapse-free stabilisation of degraded surface areas in the second step.

The advantage of using one-step PEG 4000 up to 95% concentration is that there is then a possibility to bend the distorted boat planks back into shape using heat if the boat is to be displayed. However the wood tends to be rather heavy and dark in colour.

4.4   Pumps and nozzles – spraying treatments

Spraying is an alternative to immersion in a tank for the stabilisation of a waterlogged wooden ship find, if for some reason a tank treatment is not feasible. The idea of spraying is to produce a coherent and permanent film of PEG solution on all the wood surfaces, from which the PEG can diffuse into the water in the wood. The mechanisms of stabilisation with PEG when sprayed are the same as in a tank treatment.

The spraying technique

The spraying technique depends on the premise that the treatment solution can be sprayed, i.e. its viscosity must be adjusted to the technical possibilities of available equipment. The viscosity of a PEG solution can be reduced by choosing a PEG with a lower molecular weight, by reducing the PEG concentration, or by increasing the temperature of the solution. Pure low molecular weight PEGs 200 and 400 can be sprayed without difficulty at ambient temperatures. High molecular weight PEGs 1500–4000 can be sprayed in unheated solutions with concentrations up to about 45%.

Spraying treatments at ambient temperatures can be arranged with quite simple equipment. Garden sprinkler and spraying systems are adequate, and easy to install. The ship needs to be placed in a situation where it can be sprayed from all sides, from the inside and from underneath, and where the excess sprayed

solution can be run into a catchment reservoir, from where it is filtered and pumped back into the system. Spraying solutions of higher concentrations up to 80% must be heated to 50–55°C to keep the viscosity of the solution low. Such concentrated solutions can be atomised – forming a fine mist – with compressed air being fed into the nozzles together with the solution. However, this treatment has to take place in a closed and heat insulated chamber, and all equipment and tubing must be heated to prevent the concentrated PEG solution solidifying in the system. A biocide must be added to the solution to prevent the unavoidable growth of microbes, including *Legionella*, in the warm environment. The hot atomising spray treatment is a complicated process, and it needs a permanent technical setup.

During spraying, problems with iron corrosion will turn up immediately. The low molecular weight PEGs are especially corrosive, and as there is plenty of oxygen in the spraying environment, corrosion can progress swiftly. All technical structures required to hold the ship, and the hoses and nozzles, must be made of stainless steel, galvanised steel, brass, or polymers. Even then a strong industrial corrosion inhibitor should be added for safety because some mild steel item might be overlooked. If there is iron in the ship – nails, caulking cramps, bolts, chains, gudgeons, and other applications that cannot be removed – an effective corrosion inhibitor is indispensible. Iron corrosion products on the wood are not only ugly, but very difficult, or impossible, to remove.

A first project using a spraying treatment

The conservation of the *ship from the Teufelsmoor* near Bremen was my first experience with a spraying treatment, which I carried out with the full cooperation of the building department of the town of Osterholz-Scharmbeck. We successfully carried out the treatment of the ship according to my plan. My counterparts were engineers who relished this exotic task. They also liked the prospect of having the ship in a museum in their town. We planned to treat the 21 × 5 × 1.5 m late 19th century peat freighter, built of oak and fir, in a tank containing a solution of PEG 200, and a bespoke concrete pit was built next to the local museum. When calculations showed how much it would cost to fill the tank with PEG solution, the town treasurer protested. We changed our plans, and designed and installed a spraying system of pipes and nozzles in the concrete tank. A simple roof of polythene sheet covered the tank and a submersible pump, pumping 10 m³ per hour to a height of 6 m, served the system. The nozzles got clogged up so the whole installation was exchanged for a simple garden watering system laid out under and in the ship. 10–15 fan sprayers and 3–5 full cone spray nozzles kept every part and corner of the ship covered in a film of PEG solution; 5 m³ of solution was enough to keep the system going. The local garden centre furnished replacements whenever necessary. Two years spraying with 25% PEG 200 were followed by two years of 40%. PEG analyses of several timbers then indicated that we could end the impregnation. As a word of warning it is worth mentioning that the action of spraying fragile and very soft wood surfaces over a long period can cause serious erosion and loss – as is the case of the *Hasholme logboat* in the Hull and East Riding Museum which has been sprayed since 1988 and is now a shadow of its former self. It is still being sprayed whilst on full public display, within an insulated container – another truck back – with glass viewing panels.

After five years of air drying *the ship from the Teufelsmoor*, cross-grain shrinkages ranged between 0.5 and 1.7%, a very good stabilisation result. The wood attained a natural light brown colour, and is dry and smooth. However, several ugly stripes indicate where iron corrosion products have run down from iron bolts and long vertical nails connecting the side boards to each other – I had not thought of adding a corrosion inhibitor to the system at the start of the project. During the conservation the local museum re-erected an old protected half-timbered barn from a nearby village over the concrete tank, and when the polythene sheet roofing was removed the ship stood in the centre of a new museum about the history of local peat extraction.

Spraying with an unheated solution of PEG 200 is perhaps the cheapest way to stabilise a big ship, provided the wood surface is only slightly degraded.

A project for twins – two barges from Rohrsen

The two *barges from Rohrsen* on the river Weser, which went down in 1775 laden with sandstone building blocks from the famous Obernkirchner quarries, were stabilised using a spraying treatment, in what I think is the shortest possible time for a well-preserved ship built of sturdy oak wood timbers. A joint project was established between the Weser Renaissance Museum in Lemgo and the Deutsches Schiffahrtsmuseum. I drew up a conservation plan based on wood analyses in Bremerhaven, and Eckehard Deichsel, art historian and restorer, set up and performed a spraying treatment in Lemgo. Monitoring the progress of the impregnation was my task. The barges measured about 20 × 5 × 1.50 m each. The oak wood was somewhat degraded, u_{max} varied from 120 to 250%, and a spraying treatment with PEG 200 was the only feasible method. Deichsel erected a greenhouse from commercially available modules on a concrete base with a slight inclination, so that the spray solution would collect in a catchment pit. The barges were placed on galvanised iron stanchions about 1.50 m above the ground, so that the undersides were accessible and could be sprayed. Various types of nozzles and lawn sprinklers from a garden system were used, connected to ordinary hoses. A submersible pump circulated water to first wash the ships. A filter in the line was necessary, as silt and wood splinters washed off the barges for a long time and kept clogging the nozzles. Only when the circulating water became clear could the addition of PEG begin. 3–4 m³ of PEG 200 at 20% concentration were sprayed and circulated

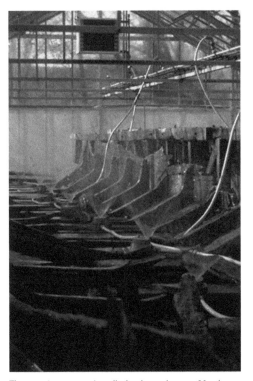

The spraying system installed to keep the two 20m *barges from Rohrsen* constantly covered with a film of treatment solution required only 3–4 m³ of PEG solution. Photograph: Eckehard Deichsel

during the first year, followed by a 40% solution for two more years.

The concrete base of the greenhouse had been lined with heavy-duty foil which was sealed to the glass walls to form a sort of trough to catch the runoff solution. This arrangement caused some problems. When loss of solution indicated a leak, it was extremely difficult to find, with dozens of stanchions standing on the plastic lining, and folds and puddles obscuring the view. Repairing the lining that had been in contact with PEG proved to be difficult. It would have been better to paint an epoxy sealant directly onto the concrete floor, and to meticulously point up the joint between the glass walls and the concrete base.

Although a corrosion inhibitor was added to the PEG solution and only galvanised stanchions and fittings were used, after three years rust began to develop which threatened to circulate and be sprayed onto the wood. It was fortunate that the PEG analysis showed that the wood was sufficiently impregnated to end the treatment. In a greenhouse the temperature easily rises to 50°C on a sunny day, even in northern Germany. The high temperatures promoted

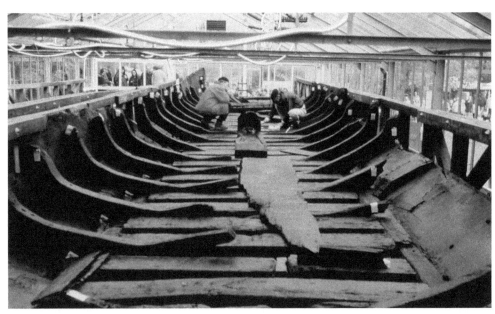

The two barges carried sandstone building blocks for building town halls, churches, castles, and forts in Holland and in the Dutch colonies to Bremen, from where they were shipped to Amsterdam. Photograph: Gabriele Hoffmann

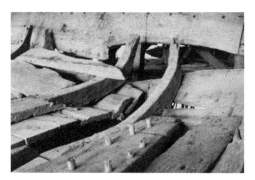

Upon air drying, the PEG 200-treated wood of the *barges from Rohrsen* have a quite natural and light look and a soft touch. Photograph: Per Hoffmann

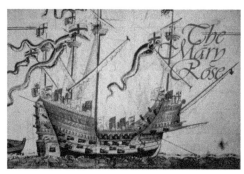

The *Mary Rose*, King Henry VIII's flagship depicted in the Anthony Roll of the King's ships, 1546. Reproduced courtesy of Magdalene College, Cambridge

the PEG diffusion, but cold winter weeks in turn retarded the process. With daylight in the greenhouse, algae grew on all surfaces but not on the wood – as long as it remained covered with a liquid film of PEG solution.

In the three years since the end of the treatment, no shrinkage has been detected, no splits, cracks, or deformations. The wood has turned a pleasant light brown colour and the surfaces are dry and smooth, and soft, like suede, to the touch. We regard the treatment a complete success.

Fighting the risk of bacteria – the Mary Rose

A spraying project of quite a different order of magnitude was the stabilisation treatment for the *Mary Rose* in Portsmouth, UK, the Tudor warship of King Henry VIII. Apart from the sheer size of the ship and its consequences for the dimensions and requirements in technical installations, manpower, and money, the project is unique in the pains that were taken to eliminate the risk of bacterial growth in the ship hall, and of infection to staff working there.

The remains of half of the hull of the *Mary Rose*, recovered in 1982 in a spectacular salvage operation from the underwater archaeological excavation site in the Solent, off Portsmouth on the south coast of England, were still more than 30 m long and 13 m high. Resting in a steel cradle it was brought into an

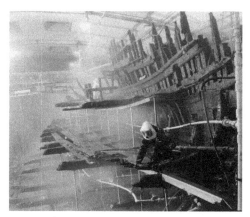

The hull of the *Mary Rose* was sprayed with solutions of PEG 200, then PEG 2000, using an elaborate system of PVC tubes and full jet spray nozzles. Photograph courtesy of The Mary Rose Trust, Portsmouth

old dry dock, which was then covered with a lightweight roof. In this space the spraying treatment commenced. The spray system consisted of 300 m of PVC pipes, with full jet spray nozzles positioned at 1 m intervals. The system worked at 2 bars of pressure, and 567 nozzles ensured complete coverage of the hull timbers. For 12 years the hull was sprayed with water. In this time mud, silt, and salt deposits were washed out, especially from the difficult to clean spaces between outer and inner planking and ribs. Filters and cyclone separators kept the circulating water clean.

The decks, knees, and other timbers, which had been removed before the lifting

73

of the hull, were then reinstalled. Where supports were needed, titanium stanchions and bolts were used. This material is light, strong, and does not corrode. The hull was studied, and the condition of the timbers assessed in order to determine a suitable conservation treatment. A Pilodyn survey revealed that most timbers were composed of slightly degraded inner parts enveloped in a layer of heavily degraded wood, up to a few centimetres thick. However, there were also timbers that were heavily degraded throughout. Having been asked for my opinion, I recommended a two-step treatment, and the chief conservator, microbiologist Mark A. Jones set up a series of pilot scale experiments with original *Mary Rose* timbers. He tested combinations of PEGs 200, 600, 1500, and 4000 in order to find the best scheme for the *Mary Rose* hull.

Throughout the period of water spraying there was a real risk of bacterial infections to staff working in the ship hall. Poorly maintained water systems provide ideal sites for the growth of many aquatic bacteria. The occurrence of *Legionella pneumophila* was considered a threat. However, the risk of Legionnaires disease from the *Mary Rose* spray system was effectively controlled by consequently maintaining the water temperature at 2–5°C, well below the optimum growth temperature of many marine and terrestrial bacteria and fungi which cause wood decay and may be a health hazard. In this way the use of large amounts of biocides could be avoided. Four industrial chilling units were necessary to act as backups in case of breakdowns and to ensure the temperature was kept low. Regular cleaning of the spray system, careful monitoring of microbial populations, and a selective application of biocides to reduce the growth of biofilms completed the safety measures. Generally, the buildup of slime on the wood was an indication of poor water flow over that area. Accelerating the flow rate over the wood prevented surface fouling by microorganisms.

The stabilisation of the *Mary Rose* hull was in two nine-year phases. The first nine-year phase involved spraying a PEG 200 solution, ending with a final concentration of 30%. It was feared that higher concentrations, 40–50%, may result in internal cracking of sound cores in the timbers due to osmotic pressure effects. In the second nine-year phase, PEG 2000 was sprayed, in concentrations up to 50%. The conservation project for the *Mary Rose* has been going on for 30 years now, and has suffered the typical difficulties occurring in projects of too long duration: wear, breakdown and replacement of vital and expensive equipment; even the roof of the ship hall had to be repaired, and then replaced. Staff have changed, and there have been times where sufficient funds were really difficult to obtain. However, the project will succeed in the end; it is being pursued with patience and tenacity. It is based on sound and advanced scientific studies, and on a tight system of monitoring of all aspects of the process. The *Mary Rose* conservation project was, from its beginning, an exceptionally large operation, comparable only to the conservation project for the Swedish Royal warship *Vasa* in Stockholm.

Worldwide first – the spray treatment for the Vasa

The *Vasa* project was the first of the big ship conservation projects. It was the first to use PEG for the stabilisation of a ship and to apply it in a spray treatment, and the experiences gained during the course of the project have been invaluable to many conservators since. In recent years the *Vasa* project has again launched a comprehensive programme of fundamental research into the occurrence of sulphur and iron, and their effects on waterlogged wood; as into the long-term stability of PEG treated waterlogged wood and the chemical processes obviously taking place in it. The results of this research will influence the design of future conservation projects.

The *Vasa* was deliberately searched for, found, and salvaged with great public acclamation, as was the case with the *Mary Rose* twenty-one years later. When the battleship of King Gustav II Adolf from 1628 broke surface in 1961, a ship of 61 m length and 12 m width appeared; the stern castle rose to a height of 20 m. Once the ship was manoeuvred into a dry dock, and onto a pontoon, a lightweight hall of concrete, steel, and glass was built around it and the public could, for the next 27 years, watch the conservation of the magnificent hull. The conservators were confronted with 1200 tonnes of waterlogged oak wood. The enormous size of the ship excluded any thought of a tank treatment. It could only be a spraying treatment. In 1961 this was a new approach to the conservation of waterlogged wood, but then the conservation of a wooden object of these dimensions had never been tried before. The team around chief conservator Lars Barkman decided to use PEG for the dimensional stabilisation of the large ship. They had no experience with PEGs, then a new material, and they had no time for extended experiments to learn about molecular weights and impregnation of wood of different states of degradation.

As soon as the archaeologists had finished the excavation of the mud-filled interior of the *Vasa*, the ship was washed down thoroughly, and sprayed with water to prevent the wood from drying. Then a manual spraying with a PEG 4000 solution was started to protect the wood surfaces. This was not a continuous treatment, so a humidifier system had to keep the relative humidity in the ship hall as high as possible. After two years, in 1964, the spraying was replaced by an automatic installation with 487 nozzles of various types. Problems with spraying a solution of PEG 4000 forced a change to PEG 1500. Investigations proved that PEG with even smaller molecules was much more effective as a stabiliser of the very slightly degraded *Vasa* oak wood. From 1971, PEG 600 was added to the spray solution. The total PEG concentration was raised from 10 to 45% in the period 1964–1976, and then kept at the final concentration for three more years. Spraying was stopped in 1979, and a surface finish of PEG 4000 was applied to the outside of the hull to fill and close the wood surface, and to give a gloss to the ship, as if it were lacquered, by brushing a paste of PEG 4000 melted with hot air blowers, onto the wood.

The need to protect the wood against microorganisms and fungi during spraying was undisputed. It was decided to use borate salts, which were popular in the commercial wood industry at that time. The *Vasa* research laboratory developed a formula that contained sufficient PEG for dimensional stabilisation and enough borates to control the growth of microorganisms: a 7:3 boric acid–borax mixture – up to 7% – was dissolved in PEG solutions of up to 45% concentration.

An important aspect of the *Vasa* conservation project was the carefully controlled slow drying of the hull timbers. The relative humidity around the upper parts of the hull was decreased from 95% in the first years of hand spraying, down to 58% in 1992. Accordingly, the mean moisture content of the outer planking dropped from 140% to about 13%. The drying of the timbers was accompanied by a cross-grain shrinkage of about 6% in the inner and outer planking, and of close to 8% in the heavy timbers of frames, knees, deck beams, keelson, stem posts, etc.

The reported shrinkage values are close to the corresponding values for sound wood. This is not surprising. The *Vasa* sank right after she was built, and came to rest in an anoxic environment where wood degradation was very slow. Considering the enormous cross-section dimensions of the timbers, one can probably say that the bulk of the *Vasa* timbers still are in the state of, and behave like, fresh oak wood. PEG analyses of wood cores taken during the impregnation treatment gave disappointing results in terms of the penetration of PEG. With today's knowledge one can confirm that PEG 1500 is not able to penetrate into sound oak heartwood. The spraying treatment, however, did stabilise the surface layers of the *Vasa* timbers wherever they needed it. The very slow reduction of relative humidity around the hull, combined with the retarded evaporation of moisture from the timbers, due to them

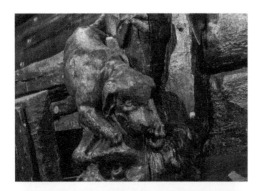

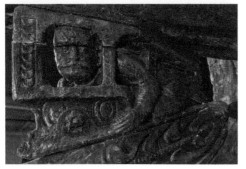

The outside of the *Vasa* hull, and the sculptures and decorations attached to it, were brushed with a concentrated solution of PEG 4000, which was then melted onto the surface as a strengthening and protecting finish. The dog and the Polish nobleman – moustache and agraffe on the cap – are found in the galleries at the stern castle. Photograph: Anneli Karlsson, Swedish National Maritime Museums

being covered with PEG, led to a uniform and stress-free drying even of thick timbers. In this way, distortion of the ship's structure, and major cracks and warping in individual timbers, have been avoided. The enormous efforts spent on the conservation of the *Vasa* by at least two generations of conservators, museums administrators, and politicians have produced an overwhelming centrepiece of Sweden's most popular museum.

In recent years the *Vasa* has gained international attention again: '*Vasa* endangered!' read the headlines. When whitish and yellow patches appeared on some timbers, and on wooden objects found with the ship, and when the patches were found to be caused by sulphuric acid in the wood, which was unexpected, a series of research programmes with international participation was launched to find reasons and remedies. A wealth of new knowledge about archaeological wood, its degradation and technological properties, about PEG, and the role of sulphur and iron compounds in waterlogged and dried wood, has since been acquired. It seems that sulphur diffuses into the wood as sulphate from seawater, and as hydrogen sulphide from anaerobic organic sediments. In waterlogged wood, sulphur will be present in various chemically harmless forms. But when the wood dries and the sulphur comes into contact with oxygen from the air, the sulphur is oxidised to form sulphuric acid. The acid will slowly hydrolyse, degrade, the carbohydrates of the wood, and as the acid is not consumed in the process, the degradation will go on and on. Timbers from several other ship finds have been analysed: among others the *Mary Rose*, the *Batavia* in Fremantle, Australia, and the *Bremen Cog*. Sulphur was found in them all except for the *Bremen Cog* which had sunk directly from the wharf in a river, and had never been in contact with seawater, or sulphur containing sediments. The *Batavia* timbers are known to have acid problems, and the *Mary Rose* seems to be threatened by the same problem as the *Vasa*.

The finding of paramount importance to conservators is that iron causes the most trouble. It is a catalyst for several of the chemical reactions involving sulphur which will damage wood components: crystalline compounds may form and grow and disrupt the wood. Iron compounds get into ships' timbers as corrosion products from nails, rivets, bolts, and from all sorts of fittings and attachments. One has to remove as much of the iron from the wood as possible while the wood is waterlogged. Once the wood has dried, it seems to be impossible to remove iron from inside the wood. This shows that the wood has to be analysed for iron before conservation begins. Should there also be relevant amounts of sulphur in the wood, then they too should be extracted together with the iron. Concentrating on iron removal is the most important preventive measure against future troubles. At the moment it is not yet clear how iron and sulphur can be extracted from waterlogged wood efficiently, and whether a method can be found to extract these noxious compounds from wood which has already dried. Intensive research is needed to deal with these problems.

The *Vasa* timbers are dry now, and at this moment there is no remedy in sight. Fluctuations of temperature and humidity cause condensation and evaporation of capillary water in wood cell walls. These changes in water content and water distribution produce concentration gradients of dissolved substances, which enhance chemical reactions. The only realistic option is to inhibit the chemical reactions taking place in the wood by reducing the temperature and the relative humidity in the museum as far as is acceptable to visitors, other museum objects, and the building itself; and then to keep the climate as constant as possible. This is not an easy task in a museum with more than a million visitors every year.

4.5 Tank treatment versus spraying – a comparison

The decision to follow a tank treatment or a spraying procedure for the stabilisation of a waterlogged ship or boat depends on the assessment of a series of scientific, technical, financial, and personnel factors with regard to the project in question. For each project, individual aspects may have greater or lesser priority, and one has to strike a balance to determine which treatment method should be chosen.

A tank treatment can be individually designed for optimal stabilisation of a ship containing wood of any quality. It is therefore the method which offers the greatest flexibility. Spraying treatments can apply low molecular weight PEG at any concentration, but high molecular weight PEG only up to about a 50% solution. With this limitation, spraying cannot stabilise heavily degraded hardwoods, such as oak, to the best possible degree. For slightly degraded wood, and wood where the great bulk is only slightly degraded, and for softwoods, the stabilisation can be optimal.

There are practical and technical limits to the size that a tank can be built, whereas a spraying system can be installed for a ship of any size. Generally, a tank is more expensive than a spraying installation for the same ship. The cost of a tank increases greatly with size; the cost for a spraying installation does not increase at the same rate.

The accommodation to house a tank can be quite simple. Electricity, water, and a gully in the floor are the only essentials. A spraying installation, on the other hand, needs to be set up on a watertight base with a slight slope and a catchment pit, and in a housing that will allow the spray solution to recirculate. Electricity, water, and a gully are, of course, also obligatory.

The amount of PEG required to fill a tank with treatment solution, and its cost, obviously increases with a larger ship and tank. The 20 m ship from the *Teufelsmoor* was planned to be immersed in a tank of about 220 m³ volume using a solution of 40% PEG 200, corresponding to 88 tonnes of PEG. When the plan changed to spraying, 5 m³ solution were sufficient, equivalent to 2 tonnes of PEG. The high cost for the disposal of spent PEG solution also needs to be considered.

The manpower necessary to run and control the stabilisation treatment is another crucial aspect when deciding on the method to use. Once a ship has been installed in a tank, one or two workers are needed to prepare the treatment solution, and later to increase its concentration. Between these activities the tank only needs to be monitored and inspected for leaks, and checks need to be made to ensure that the top cover is in place – to avoid evaporation of water – and that there are no exposed timbers floating on the surface. One person inspecting the ship once or twice a week is sufficient. A heating system, however, must be checked more often unless it is part of the central heating of the building, in which case it will need little attention. Although the temperature of a heated bath must be checked several times a

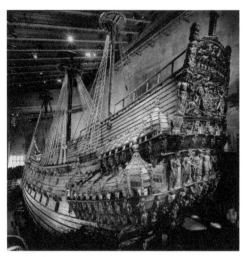

A ship like the *Vasa* was definitely too big for a tank treatment. The hull was spray treated for 27 years, the sculptures and decorations were tank treated separately. Today she stands in her own museum. Photograph: Hans Hammarskiöld, Vasamuseet

week, this can be run alongside other duties of the staff. A spraying installation, on the other hand, needs daily maintenance. Pumps fail, filters and nozzles get clogged and have to be exchanged and rinsed, hoses and connections must be checked for leaks. The flow of treatment solution must be constantly checked, and also whether the wood is covered with solution on all surfaces, also undersides, and in all corners and crevices. Maintaining a spray treatment even of a medium sized ship is a full time job for one person. A big ship will need more personnel.

In the long run, salaries may easily consume the cost advantage of a spraying installation compared to a tank and its contents. One therefore needs to know which type of funding is easier to obtain: a one-off large sum (capital funding) – this could also be a donation in kind, or a commitment to smaller but regular support (revenue funding). Either way, resourcing must cover the cost of employing staff.

Even when the decision is made to stabilise a ship using a spraying treatment, it can still be advisable to impregnate non-structural individual wooden timbers and objects in a tank. They may need an optimal stabilisation

because of their value, as was the case with several hundred carved figures and ornaments from the stern castle of the *Vasa*, or they may need an extended impregnation time because of their thickness, as could be the case with a capstan, a mast step, a figurehead, and the like. After cleaning and drying, the appearance of the wood will not show which treatment was applied. One should consider using alarm systems built into the heating and circulating circuits, in case of a breakdown. Such alarms can be connected to a call centre, or directly to a mobile telephone or a computer. This might be especially important if the facility is in a museum gallery, or situated at a remote location which is not visited daily.

Notes to §4.1 Some surprising laboratory experiments on wood

– The comprehensive and richly illustrated monograph on the *Bremen Cog* edited by G. Hoffmann and U. Schnall, 2003, is the best for reading about all aspects of this ship: salvage, reconstruction and conservation, and the archaeological interpretation of the type 'cog', historical background, and life on board the medieval ship.
– The conservation of the *Roskilde Viking ships* is described by B. Brorson Christensen, 1970, and the conservation of the *Vasa* by B. Håfors, 2001.
– Some colour reactions for the detection of PEG in wood are described in P. Hoffmann, 1983.
– For the laboratory experiments leading to the formulation of a two-step conservation proposal for the *Bremen Cog*, see P. Hoffmann, 1984, and P. Hoffmann, 1986.
– Stabilisation experiments with oligomer PEG are published in P. Hoffmann, 1988.

Notes to §4.2 Scaling up – ships in tanks

– PEG determinations using HPLC are given in P. Hoffmann, 1989, the method using TLC by A. Crawshaw, 1994.
– PEG analysis in wood using a combination of extraction, ATR-FT IR, and MALDI-TOF MS has been demonstrated by Tjelldén *et al.*, 2009.

The stabilisation of waterlogged softwoods from several species – *Pinus massoniana* (Chinese red pine), *Pinus densiflora* (Japanese red pine), *Cunninghamia lanceolata* (Chinese fir), and *Cryptomeria japonica* (Japanese cedar) – was investigated in a joint project with Korean colleagues Choi K.-N. and Kim Y.-H. with the aim of developing a conservation concept for the *Shin An ship*, a medieval Chinese junk salvaged 1976–1984 with its cargo of 20,664 pieces of ceramic, 28 tonnes of Chinese copper coins, 1,017 trunks of sandalwood, and 2,118 other objects (P. Hoffmann, 1990; P. Hoffmann *et al.*, 1991). Today the ship is the central exhibit in the Korean Maritime Museum, built right on the shore of the Yellow Sea. The experimental results for the four softwood species are very consistent, and this is no surprise. The structure on the cellular level and on the cell wall level is very much the same in all softwoods. Hence it is justified to present the results as valid for softwoods in general.

Notes to §4.3 One-step or two-step – the range of tank treatments

– For a detailed description of the conservation of the *boats from Pommeroeul* see De Witte *et al.*, 1984.
– G. Kaenel, 1994, gives a comprehensive account of the *Barge II from Yverdon-les-Bains*, and of its conservation.

– An interesting description and interpretation of the *ship from the Teerhof* is published by D. Zwick, 2010.

Notes to §4.4 Pumps and nozzles – spraying treatments

– An effective corrosion inhibitor widely used in conservation with PEG is 'Hostacor IT', a product of Clariant Ltd. It is a triethanolamine salt of 'Hostacor H', which is an arylsulphonamide carboxylic acid. A test of its effectiveness has been published by V. Agyropoulos *et al.*, 1999.
– The 'Hot Atomisation' treatment was developed, and is routinely run at the Atelier Régional de Conservation – ARC-Nucléart in Grenoble. For details see D. Bouix *et al.*, 2005.
– The story of the *Mary Rose* and her salvage has been told many times. One of the best narratives is found in G. Hoffmann, 2001, in a book on the history of underwater archaeology.
– The conservation not only of the *Mary Rose* hull, but also of the thousands of objects found in the hull, is described by M. Jones, 2003.
– Details of the conservation of the *ship from the Teufelsmoor* can be found in P. Hoffmann, 1998.
– A comprehensive report on the salvage and conservation of the *Vasa* is given by B. Håfors, 2001, chief conservator of the project for many years.

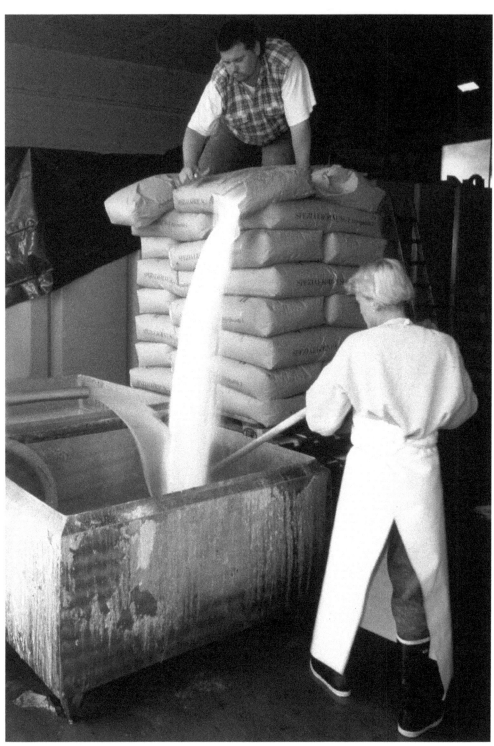

The state archaeologist decided to apply the cheap sucrose treatment to the *ship from Friesland*. He was lucky: the method could also have failed, and then the costs would have soared. Photograph: Linda Hermannsen, Archäologisches Landesamt Schleswig-Holstein

5   The sucrose method

5.1   Sugar in wood – laboratory experiments

Since James Parrent published his thesis on the conservation of waterlogged wood using sucrose in 1985, several laboratories, mostly in Europe and Japan, have worked with sucrose and many papers have been published – predominantly success stories. The advantages of using sucrose – beet or cane sugar – compared to other methods, especially those using PEG, were listed as follows:

- sucrose is cheap and available everywhere;
- it is non-toxic, non-corrosive, and only slightly hygroscopic;
- no sophisticated equipment is needed;
- no heating is necessary;
- degraded and non-degraded wood can be treated alike;
- the dimensional stabilisation achieved is good;
- the wood keeps its natural colour;
- sucrose treatment is much cheaper when compared with a two-step PEG treatment.

However, talking privately to colleagues has confirmed my own experience: caution is required when considering a treatment with sucrose. Numerous failures seem to indicate systematic weaknesses in the method. In particular, large scale operations with sucrose solutions may pose unforeseen problems. For about twelve years I investigated the potential of sucrose treatments in both laboratory experiments and in full-size conservation schemes for waterlogged ship finds. My intention was to find out where this method would fit in the conservator's tool box.

Dimensional stabilisation

The first result from a series of laboratory experiments showed that the dimensional stabilisation of all waterlogged woods increased with the amount of sucrose incorporated in the wood by increasing the concentration of the treatment solution. However, the limit of solubility for sucrose in water is around 67–70%; a higher concentration cannot be achieved, even heating the solution will not increase the solubility significantly. One has to work with saturated solutions at room temperature. Looking at the stabilisation achieved in six hardwoods and three softwoods covering a wide range of degradation – maximum water contents varied from 140 to 1300% – a few general observations could be made. Despite thorough impregnations there is residual cross-section shrinkage upon drying, with values ranging from 0 to 25%. This span of results seems to be independent of the quality of the wood – there is no correlation with the degree of degradation. In other words, degraded and non-degraded woods respond in the same way to a sucrose treatment so there is no need to divide timbers into groups for different treatments. All wood qualities can be treated together and in the same way. The range of results, however, is wider than the comparable ranges of results for other established stabilisation methods.

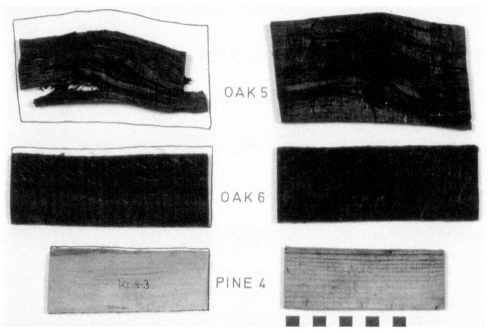

OAK 5

OAK 6

K: 4-3   PINE 4

Left: small boards of waterlogged oak and pine, air dried without treatment; right: after a sucrose impregnation. The treated boards have maintained their wet dimensions, no shrinkage occurred. Photograph: Per Hoffmann

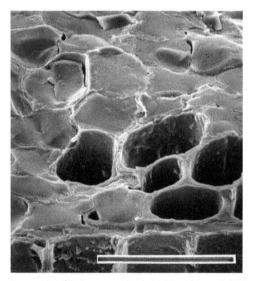

Sucrose has filled most tracheids in this oak wood. SEM micrograph: Uwe Schmitt, Federal Research Centre for Wood and Wood Technology, Hamburg. Scale bar = 50 μm

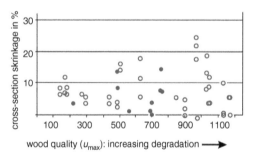

wood quality (u_{max}): increasing degradation →

The stabilisation with sucrose of the cross-section of six hardwoods (open circles) and three softwoods (filled circles) is quite irregular and independent of the wood quality. Shrinkages on drying vary considerably, from very low to unacceptably high values. Illustration: Per Hoffmann and Reinhold Breden, DSM

Splitting up the cross-section shrinkage of stabilised woods into their radial and tangential components reveals an interesting picture. The radial shrinkages are quite low, from 0 to 3%, whereas in the tangential direction shrinkages can be higher than expected, up to 10%. This holds for woods which are not extremely degraded. In all woods the longitudinal shrinkage was completely suppressed by a sucrose treatment.

Warping and collapse

The great difference in shrinkage behaviour between the radial and tangential directions in sucrose-treated wood is the reason why this method will not suppress warping tendencies in wooden objects. On the contrary, it rather enhances such tendencies. Another failure occurring in sucrose-treated wood on drying is the collapse of smaller or larger portions of

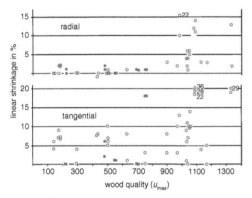

Radial shrinkages of hardwoods and softwoods on drying after a sucrose treatment are low, except for extremely degraded wood, whereas tangential shrinkages vary from zero to unacceptably high values. Illustration: Per Hoffmann and Reinhold Breden, DSM

tissue. Such collapse results in depressions on plane surfaces; cavities opening up in the interior of the wood; washboard surfaces on radial-cut specimens; and in heavy shrinkage or warping. Heavily degraded wood is more susceptible to collapse and warping, and hardwoods suffer more from these failures than softwoods. Of 24 small boards of postcard size, cut from heavily degraded hardwoods, not one dried without substantial failure of one kind or other. Warping and collapse are not normally mentioned in publications. However, colleagues who have worked with the sucrose method agree that these phenomena are quite common.

Judging from available laboratory experiments, the results of stabilisation using the sucrose method are rather unpredictable within a wide range. This does not mean that the method has to be rejected in every case, but the conservator must carefully look at his objects, how the anatomical planes of the wood are positioned within them, and then decide which magnitude of shrinkage he would be willing to risk. With strictly radially cleft boards the risk of heavy shrinkage and warping is not very high; but with tangentially sawn boards in a degraded state, the risk is much too high to accept. Woods may react favourably, or not so favourably, to sucrose stabilisation, and it is not possible to predict which timbers would fall into which category.

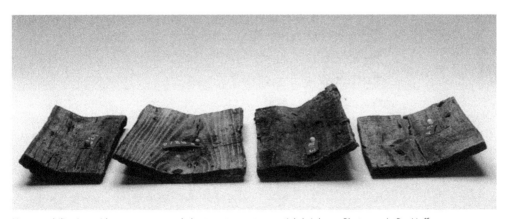

How a stabilisation with sucrose may end, due to extreme tangential shrinkage. Photograph: Per Hoffmann

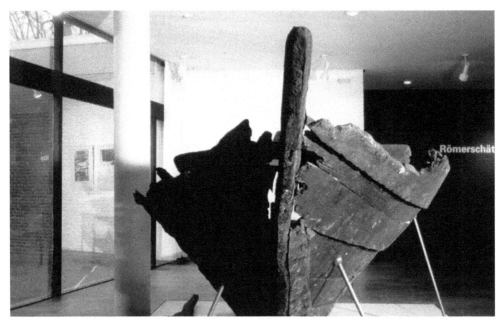

The late medieval *Beck's ship* was the product of very poor craftsmanship, as our shipwright stated, but it came out of a sucrose treatment excellently stabilised. Photograph: Per Hoffmann

5.2   Ships in sugar – case studies

A good stabilisation may or may not be achieved when using a sucrose treatment. Laboratory tests indicate that there is an equal probability of having a good or bad outcome. However, the golden promises attributed to the method – its simplicity, low cost, and good results – are so tempting that several archaeologists have decided to use this method for the conservation of their ship finds, knowing and accepting the high risk of failure.

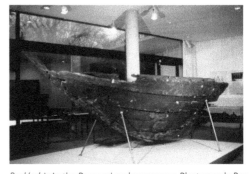

Beck's ship in the Bremer Landesmuseum. Photograph: Per Hoffmann

An excellent result – the Beck's ship

When the bow section of a small medieval ship, dated by dendrochronology to about AD 1489, was excavated on the premises of a well-known brewery in Bremen, the management decided to conserve it. Being an innovative company, they wanted to apply the new sucrose method which they had just heard about and were attracted by the simplicity of the method and the aesthetically pleasing appearance of the final product. The development

of a conservation scheme and the monitoring of the process were to be undertaken by our museum; the actual work would be done at Beck's brewery under the auspices of the master brewer.

This was an encouraging joint project: means and funds were ample, and the technical and microbiological know-how of my counterpart most adequate.

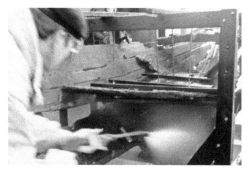

Steam washing is the best way to clean sticky sucrose-treated wood before the sucrose crystallises. Photograph: Gabriele Hoffmann

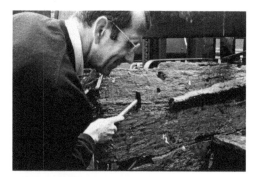

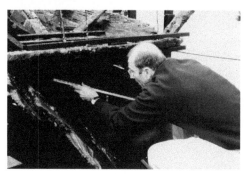

Immediately after the impregnation treatment, reference marks for measuring shrinkages must be checked, or new ones fixed. Photographs: Gabriele Hoffmann

All the ship's timbers were of oak, and they were only slightly degraded. The ship was fixed to a wooden cradle, and was lowered into a painted steel tank of 14 m³ volume. The impregnation started with a 35% sucrose solution for eight months, followed by a 55% solution for four months, and finally a saturated 74% solution for five months. During the process the tank temperature was held at 50°C. If the temperature were much higher, the sucrose would break down via caramelisation reactions. The big brewery, which also produced soft drinks, had no problems applying heat or providing sugar solutions of any particular concentration. Best of all, they were very competent in the use of biocides to maintain the sterility of sweet liquids, pipes, pumps, and other technical equipment. However, even for them, it proved difficult to keep 14 m³ of a sucrose solution sterile in an open tank for 17 months. The biocide they used, and in what amounts and how often, they kept to themselves – a trade secret. But they knew that the greatest risk of working with sucrose solutions over long times was microbial infection. Omnipresent microorganisms would feed on the sugar, and degrade it to evil-smelling and sticky products. The sugar would be consumed, no stabilisation achieved, and the wood would become dark and sticky; it would never dry. Anyhow, after 17 months the *Beck's ship* was lifted from a pristine golden syrup, washed with a cautiously handled steam jet, and left to dry.

The end of the impregnation had been determined by analysing wood cores taken with a 5 mm core drill. The cores were cut into 5 mm increments, extracted, and the sucrose content determined with a refractometer. Calculations gave the concentration of sucrose in the water in the wood. When equilibrium with the impregnation solution was obtained throughout the timbers, the treatment could be finished. Another method would be to monitor the weight of a representative piece of wood. Sucrose has a density of 1.5 g/cm³, and the wood will increase in weight as long as it continues to take up sucrose. The size of sucrose molecules (gram molecular weight M = 342), and their polarity, are comparable with those of low molecular PEG, and the impregnation times are also comparable. Even for thick timbers a treatment of 2–3 years will bring sufficient sucrose into the wood structure.

After four years of drying, cross-grain shrinkages ranged from 0 to 2.5%, with an average of 0.8%. The stabilisation was perfect. No collapse or warping had occurred and the wood looked dry and sun-bleached. Today the ship stands exposed in the Bremer Landesmuseum. On a rainy summer's day when the doors to the museum stay open for hours for visitors to shelter from the rain, the ship becomes damp and even moist. However, it dries again when the doors are shut and the normal museum climate takes over again.

Undefeatable microbes – the case of the Schlachte ship *from Bremen*

A conservation treatment which unexpectedly turned into a slight disaster was the sucrose treatment of the *Schlachte ship* from Bremen. The keel/stern transition part of a medieval middle-sized ship seemed to have been fashioned from one half of a logboat, from which heavy bottom strakes protruded in order to support the upgoing sides. Attached to it was the oldest iron gudgeon found in northern Europe, dating to the first part of the 11th century. The presence of already corroded iron had suggested that it might be preferable to employ sucrose instead of corrosive PEG. As a safeguard, I added 2% of the corrosion inhibitor Hostacor KS1 to the sucrose solution. The degraded oak wood, it turned out, was heavily infested with highly resistant microorganisms which were impossible to kill off. I tried quaternary ammonium compounds and high doses of isothiazolinones, but only succeeded to keep the sucrose solution clean for a few weeks. Then it started to ferment furiously. Within one year the treatment solution had to be exchanged twice. After three more months and a discussion with a microbiologist, I broke off the treatment, nothing more could be done. I found that the microorganisms had reacted with the biocides and produced slime and hard gels on and in the wood to protect themselves. No impregnation had been possible. As a result, the outer parts of the wood collapsed and formed deep longitudinal cracks. The logboat

now looks as if it is still covered with old bark. Only an extensive filling of these cracks can give an idea of how the ship looked when found. The hull itself, however, has not split or distorted; it has kept its basic form.

The fact that this treatment went wrong was not initially caused by the sucrose method; the resistant microbes might have impeded any impregnation. But the sucrose solution was an excellent nutrient, and maybe it enhanced the microbial activity and allowed it to proliferate, leading to the total blockage of the wood.

The sucrose treatment on a grand scale – the ship *from Friesland*

The *ship from Friesland* is the largest object so far treated with sucrose. To show how precarious a large-scale sucrose treatment can be, the project is described in detail.

The ship, a 12 × 5 × 1.5 m Renaissance coastal cargo ship, which sank around 1600, was found in a reclaimed polder on the North Sea near Husum in northern Germany. The state archaeologist of Schleswig-Holstein wanted to transform this rare find into a major museum exhibit; but, due to the high cost, he was not prepared to pay for a two-step PEG treatment which I had recommended in light of the degradation pattern of the ship's timbers. He asked me to consider a sucrose treatment, which would cost half as much. He accepted the uncertainty about the quality of the stabilisation, and the chance of even a complete failure in case of uncontrollable microbial growth in the solution or in the wood. The necessity of intensive care, control, and maintenance of the process by skilled and reliable people was acknowledged, and the personnel would be provided. The deputy archaeologist Hans Joachim Kühn would organise and lead the practical conservation work in Husum, and I would design the treatment process and its monitoring. I would also do the wood analyses during the impregnation. We then embarked on a sucrose treatment project on a scale we felt a little breathtaking. We would have to handle a tank holding about 90 m³, and all the

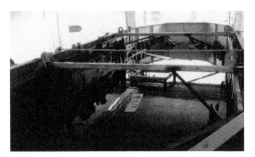

The conservation tank with the *ship from Friesland* was filled with 90 m³ of sucrose solution. Photograph: Per Hoffmann

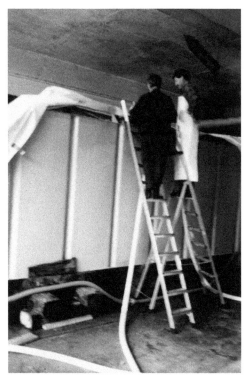

A journalist interviewing the archaeologist, trying not to get her microphone stuck in the omnipresent sucrose solution. Photograph: Per Hoffmann

unforeseen complications normally associated with the scaling-up of chemical and technical processes.

The archaeological excavation and documentation had taken nine weeks. During this time the exposed ship was kept wet: by spraying by hand, by covering with wet cloth, and by sprinkling with hoses. A steel support was built around the ship in situ, and lifted a little. The hull was washed and cleaned of the sticky clay as far as possible then lifted and lowered into a tailor-made steel conservation tank waiting on a lorry, and brought to an empty army garage in nearby Husum.

Three more rinses removed considerable amounts of clay from the interior of the hull. A disinfection step followed: the tank was filled with water, and 15 ppm isothiazolinones added, a concentration that should kill any microbes present on and in the wood. The ship sat in this solution for ten days. By whatever means, we had to suppress fermentation of the sucrose solution, as it would be too expensive to buy 100 tonnes of sugar for a second try, should we have to discard a fermenting bath.

The treatment solution was made from warm tap water and fine grain crystalline sucrose of foodstuff quality. On a microbiologist's advice, we rejected the offer from the refinery to take very cheap sugar collected from spillages, because this would undoubtedly infect our solution with large amounts of omnipresent microbes. The sugar was dissolved in a separate tank and then pumped into the treatment tank with a centrifugal pump. Pumping high viscosity sucrose solution requires strong pumps, which in turn build up substantial pressure in the outgoing line. Only pressure-resistant hoses will stand this, as we soon learnt.

The impregnation started with a 20% sucrose solution, again with 15 ppm isothiazolinones added. A black polythene floating cover on the surface excluded light and reduced the access of oxygen. The concentration was raised to 40% after three months, and to 67% after eight months. Each time some solution was pumped off and sucrose added to raise the concentration. With the last concentration increase another dose of biocide was added; we assumed that the first dose had been consumed or inactivated.

We monitored the colour, smell, and pH of the bath once a week. Four times during

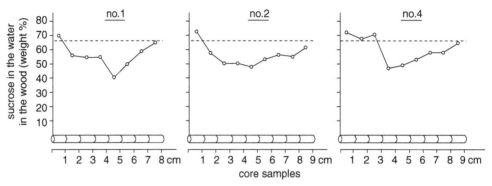

Concentration profiles for sucrose in the water in the wood of three futtocks from the *ship from Friesland* after 20 months of impregnation. Illustration: Per Hoffmann

the impregnation period the pH dropped from neutral to acidic, and on advice from the chemists at the sugar mill we neutralised the solution with lime water – a slurry of calcium hydroxide. An acid solution would cause hydrolysis of sucrose and support microbial growth with all its implications.

After 20 months the sucrose concentration in the central parts of the timbers had not yet reached equilibrium with the treatment solution, and we continued the impregnation.

Initially, the solution was circulated in the treatment tank once a week to keep the concentration uniform. We stopped this when fungi and bacteria were found in the 67% solution, in spite of the additional dose of isothiazolinones. Floating islands on the solution surface were identified as fungal and bacterial colonies. Their occurrence on the strong sucrose solution (which had been dosed with biocide) was tentatively explained: the cover on the tank was not in contact with the surface everywhere due to protruding parts of the ships cradle. In these areas water evaporated, condensed on the cover, and dripped back, forming pools with lesser sucrose and biocide concentration – ideal habitats for microbes. Continued circulation of the solution would further disperse these local colonies into the whole of the tank.

When finally the solution became turbid and its colour changed, after 26 months, a microbiologist from the Saxony State Institute for Agriculture in Leipzig analysed the situation.

She found an osmotolerant yeast, *Citeromyces matritensis* (Santa Maria), a xerophilic fungus *Wallemia sebi* (von Arx), and an osmophilic penicillium species, all living in the surface layer of the sucrose solution. These microbes are ubiquitous and they are known to grow in very high sucrose and salt concentrations in products such as honey, marzipan and chocolate. *Wallemia sebi* also thrives in dry matters such as bread, hay, earth, textiles, salted fish, and bacon. The microbiologist judged the solution to be in a state of progressive degradation and recommended that we stopped the treatment before it went completely out of control.

Meanwhile, the wood had reached equilibrium with the solution and the impregnation could be ended. However, the ship was scheduled to stay in the solution over Christmas and a few weeks into the New Year. But two days before Christmas Eve the solution developed a sweet–sour smell and started to ferment. It had to be pumped off immediately. After some delicate negotiations with the district administrator and the department of the environment, deputy archaeologist Kühn was allowed to spread the 90 m³ of sugar solution mixed with manure on some meadows, but only after he had destroyed the isothiazolinone in it with a dose of bisulphite. The tank was drained and the ship steam-washed.

Air drying at ambient conditions for 20 months led to a shrinkage of 1.5 to 7.5% across the grain, with an average of 4.9%.

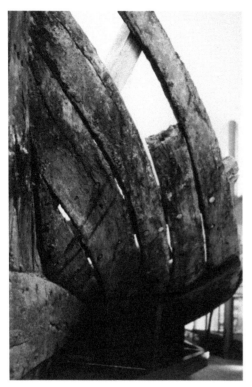

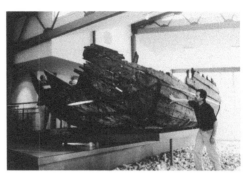

The archaeologist with his *ship from Friesland* at the end of a successful project. Photograph: Per Hoffmann

Seams have opened only a little due to moderate shrinkage on drying. Photograph: Per Hoffmann

Some timbers had warped a little, and both the keel and the stern post – which had heavy degradation in their interiors –showed a slight torsion. Some timbers were still moist in their inner parts. Many treenails – 3 cm diameter wooden pegs – had shrunk and fallen out of their holes. They were replaced by new oak treenails. The surfaces of the wood now looked very agreeable – dry and of a natural colour, and no cross-grain cracks had developed. Remnants of original paint on the inner planking were not affected by the treatment.

Hans Joachim Kühn has kept a detailed log of the number of men and days his crew worked on the conservation of the ship. For the preparation of sucrose solution: (6 days × 12 men) + (2 days × 8 men) + (1 day × 7 men); to rinse the ship and the tank: (6 days × 6 men); to attend to the ship: (1 day × 4 men) + (10 days × 3 men) + (121 days × 2 men). For a ship conservation project, the crew was exceptionally numerous.

Two men, as would be the usual crew, would have despaired. One would have had to constantly clean away sucrose solution: everyone and everything is always sticky, even without coming into contact with the solution.

We consider the project to be a success for several reasons. First of all, we succeeded in keeping the huge volume of sucrose solution stable for two years, just long enough for a sufficient, but not ideal impregnation. Secondly, the costs of the project stayed within the anticipated and accepted range due to generous donations of money, materials, and manpower. Thirdly, the stabilisation succeeded, and the visual appearance of the ship, now standing in the maritime museum in Husum, is agreeable and satisfying. Only once, when the roof of the gallery was open for construction reasons and the relative humidity rose above 85%, did the timbers of the ship become moist, and solution even dripped from the seams. In normal museum conditions, however, the hygroscopicity of the sucrose-treated wood is not a problem.

For future projects the microbiologist Henriette Mietke from the Saxony State Institute for Agriculture in Leipzig provided a set of indispensable guidelines for the handling of sucrose solutions:

– only use microbiologically clean sucrose;
– strive for highest possible cleanliness: sterilise tanks, equipment and wood surfaces;

- reduce dust and turbulence in the air;
- prohibit the access of insects to the solution. Bees, wasps, flies are known to transport osmophilic yeasts in their intestines, and to transfer them to nectar, honey, and fruits. Cover the bath with mosquito netting;
- avoid the formation of 'sweet water pools' from condensed water on the surface of your solution;
- keep the solution at ambient temperature – do not heat or cool;
- keep the pH between 7 and 8. When the pH drops, add biocide immediately, and neutralise the solution with lime. Microbiologists would prefer a pH between 8 and 9, but this alkalinity will dissolve hemicelluloses and degraded cellulose from the wood.

Both the archaeologist and the conservator had nights with bad dreams, especially towards the end of the project: how will the bath look like – and smell – tomorrow? We can only emphasise that a large-scale sucrose treatment is an ambivalent affair. One never knows if it will turn out to be a success or a disaster, and if the latter, why did it go wrong? However, should such a treatment be considered, then it can only be run if it is tightly monitored by a crew of skilled people who really understand what is going on.

It is worth emphasising that any infection in the sucrose solution will cause it to hydrolyse and invert to lower sugars, especially glucose and fructose. In theory, wood stabilised with pure, undegraded sucrose will, once dried to equilibrium moisture content in normal museum conditions, be stable across a broad range of humidities. It will absorb only 5.5% of its weight of water at 81% RH and will not deliquesce until the conditions have reached almost 90% RH. Glucose is more reactive to changes in RH and at 60% RH will have absorbed up to 9% of its weight of water but will only start to deliquesce at 98.8% RH. Fructose is more hydrophilic still, and will absorb up to 22% of its weight in water in an environment of 63% RH, at which point it will also deliquesce. So, depending on where the various sugar products are in the wood, the wood could be very reactive to changes in relative humidity and start deliquescing at around 65% RH – well within the range of normal museum conditions. Surfaces that become damp and sticky will become discoloured and attract dust and dirt, and be attractive to insects, especially wasps.

Notes to §5.1 Sugar in wood – laboratory experiments

- A bibliography on conservation with sugars has been compiled by A. Morgos, 1994.
- To broaden the basis of laboratory results, four European institutions joined in a research project on the stabilisation with sucrose. The results are published in P. Hoffmann et al., 1994.

Note to §5.2 Ships in sugar – case studies

- The meticulous minutes of the conservation of the *ship from Friesland*, written by the archaeologist, also list the many man-hours spent on the project. The minutes are found in P. Hoffmann and H. J. Kühn, 1999.

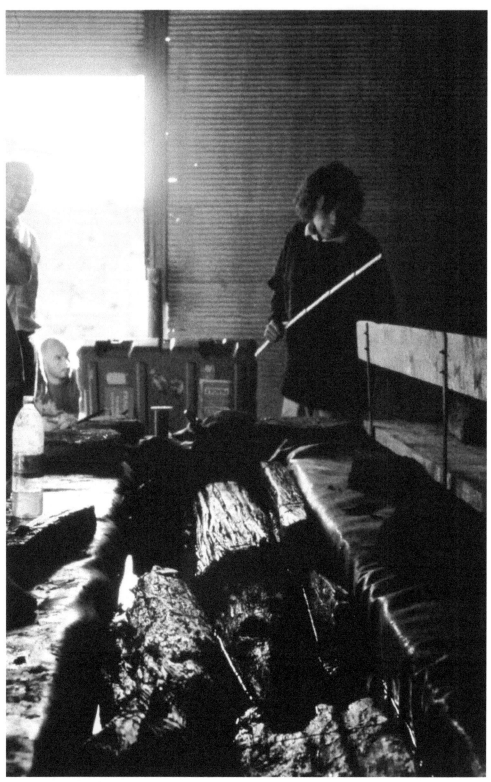

A Lactitol treatment is ideal for a hot and humid climate: Lactitol will not melt at temperatures around 55°C – as will PEG – and it is less hygroscopic. The conservation on site of these construction timbers from a Bronze Age royal palace in Qatna, Syria, are unfortunately not yet finished. Photograph: Gabriele Hoffmann

6   The Lactitol method

6.1   Lactitol in wood – laboratory experiments

The conservation of waterlogged wood with Lactitol and trehalose was developed by Setsuo Imazu and András Morgós to overcome some of the deficiencies of the sucrose method. The authors were particularly looking for better stabilisation of heavily and extremely degraded hardwoods. To this end they needed a stabilising agent with a higher solubility than sucrose. The work with sucrose had clearly indicated that the dimensional stabilisation increased with the amount of sucrose brought into the degraded wood. A mixture of 9:1 parts of Lactitol, an artificial dimeric sugar alcohol, and trehalose, a natural dimeric sugar, is soluble in water to a much higher concentration than sucrose, up to about 90%. This mixture promised other advantages, too, when used for conservation:

– the stabilisation of degraded hardwoods would be better than with sucrose;
– the new saccharide mixture had a better thermal stability; solutions could be heated without browning and caramelisation;
– the mixture was more resistant to microbial attack, and it was not corrosive to metals;
– wood treated with Lactitol and trehalose was less hygroscopic than sucrose-treated wood.

Lactitol was quite expensive, but due to the increasing application of Lactitol as a low

Structural formula of Lactitol: (4–0-β-D-galactopyranosyl-D-glucitol) monohydrate

calorie artificial sweetener in the food industry, the availability and price of the product promised to come down to a reasonable level.

In the light of my somewhat unnerving experiences encountered during the conservation of ship finds with sucrose, the prospect of a microbiologically more stable, and better stabilising, non-corrosive new agent sounded tempting. I conducted several series of stabilisation experiments, as recommended by the authors, on 28 postcard-sized specimens from the three degraded wood species which I had used in former experiments with PEG and sucrose. They produced results which allowed me to draw some general conclusions.

The dimensional stabilisation achieved in pine and oak was not significantly better than with sucrose, nor was the reliability. However, in heavily degraded beech wood the formation of Lactitol crystals expanded the wood tissue, and caused numerous longitudinal splits along the rays to open. The addition of trehalose to the Lactitol was meant to prohibit this growth

Structural formula of trehalose: (α-D-glucopyranosyl-α-D-gluopyranoside) dehydrate

of Lactitol trihydrate crystals during the drying of the wood. In my experiments, however, it did not work. In all three woods tested, warping and collapse occurred: some slight warping in pine wood, slight warping and some collapse in oak, and substantial warping in nearly all the specimens of degraded beech wood.

The fact that Lactitol is more stable against microbial degradation does not mean that a biocide can be omitted from the treatment solution. Trehalose, a disaccharide, is widespread in nature, and many microorganisms can attack and metabolise it; also, Lactitol is not completely safe from biodegradation. The necessity to handle biocides and toxic impregnation solutions remains.

The authors recommend practising this method again and again in order to become acquainted with it. When confronted with a ship or boat to treat, the conservator, if not already experienced in this method, will probably not have time for exercises or experiments.

Two positive features of the Lactitol method remain to be considered. The treatment solution is not corrosive to metals; the method can thus be an option for the stabilisation of wood–metal composite objects. More importantly, wood treated in this way reportedly has a quite low hygroscopicity. It can be kept at relative humidities of up to 90–95%, as is often the case in museums with poor climate control. This is often the case in subtropical and tropical countries. For conservators working in such conditions it could be worth getting acquainted with the Lactitol + trehalose method.

6.2 Lactitol treatments for large objects

To date, no archaeological ships or boats have been treated using either Lactitol + trehalose as the stabilising agent, or Lactitol on its own. However there are two reports from Japan on the successful treatment of some larger objects made from softwoods: a waterlogged 6 m timber coffin made of Umbrella pine (*Sciadopitys verticillata*), and three 4 m elements of a wooden pipeline made of Japanese cypress (*Chamaecyparis obtusa*). In both cases the softwoods were medium to heavily degraded. The coffin was impregnated with a 60% Lactitol solution at 50°C, whereas the pipeline elements were impregnated with a 50% Lactitol solution at ambient temperature – the maximum concentration at that temperature. Impregnation times were 13 and 39 months respectively, and 0.02% isothiazolinones were added as a biocide. After impregnation, the wood was dusted with Lactitol powder to initiate crystallisation in the wood, and then dried at 50°C to prevent the formation of large Lactitol–trihydrate crystals, which would form at lower temperatures. When drying was complete, the Lactitol powder had to be washed off all the surfaces with warm water. Following completion of these projects the authors improved the method by adding trehalose to the impregnation solution.

Some general comments on the Lactitol method, applied on a large scale, may be made here. Solutions of Lactitol + trehalose, and also Lactitol alone, are vulnerable to microbiological attack. Handling a large volume over a long impregnation time will be as difficult and insecure as has been described for sucrose solutions. The use of a biocide is absolutely necessary.

The sizes and dimensions of Lactitol and trehalose molecules are the same as those of sucrose, hence impregnation times must be expected to be the same for both methods. Monitoring the progress of the impregnation can be carried out as for a sucrose treatment, by analysis of wood cores taken from the thickest timbers.

The laboratory experiments and discussions with the authors of the Lactitol method indicate that the stabilisation of degraded, and especially extremely degraded, hardwoods is a weak point of the method. In practice, it is apparently not as easy to prevent the growth of large crystals which disrupt the delicate wood as the chemical theory tells us. Much more work will be necessary to define the potential and limits of the Lactitol method, and to prescribe successful procedures for the optimal treatment of different wood species and wood qualities of large dimensions. For the moment, such work is made more difficult in our part of the world, as Lactitol is no longer produced in Europe; it has to be imported from Japan.

Note to §6.1 Lactitol in wood – laboratory experiments

– The publications introducing the Lactitol method, and then the improved method with Lactitol + trehalose, contain valuable theoretical information on the chemical properties of the saccharides; however, the experimental basis presented is rather narrow with regard to both wood species and to states of degradation of the woods tested. In addition, the numbers of parallel tests are insufficient to give a satisfactory impression of the potential of a new stabilising agent (S. Imazu and A. Morgos, 1997 and 2001). These deficiencies led me to conduct some more extended stabilising experiments, the results of which are discussed in this chapter, and in Chapter 9.

Note to §6.2 Lactitol treatments for large objects

– The conservation of the timber coffin, and of the pipeline segments are described in S. Imazu and A. Morgos, 1999(1) and 1999(2).

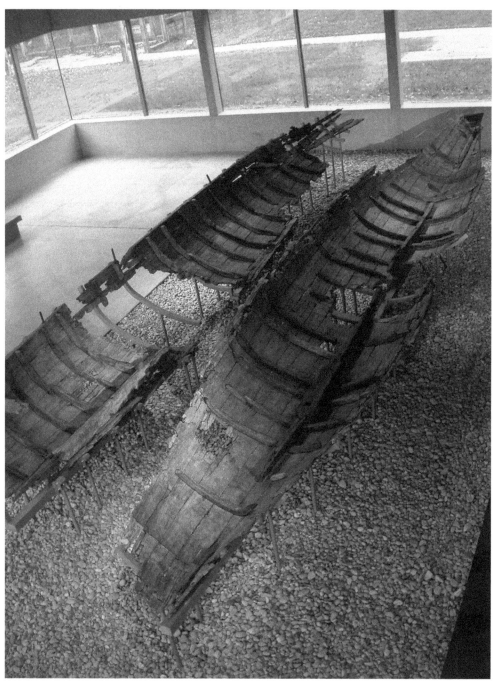

Two ships from *Oberstimm* in Bavaria stabilised with Kauramin. In the 2nd century the light and fast ships were part of the defence fleet of the Roman Empire on the Danube. Photograph: Wolfgang David, Kelten und Römer Museum, Manching

7 The Kauramin method

by Per Hoffmann and Markus Wittköpper

7.1 Melamine in wood – laboratory experiments

The stabilisation of waterlogged wood with Kauramin consists of an impregnation with a low molecular weight melamine formaldehyde prepolymer dissolved in water, which then condenses to a three-dimensional, hard, and insoluble polymer – a melamine resin – in the wood. The Kauramin method is a modern version of the old Arigal C and Lyofix treatments, which have been used since the 1950s for the stabilisation of predominantly smaller objects, but also for the treatment of a group of Roman shipwrecks at Mainz on the Rhine.

The modification of the method described here is the use of an improved resin, produced by BASF in Germany, known as 'Kauramin impregnation resin 800'. It comes as an aqueous solution with 70–90% resin content and is mainly used in the wood and furniture industry. It has a low viscosity and good penetration ability due to the small size of the melamine molecules. Their molecular weight is only 140, and their diameter is given as approximately 0.5 nm. The product contains small amounts of low molecular weight ethylene glycol added by the supplier to reduce the brittleness of the cured resin and also to reduce the tendency of impregnated wood to develop cross-grain cracks. The polycondensation reaction is acid-induced, and is enhanced by heat.

The Kauramin method has several advantages:

- the technology is simple. No heated tanks are necessary, any watertight container will do. No pumps or dissolving tanks are needed, the liquid resin product is easily diluted in water;
- wood of all qualities can be stabilized;
- the impregnation time is short compared to PEG impregnations with high molecular weight PEG;
- excellent dimensional stabilisation can be achieved, and the preservation of the finest surface details is routine;
- the weight of the treated wood is low, and this can be very useful when considering the reconstruction of large objects like ships and boats.

However, there are some inherent drawbacks and problems in the method:

- there can be a tendency for timbers to warp, and to suffer from depressions in the surface due to local collapse of the structure of the wood;
- deep cracks can develop across the grain. Often they are very fine, but nevertheless they reach far into the wood;
- the colour of the wood often becomes light greyish to beige and cream.

To obtain the best possible results with the Kauramin treatment, each step of the procedure must be optimised – the cleaning of the wood, the impregnation, polymerisation, and drying. In laboratory experiments, and in years of practical work with the method at

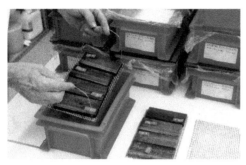

Test series for optimising the Kauramin concentration of the treatment solution were conducted with small boards of several wood species. Photograph: Gabriele Hoffmann

the Museum für Antike Schifffahrt in Mainz, we have tried to find the best parameters for the process and to overcome the drawbacks of the method. Very degraded hardwoods are difficult to stabilise with most conservation treatments. Therefore we focused our attention on this material and incorporated several heavily degraded hardwood species in our investigations, alder (*Alnus sp.*), ash (*Fraxinus spp.*), beech (*Fagus sp.*), and European oak (*Quercus sp.*) with degraded outer layers but solid cores.

The amount of melamine resin incorporated into the wood governs not only the dimensional stabilisation, but also the tendency to warp, and the development of cross-grain cracks. Optimal amounts of resin will diffuse into the wood from impregnation solutions with melamine concentrations of 25–35%. The resulting stabilisation is near-perfect: there is no residual shrinkage, at most a very slight swelling may occur, and warping and crack formation can be minimised if the drying of the wood is very slow.

At the end of the impregnation and polymerisation of the resin, the wood is still waterlogged. The mode of the final drying has perhaps the most decisive influence on warping and crack formation. The drying regime must prohibit the development of a steep moisture gradient from the surface layer to the inner parts of the wood. Testing several drying temperatures, combined with normal or reduced air pressures, we found

that vacuum freeze-drying is an acceptable way of drying impregnated objects in a relatively short time – from days to weeks. Even better results, however, with fewer or no cracks at all, can be obtained with very slow air drying at ambient temperature and pressure.

Kauramin treatment procedure

Building on more than 20 years of working with melamine resins and wet wood, we have developed the following procedure for the stabilisation of waterlogged wood with Kauramin 800.

Cleaning of the wood

The curing of Kauramin is initiated by acids. Impregnation baths contaminated with acids will not be stable and polycondensation will start too early – before the wood is fully impregnated. Therefore, thorough cleaning of the wood is essential in order to extract and remove, as far as possible, any acid compounds originating from the groundwater, humic substances, organic residues from garbage pits, wells, etc. The washing process can be monitored via pH measurements – neutral pH is desirable, and via conductivity measurements for the presence of salts.

Impregnation

- A Kauramin solution of 25–35% is prepared with deionised water. Kauramin 800 comes as an aqueous preparation of 70 or 90%;
- Triethylene glycol is added (10% by weight of the Kauramin resin) to the Kauramin solution to enhance the solubility of the prepolymer;
- 0.5 wt % triethanolamine is added as an alkaline buffer to prolong the service life of the solution to 12–14 months. Not more than 1% maximum should be added, otherwise curing may be totally inhibited. Without triethanolamine the service life of the solution will only be 2–4 months;
- about 5 wt % urea is added to reduce the viscosity of the solution and thereby enhance

the penetration of the resin into the wood. Urea also binds free formaldehyde from the resin preparation, and so reduces the health hazard of formaldehyde in the air.

The impregnation bath is covered and sealed with plastic film to prohibit the evaporation of water and formaldehyde, and the access of oxygen. Oxygen can react with formaldehyde to form formic acid, which would shorten the service life of the solution.

So far no exact investigations have been made into the penetrability and diffusion process of Kauramin 800 into waterlogged wood. The impregnation times applied to objects of different dimensions are governed by experience; they are chosen by comparison with the impregnation times for low molecular weight PEGs: from a few weeks for thin objects to more than a year for thick timbers. Good results seem to justify this approach. Until now no simple method to determine quantitatively the presence of Kauramin in wood has been published. The impregnation can, however, be monitored by regularly analysing core samples for nitrogen. Nitrogen in the wood will stem from the melamine resin present, and the amount of resin in the water in the wood can be calculated.

The pH of the solution is measured once a week and will drop slowly from an initial pH of eight or nine. When the pH decreases to values of seven or six, polymerisation will commence. Also once a week, a few drops of the solution are added to clear water in a test tube: if the mixture becomes cloudy the polymerisation of the resin in the solution is imminent. In that case the impregnation solution must be replaced by a fresh one, or the impregnation must be ended.

Terminating the impregnation and curing the resin

If the impregnation is completed, but the pH of the solution is still alkaline and the 'cloud test' is negative, then one must wait until the pH drops to about six, and the 'cloud test' is positive. The wood is left in the acid solution for a few days. It is then removed and rinsed

thoroughly with water. Wood without any surface coating is wrapped tightly in wet tissue, and then plastic film, and placed in an oven at 60°C to enhance the polycondensation of the melamine resin. The purpose of the household tissue under the cling film is to take up any resin leaking from the wood, and to prevent it from curing on the wood surface as a greyish deposit. However, if the wood has a coating of paint or lacquer, the tissue may be glued irreversibly onto this coating if it is not wet. In this case it should be omitted. The painted wood should be washed, and then dabbed dry, and air dried 10–20 minutes before being wrapped in plastic film and cured. The film is applied to prevent the wood from drying before the resin is cured. A sample of the treatment solution is placed with the wood in the oven in a sealed tube to indicate the progress of the polymerisation. This will normally take 2–4 days, but may take longer. With large objects the tissue coating is omitted.

Even with heating, the curing of melamine resin is a slow process; without, it may take an intolerably long time. Therefore the application of heat is indispensable. It is not so difficult and expensive to construct and install a tailor-made heat chamber for a boat or ship; it only has to serve for a few weeks. Consultations with a firm that applies hot air treatments to fight wood-boring insects in houses and roof constructions will help to find a practical solution.

Drying

One way to arrange a very slow air drying is as follows. The wood is wrapped in plastic film, and when water has condensed on the inside of the film, it is changed. This procedure will take a very long time with timbers of some thickness, but the result is worth waiting for. For a larger or complicated structure it would be easier to construct a sort of humidity chamber and keep the ship at more than 90% RH, as long as appreciable amounts of water evaporate from the wood and condense on the walls, or are caught in the condenser of the climate control unit.

More compact objects can be pre-dried in a commercial microwave oven, which is controlled by a temperature probe in the middle of the thickest part of the wood. The temperature in the wood should be 35°C maximum. Microwaves apply the heat where there is free water, so no portions of the wood are overheated. When the moisture content has dropped to about that of fibre saturation, the water content u being about 30–40%, the process is stopped, and slow air drying takes over. The installation and running of a large microwave oven is very expensive, dangerous, and requires official permission. It is perhaps not an option for a one-off conservation project for a large ship.

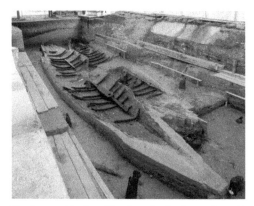

The *Roman ships from Oberstimm* in situ. As so often with archaeological ship finds, a dredge had gone right through them before they were noticed. Photograph: Museum für Antike Schifffahrt, Mainz

Finishing

The surface of treated wood is dry, light in colour, and may be soft and look chalky. Applying a finish will improve the colour, and it can consolidate and harden the delicate surface against abrasion. Acrylic solutions will harden, but not alter the colour or appearance of the surface; drying oils will consolidate and give some more natural transparency and depth to the surface, and enhance the colour a little; wax dispersions in petrol – furniture polish – will enhance colour and depth, and consolidate; high molecular weight PEGs dissolved in ethanol act like waxes, and their application would be reversible. All these finishes could be dyed to the natural colour of the wood.

7.2 Two ships in Kauramin – a case study

by Markus Wittköpper

Two shipwrecks were discovered in the course of a survey excavation at the Roman castellum at Oberstimm in Bavaria. They were dated to the beginning of the second century AD. The boats were built in the Mediterranean fashion: the hull assembled using a mortise and tenon technique, and thereafter stabilised with interior timbers. The number of thole pins suggested a rowing crew of about twenty; mast steps

in the keelson showed that the boats could also be sailed. The slender ships were probably used as part of the defence system of the Roman Empire along the Danube.

A falling groundwater table threatened the preservation of the wood in situ, and therefore, in 1994, it was decided to excavate and salvage the two ships in a joint campaign of the Bavarian Antiquities Authority, the Roman Germanic Commission, and the Roman Germanic Central Museum (RGZM) in Mainz.

Both ships were approximately 15 m in length and 2.50 m wide. Ship 1 had its complete starboard side preserved and on ship 2, only the top strakes on both sides were lost. The planks and keelsons were made of pine, whereas the frames, keels, and cross-beams were of oak. The ribs were fastened to the hulls with treenails.

The state of preservation of the wood varied. The prows were heavily degraded, their consistency resembled peat. The pine strakes amidships were somewhat less degraded. The pine keelson in ship 2 was quite well preserved in its core. The oak timbers, however, were heavily degraded. Only in a few parts did the keel still show wood fibres of some strength.

Lifting the two overlapping ships *en bloc* was impossible in view of the size, and

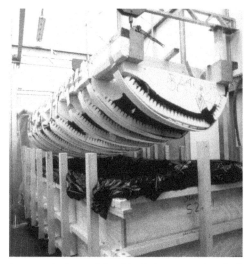

A segment of one of the ships in its transport cradle is lowered into the wooden treatment tank. The cradle was then exchanged for a new construction with less buoyancy. Photograph: Museum für Antike Schifffahrt, Mainz

dismantling the ships would have meant destroying the typical wooden joints of the timbers. To salvage the two ships in segments seemed to be the most reasonable approach. Some years before, a mechanical excavating machine had already cut the hulls in two, and as the prow parts were so extremely degraded, they had separated from the midship sections. Each ship now consisted of two midship segments of about 6 m in length, and two prow segments of 2–2.5 m in length. In order to raise them, the segments were sandwiched between Styrofoam ribs and protective sheets, and securely fastened to wooden frames and cradles. They were then transported on trucks to the waterlogged wood conservation department at the RGZM.

The segments were cleaned, and wooden tanks were built around each of them and lined with heavy-duty foil. This preparatory work took four men about eight months. The largest tank had a volume of 6.5 m^3. Now that the ships sat in water, the Styrofoam ribs, which gave too much buoyancy, could be exchanged for PVC ribs, cushioned where they touched the ship. The new ribs were tailored in such

a way that hull planks, which, when underground had been displaced by the pressure of the earth, could be placed in their original positions.

During this work the wood was kept in changes of de-ionised water to remove dirt and substances which had been absorbed during burial. Five baths were needed until the pH and conductivity remained constant in the washing water. In September 1996 the Kauramin treatment of ship 2 began.

Wood of all states of degradation was treated in the same bath. The resin prepolymer impregnates even non-degraded wood, and the same Kauramin concentration is optimal for the stabilisation of different wood qualities. Working with the resin solution was unproblematic: it was not corrosive, and was handled at room temperature. With an ordinary garden pump the components were poured into a 2,000 litre vat, mixed, and pumped into the impregnation tanks. To make 12,000 litres of a 25% solution, about 3,000 litres of Kauramin 800 were diluted with 8,000 litres of de-ionised water; 5% urea was added to lower the viscosity, and 1% triethanolamine added as an alkaline buffer to prolong the stability of the solution. Without triethanolamine, a Kauramin solution is only stable for about 2–4 months. As we planned an impregnation of 7–9 months, the addition of a buffer was necessary.

The impregnation time is governed by the thickest timber, in this case the keelson of ship 2 with a diameter of 16 cm. Since nitrogen analyses indicated that melamine resin molecules penetrate degraded wood at a rate of about 1 cm per month, in eight months the keelson should have been impregnated to its core. Once a week the density of the bath solution and its pH were measured, and the 'cloud test' done. The change of density helps to assess the impregnation; the pH value and the 'cloud test' are indicators of the stability of the solution. Melamine resins are acid-cured; hence the pH has to be kept alkaline during impregnation. Otherwise, polyaddition starts, and the resin is no longer water soluble and the treatment solution is spoilt.

After nine to ten months, the segments of ship 2 were lifted from the tanks, the pH had dropped to 7.5–7.0, and the 'cloud test' was positive. In this state, resin residues can still be easily washed from the wood surface. If this point is missed, a sticky resin layer may form, which can only be removed with great effort.

A heat treatment followed the impregnation in order to cross-link the resin in the cell walls. A large heat chamber was built, 6.8 × 3.3 × 2.3 m, which could be heated to 70°C by two heating units. Six microwave transmitters of 1,000 W each, placed evenly under the ceiling, could supply microwave energy. The wood surfaces were covered with moist tissue paper to prevent resin from the wood sticking to them. The ship segments were then packed in polyethylene film to prevent the wood from drying during the heat curing. The segments of ship 2 were treated, one by one, at 50°C. Within a week, the resin was totally cured. A sample of the impregnation solution served as an indicator. When it had solidified, the curing was finished. After complete cooling, the foil and tissue were removed. Kauramin contains about 0.5% formaldehyde; if the wood is unpacked while still hot, this will irritate eyes and noses.

At the end of the curing, the wood is still waterlogged. A rapid and uncontrolled drying can, even in this state, result in shrinkage, warping, and crack formation. For a controlled drying, we packed the ship segments in plastic film again. To reduce the drying time for the four parts of ship 2 and to obtain a good stabilisation, we dried the plastic-wrapped wood using microwave energy. This energy penetrates the dry wood substance without warming it too much, but heats up any water in the wood and makes it evaporate. The evaporation energy does not have to be transported by the wood substance from the outer, already-dry portions of the timbers to the still water-filled interior. In this way, the dry wood is not overheated, and no dangerous moisture gradient builds up.

The microwave setup was regulated to 35°C via sensors in the wood, and worked in time intervals. After 3–4 hours it was turned off, the wood unpacked, and the condensed water on the foil and on the wood left to dry for one to two hours. The microwave drying was carried out until the moisture content of the wood had come down to about 40%, the approximate fibre saturation point (FSP) of degraded wood. This procedure took nine months for the segments of ship 2. The segments were then covered with foil and slowly dried in ambient conditions to 12–15% moisture content.

The melamine impregnation of ship 1 required about 5,000 litres of resin solution. The timbers were thinner than those of ship 2, and the impregnation time of each of the four segments could be planned for only six months. Only 0.5% triethanolamine buffer was added.

The microwave drying of the last segment was finished in early 2001; the stabilisation of the two ships had taken four years and three months.

All wood surfaces were brushed twice with a natural oil. The stabilisation with melamine resin adds only small amounts of resin to the wood structure. The objects remain relatively light, in both weight and colour. A surface treatment with solvent-based natural or synthetic resins, oils, or waxes, can adjust the colour to that of recent wood. At the same time, the surface is strengthened, and the wood is protected a little against fluctuations of relative humidity.

Shrinkages of up to 0.5% were measured in the direction of the fibres and less than 1% across the grain. The seams between hull planks only opened a few millimetres.

The ships were put on exhibition in the RGZM until a new museum could be erected near the place where they were found. The segments were mounted on individual bases, which later on could serve as transport cradles. The new Kelten Römer Museum, Manching, however, wanted to present the ships in aesthetically pleasant, unobtrusive steel supports. This meant that in addition to the temporary transport cradles, a lifting

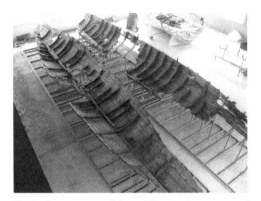

The final arrangement of the stabilised and reconstructed ships on steel supports. Photograph: Museum für Antike Schifffahrt, Mainz

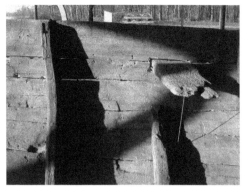

A close view of the Kauramin-treated ship's side. Photograph: Wolfgang David, Kelten und Römer Museum, Manching

system was necessary which could lift the ship segments from the cradles into their final support structure. We used the same technique – with wooden frames, Styrofoam ribs, temporary templates, and tightening belts – as was developed for the lifting of the ships from the excavation.

The construction of the large microwave 'oven' was very expensive. However, in recent years it has been quite useful in the conservation of other large wooden objects, and we feel the expense was justified. Nevertheless, the application of the Kauramin method on very large objects reaches its limit when it comes to the drying stage.

Positive aspects of the conservation of the *ships from Oberstimm* with Kauramin 800 are the first class stabilisation and visual appearance. The light weight of the stabilised timbers made working with the reassembly and presentation of the ships easy. The wood is still porous, as only small amounts of resin have been introduced. Should a strengthening or restabilisation of the timbers become desirable at some point, then such a treatment will

be possible, even if the melamine resin cannot be extracted again.

Note to §7.1 Melamine in wood – laboratory experiments

– Stabilising waterlogged wood with melamine resin has become the speciality and routine of the conservation department of the Roman Germanic Central Museum in Mainz, Germany. A microwave oven the size of a garage has been constructed for the stress-reduced drying of Kauramin-impregnated and cured ship finds. Markus Wittköpper has published a detailed description of the practical Kauramin procedure on the internet. http://www.rgzm.de/kur/index.cfm?Layout=holz&Content=kauramin

Notes to §7.2 Two ships in Kauramin – a case study

– The archaeological report on the ships from Oberstimm is given by R. Bockius, 2002.
– The salvage operation of the ships from Oberstimm is described in detail by A. Kremer, 1997.

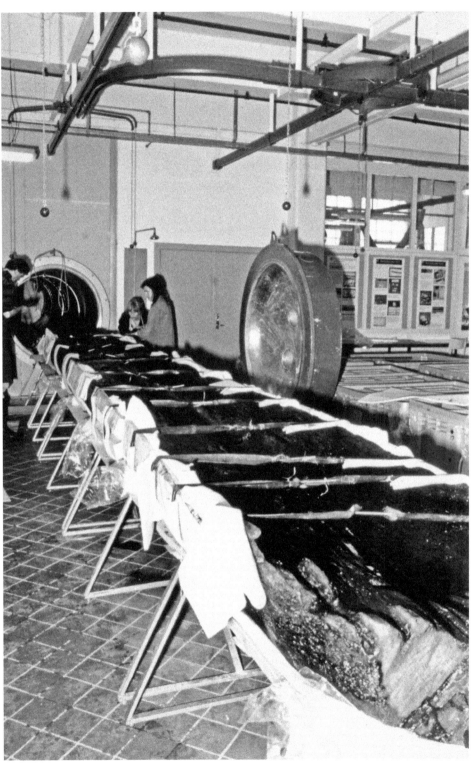

The conservation department of the Danish National Museum operates the largest vacuum chambers for freeze-drying waterlogged timbers and whole boats. The laboratory is a worldwide leader in both theoretical and practical handling of this method. Photograph: National Museum of Denmark, Copenhagen

8 Freeze-drying of archaeological waterlogged wood

by Poul Jensen, Kristiane Straetkvern, Inger Bojesen-Koefoed and David Gregory, National Museum of Denmark

8.1 The theory of freeze-drying

Vacuum freeze-drying is very well suited for most kinds of degraded or semi-degraded wooden objects with a tendency to heavy shrinkage and collapse, provided they are not too big. If vacuum freeze-drying is applied on voluminous objects, the method can be combined with vacuum-drying at room temperature. Vacuum freeze-drying requires expensive and relatively complex equipment; the process is energy intensive and needs to be run by trained personnel. The construction of most drying chambers permits the most efficient drying when the wood is placed in one layer only. As the freeze-drying process is lengthy and demanding of resources, the end use of the object has to justify the conservation costs.

The basic idea

The principle of using freeze-drying for the conservation of waterlogged archaeological wood is to reduce the capillary forces which normally develop when water evaporates from the water menisci in the small pores in the wood. These contractile forces can result in collapse if the cell wall cannot withstand the suction pressure.

These forces are avoided by freezing the water to ice and drying through sublimation, thus avoiding the liquid phase of water. The sublimation, and thereby the freeze-drying, starts when the partial pressure of water vapour around the object falls below the partial pressure of saturated water vapour over the ice. Freeze-drying from pure water can take place at temperatures below 0°C and partial water vapour pressures below 610 Pa.

The sublimation takes place from a retreating front, parallel to the surface of the object, dividing the object into an outer dried zone and an inner core of wood and ice. As energy must be transferred from the surface to the ice front, and water vapour transferred from the ice front to the surface, both through the dried zone, the speed of the freeze-drying process is inversely proportional to the depth of the ice front. Consequently, the thicker the object, the longer and more resource-demanding the drying process. The illustration below shows the drying of waterlogged wood in two dimensions.

Freeze-drying of waterlogged wood without impregnation

Although freezing the water in the wood fixes the cell wall in the water-swollen state to a

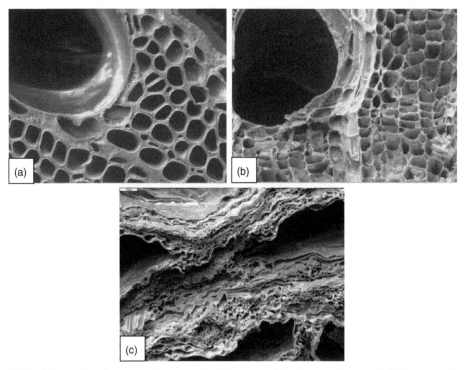

(a) Air dried non-degraded wood with intact cells; (b) freeze-dried, heavily degraded wood with degraded cell walls but intact cell lumen; (c) air-dried, heavily degraded wood. The cell lumen collapsed and flattened
Photographs: Conservation Department, National Museum of Denmark.

certain extent, freeze-drying is not normally done when the wood contains only water, as this will result in expansion and cracks in the object when the free water in the cell lumen freezes. Additionally, shrinkage, disintegration, and cracks occur when the hygroscopically bound water in the expanded water-swollen cell wall is removed.

Freeze-drying of waterlogged wood after impregnation with water soluble agents

To prevent or reduce shrinkage of a freeze-dried object, the waterlogged object is impregnated with a water-soluble bulking agent which is able to replace the bound water in the cell wall. As dried degraded objects frequently have a low compression and tensile strength, they can be impregnated with a consolidating agent too, which, after drying, adds strength to the objects by partially filling the pores i.e. cell lumina. Both bulking and

consolidating agents can act as cryoprotectors by reducing the amount of cracks caused by the expansion of water during its transition to ice.

The introduction of water-soluble impregnation agents lowers the freezing point of the aqueous solution, and as experience has shown that a successful freeze-drying process requires total solidification of the solution, the process temperature must normally be kept below the eutectic (collapse) temperature of the solution. The eutectic structure is formed at the eutectic temperature. At this temperature, both water in which the PEG is dissolved, and the dissolved PEG, solidify, forming ice and solid PEG respectively. The illustration below shows the eutectic structure of freeze-dried PEG 2000.

A consequence of the ice sublimating from a retreating ice front in the wood is that the speed of the freeze-drying process is nearly proportional to the water vapour pressure

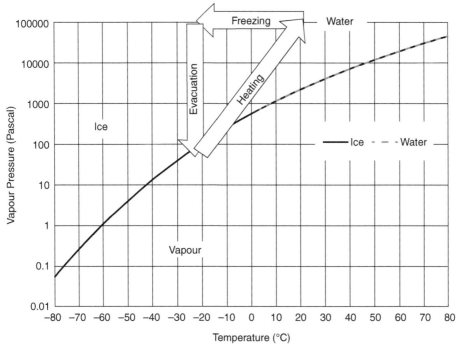

Principles for freeze-drying in relation to the liquid, solid and gas phases. The water in the porous structure (wood with solidified PEG) changes from water to ice through cooling. The partial pressure around the waterlogged porous structure is then lowered, so that the water passes from ice to water vapour by sublimation. The water in the porous structure is removed without the development of destructive capillary forces. Finally the vacuum is released and the temperature of the objects is raised to ambient. (The data for water vapour pressure over ice is from Lide (1995). 100 Pa = 1 mbar)

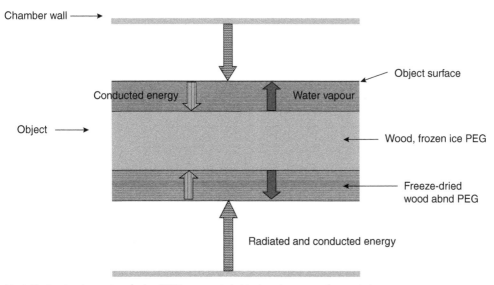

Model for heat and mass transfer in a PEG impregnated object under vacuum freeze-drying over ice at the freeze-drying temperature. The lowering of the freeze-drying temperature to the collapse temperature reduces the water vapour pressure over the ice and subsequently slows down the process.

The concept that the aqueous impregnation solution must have a eutectic temperature and structure means that the original pores of the wood will be filled with a solidified impregnation agent, also forming a porous structure. The permeability of the wood in the dry zone will be inversely proportional to the

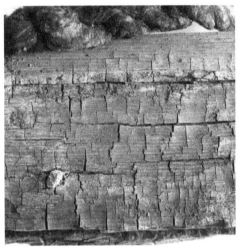

Wooden object freeze-dried directly from water, showing transverse cracks due to shrinkage caused by removal of the hygroscopic water in the cell wall
Photographs: Conservation Department, National Museum of Denmark.

concentration of the impregnation solution, and as the drying time is proportional to permeability, the drying time will be increased by increasing the concentration of the impregnation agent. Importantly, concentrations higher than the eutectic concentration will hinder the transfer of water vapour from the ice front to the surface, as no pores are formed in the solidifying impregnation agent which is not part of the eutectic mixture.

Therefore, the freeze-drying process is a compromise of many parameters such as type and concentration of impregnation agent, eutectic temperature and structure, and process temperature. Irrespectively, all freeze-drying processes can be divided into three phases: impregnation, freezing and finally freeze-drying, either under vacuum or at atmospheric pressure. As impregnation is the same for freeze-drying under either reduced or atmospheric pressure, it is dealt with in a separate section.

Selection of water soluble impregnation agents prior to freeze-drying

The purpose of an impregnation agent in relation to freeze-drying of a waterlogged wooden object is to ensure that the process can be performed with an optimal result, and that the dried object will be suitable for storage, exhibition and scientific analysis. The impregnation agent has to reduce the shrinkage, strengthen the object, and reduce the damage caused by

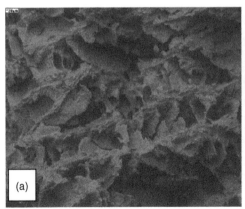
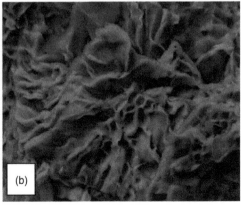

(a) Eutectic structure of PEG 2000 (75×); (b) close up of the same eutectic structure (500×). Photographs: Conservation Department, National Museum of Denmark.

the expansion of water when transformed into ice, by acting as a bulking agent, stabilizing agent and cryoprotector. At the same time, the impregnation agent must possess a not too low solidifying (eutectic/collapse) temperature and a porous solid (eutectic) structure. Finally the impregnation agent must be water soluble and able to diffuse into the waterlogged wooden structure at a reasonable speed.

As these demands for an impregnation agent can be in conflict with each other, a variety of water-soluble impregnating agents such as glycerol, sucrose, glucose, mannitol, sorbitol and polyethylene glycol (PEG) have been tested.

At the moment, PEG is the impregnation agent which has had by far the most use. PEGs are available with molecular masses from 200 to more than 100,000, they are water soluble, can diffuse into waterlogged wooden objects, and can replace bound water in the cell walls. They have eutectic properties at not too low temperatures and are able to strengthen degraded wood. The two most conflicting requirements are the necessity of a small molecular mass in order to facilitate fast diffusion and a high eutectic temperature, which is equivalent to a high molecular mass. The illustration below shows the eutectic temperature of PEG as a function of the molecular mass. Normally PEGs with molecular masses above 1,500 are chosen as those with lower molecular masses are not solid at room temperature

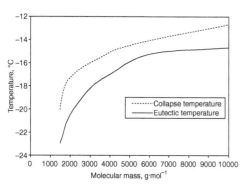

Eutectic and collapse temperatures for aqueous PEG solutions (Schnell and Jensen 2007)

and their eutectic temperatures are very low, making freeze-drying difficult. Likewise, PEGs with molecular masses above 4,000 are not used due to their slow diffusion and lack of ability to penetrate well-preserved wood.

8.2 Freeze-drying processes

In addition to freeze-drying under reduced pressure, it is possible – under specific conditions – to conduct freeze-drying at atmospheric pressure. However, both processes require the waterlogged wood to be impregnated with a stabilising agent.

The impregnation process

The objective of the impregnation process is to ensure a correct, pre-defined concentration distribution of the impregnation agent in the object.

If PEG is chosen as an impregnation agent, a high molecular mass PEG (1500 to 4000) is selected as the primary agent with an end concentration of the treatment solution of 30 to 45% w/w. This concentration can stabilize the object by filling cell lumina and 'gluing' disintegrated wood together. The less degraded the wood, the lower the molecular mass that can be selected.

For very well-preserved wooden objects a low molecular mass PEG (200 to 600) can be added to the solution in concentrations of between 3 and 10%, as these small molecules have a better ability to penetrate the cell wall, and to exchange the hygroscopically bound water – thereby preventing shrinkage. If the low molecular mass PEG is not absorbed into the cell wall or the eutectic structure of the high molecular mass PEG, collapse can occur. In order to minimize the concentration of low molecular mass PEG in the outer, often more degraded, zone of the wood, the two-step impregnation method can be used.

The impregnation normally takes place in tanks at room temperature. The initial concentration is usually 10% and increased in steps of 5 to 10% w/w until the final concentration is reached. The impregnation time varies from a few months to many years depending on the type of wood, the dimensions, the state of degradation and the molecular mass of the PEG. Experience and models for diffusion are used to determine impregnation schedules. The concentration of the impregnation baths has to be monitored during the impregnation process. For further information on impregnation processes see Section 4.3 on the one- and two-step methods.

Problems with microorganisms can occur, but may be reduced by heating or adding biocides. More information on the handling of microbes can also be found in Section 4.3 in connection with the *Bremen Cog* project.

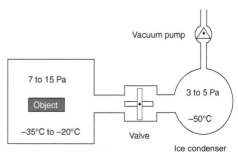

Vacuum freeze-dryer for drying waterlogged objects pre-impregnated with PEG. 100 Pa = 1 mbar

The process of vacuum freeze-drying waterlogged wood

The idea behind vacuum freeze-drying is that after freezing the impregnated wood in the chamber, all the air is pumped out of the drying chamber so only water vapour at a very low pressure is left. This condition will enable very fast transfer processes – flow – of water vapour from the ice front through the dried region of the object to its surface, and then further to the ice condenser, thereby giving very short drying times. However, the physics of freeze-drying makes it difficult to dry thick objects, and drying times for objects thicker than 10 cm can take more than six months. As vacuum-freeze dryers have a limited size, the shape and dimension of the objects have to be taken into consideration.

Specification of equipment for vacuum freeze-drying

Vacuum freeze-driers for processing waterlogged archaeological objects, pre-impregnated with PEG, typically consist of a vacuum chamber with walls that can be cooled, a connection between the vacuum chamber and the ice condenser fitted with a valve, and an ice condenser connected to a vacuum pump. The chamber must be able to

reach temperatures below the eutectic temperatures of the aqueous PEG solution, and attain a pressure where the ice in the object can sublimate. The temperature in the ice condenser must be low enough to condense the water vapour sublimed from the object to avoid overloading the vacuum pump.

Vacuum-freeze-dryers must be equipped with temperature sensors able to measure the temperatures of the chamber wall, the ice condenser, and the objects being dried. There must be pressure gauges to measure the water vapour pressure in the tank and at the pump, and scales to follow the weight loss of objects while drying.

Freezing

As vacuum-freeze dryers for waterlogged archaeological wood normally have coolable chamber walls, freezing of the impregnated objects prior to the sublimation process can take place inside the chamber. Alternatively, objects can be frozen in ordinary freezers or freezing rooms prior to the freeze-drying. During the freezing of objects they must be covered with vapour-tight foils or bags to avoid the evaporation of water from the surface in the period where liquid aqueous solutions are still present, otherwise collapse and cracks can occur.

Vacuum freeze-drying

The temperature of the chamber walls of the freeze-drying tank is lowered to below the eutectic temperature to ensure full solidification of the aqueous impregnation agent in the objects. The sublimation, and thereby the freeze-drying of the impregnated objects, starts when the pressure in the tank is lowered below the pressure of saturated water vapour over the ice (see figure on page 107 with the caption: *Principles for freeze-drying ...*). The freeze-drying is controlled by monitoring the temperature of the object, the pressure in the tank, the temperature of the chamber wall, the weight loss of the objects, and the amount of condensed ice in the ice trap. The freeze-drying process is optimized by keeping the pressure in the tank as low as possible, and the temperature in the objects just below the eutectic/collapse temperature by regulating the chamber wall temperature.

Depending upon the density, porosity and thickness of the object, the freeze-drying can take up to six months, or even longer.

Advantages

Since freeze-drying is a very safe process in terms of the preservation of original volumes and surfaces, it is a method which can be recommended for objects to be conserved for exhibitions and for studies of technology, e.g. carvings, runes. If deformed objects or planks require reshaping by clamping or blocking, this can take place while the wood still is in a wet, impregnated condition, provided that the original shape of the object is known. Similar useful procedures are possible when drying fragmented objects, as even complicated fractures can be assembled while the wood is still wet and flexible. Shapes and positions are fixed before freezing and are kept fixed throughout the drying process, thus only minimal processing is required when later mounting for display.

Disadvantages

The equipment is expensive and relatively complicated with high running costs. If objects have not been shaped prior to freeze-drying, the dried objects must be heated and humidified in order to shape them. The PEG used for impregnation does not always add strength to the object, so a suitable support may be required. Objects thicker than 10 cm are difficult to dry and they take longer.

The process of freeze-drying waterlogged wood at atmospheric pressure

The use of freeze-drying at atmospheric pressure has only been reported in a few cases, and the method has not been developed to a level where it can be considered a standard method. However, it might be an inexpensive alternative to vacuum freeze-drying for both small and large objects.

The principle is to place the frozen impregnated object in a cold chamber with a low relative humidity (RH), so that water vapour will be transferred from the ice front to the area with the lower RH.

The removal of the water vapour from the surface of the object takes place by convection – a fast process – but as the normal atmosphere is present inside the object, the transfer of water vapour from the ice front to the surface takes place by diffusion – a fairly slow process – thus making the drying process at atmospheric pressure much slower than vacuum freeze-drying.

Unlike vacuum freeze-drying, the wood should not be much thicker than 2 cm if the objects are to dry in a reasonable time. However, as large freezing rooms with adequate RH can be used, dimensions might not be a limiting factor.

Specification of equipment for freeze-drying at atmospheric pressure

In principle, freeze-dryers for freeze-drying waterlogged archaeological objects at atmospheric pressure consist of a chamber which can be cooled, a dehumidifying unit to remove moisture from the atmosphere and, in some cases, ventilators to generate a reasonable airspeed over the objects and facilitate the deposition of ice/water at the dehumidifier.

Freezing cabinets with directly cooled shelves can be used for freeze-drying. The shelves serve two purposes: (i) to cool the cabinet; (ii) to act as dehumidifiers, as the cooling coils are colder than the air temperature in the cabinet. Relative humidities between 20 and 80% can be achieved.

Freezers with cooling coils in the walls can also be used, but the RH is often higher than 75%, making the drying slow. The RH can be lowered by inserting 'cold fingers' for deposition of ice, or trays with dehumidifying agents.

Larger freezing rooms and containers can be very useful for big finds. Depending on the construction, dehumidifiers must be installed.

All types of freeze-dryers must be provided with temperature sensors to measure the temperature of the chamber wall, RH sensors, and weight sensors to monitor the weight loss of objects while drying.

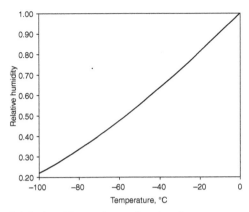

Relative humidity over ice as a function of temperature

Freeze-drying at atmospheric pressure

The temperature in the freeze-dryer is lowered below the eutectic temperature to ensure full solidification of the aqueous impregnation agent. The sublimation, and thereby the freeze-drying of the impregnated objects, starts when the RH in the chamber falls below the value at the ice front. The figure shows RH over ice as a function of temperature.

The freeze-drying process is controlled by monitoring the temperature and weight loss of the objects, the RH in the chamber, and the amount of condensed ice at the ice trap or water absorbed by the dehumidifying agent. The drying process is optimized by keeping the RH at the surface of the objects as low as possible and the temperature in the objects just below the eutectic/collapse temperature by regulating the chamber temperature.

Depending on the density, porosity and thickness of the objects and the efficiency of the equipment, the freeze-drying can take up to six months or more.

Advantages

The method is simple with the equipment being readily available and relatively inexpensive. The drying time for objects up to a thickness of 1.5 cm is quite fast.

Disadvantages

The method is not well documented. The drying time can be long for objects with a thickness of more than 2 cm and therefore resource demanding.

Alternative freeze-drying processes

The safest way of freeze-drying waterlogged objects is at a temperature below the eutectic/collapse temperature. However this practice is not always followed.

Low concentration of PEG

Low concentration solutions of impregnation agents in aqueous solutions will, if cooled, initially have water freezing as ice from solution. If enough ice is formed, a coherent ice structure is produced which is able to withstand collapse pressure. Therefore objects can be held in the water-swollen position during freeze-drying, even if the eutectic solution concentration has not been reached when at a single temperature (the eutectic point) the water and impregnation agent solidify together. This can be the case if the impregnation agent is only used in a very low concentration, 3 to 5% w/w, and if it is absorbed into the cell walls of the wood during the drying process while it is still unfrozen.

The advantages of this type of process are that the freeze-drying can take place at higher temperatures, and therefore at higher speeds; and also that impregnation agents with small molecules and low eutectic temperatures, well able to penetrate the cell walls and replace the bound water, can be used.

The two-step method

The two-step method, where the outer zone of the wood is impregnated with PEG with molecular masses over 2,000 and the inner zone is impregnated with lower molecular weight PEGs, can also, if used carefully, be beneficial for wood with an outer degraded zone prone to collapse and an inner well-preserved zone which does not collapse. The outer zone is freeze-dried at temperatures below the eutectic temperature of the high molecular PEG, and the inner zone air-dried at room temperature.

Exhibition and storage requirements for conserved objects

All the conservation methods and impregnation agents mentioned are safe to use as long as the requirements for normal museum/storage conditions are met: temperature (15 to 25°C), relative humidity (30 to 55%), physical, chemical and biological threats. As impregnation agents do not always add strength to conserved objects, support is often necessary both for exhibitions and storage.

8.3   Ships in a vacuum chamber

The following case studies are selected examples of how vacuum freeze-drying processes have been successfully applied to archaeological ship finds at the National Museum of Denmark.

A plank-built ship – Roskilde 6

The Roskilde ships were excavated in the harbour of Roskilde in 1996–97. The excavations exposed wrecks of nine ships dating from 1025 to 1336, eight of them were cargo ships, but the oldest one, the *Roskilde 6*, was a warship built for about 100 men. All ships were clinker-built; however, the dimensions of the vessels varied as well as the dimensions of the timbers applied in the constructions. After in situ documentation was written, all the ships were dismantled before being lifted and transported to water storage tanks. After cleaning and documentation of the individual pieces, all the timbers were brought to the conservation department for conservation. The majority of the timbers were of oak; some of them were only degraded on the surface with very little degradation at the centre of the wood, whereas others appeared more evenly degraded throughout the wood. Nevertheless, they were all immersed in tanks with PEG 2000 solutions, intended for vacuum freeze-drying.

The plan for the ships in 2011 was that the cargo ships would be conserved for study purposes without being assembled. However, the long war ship, *Roskilde 6*, would be conserved for display in a travelling Viking Age exhibition. This end use had an impact on the freeze-drying process, as it was important that each of the three-dimensional ship timbers would fit into its original place when the ship was reassembled in a support after conservation. Deformation of the ship timbers might have occurred during the period of burial or during the years of impregnation in the tanks. Therefore the original shape of the ship was reconstructed in order to produce individual frames, supports and moulds to be employed during the drying processes. The reconstruction was also used when building the framework to support the ship in the exhibition.

Although only 25% of the original *Roskilde 6* ship was preserved, six freeze-drying operations were required to dry all the pieces in our large freeze-drying vacuum chamber – 8 m long and 2 m in diameter. As each freeze-drying operation lasted about five months, the total drying

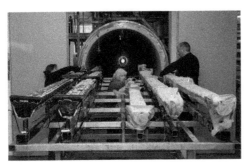

Keel parts fixed in forks on iron bars before freeze-drying. Photograph: Conservation Department, National Museum of Denmark.

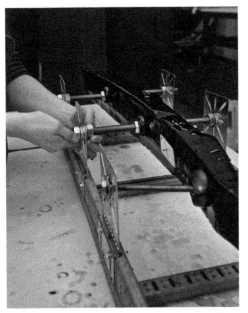

Frame timbers mounted in frames before freeze-drying. Photograph: Conservation Department, National Museum of Denmark.

time was almost three years. The keel, consisting of five parts mounted in forks on iron bars, was the first to be dried. Then, the frames and similar timbers fixed in special frameworks were processed. Finally, planks with individual supports were processed in three batches.

In order to follow and control the process in the vacuum chamber, temperature sensors were placed in selected pieces before starting the drying process. The temperature was used as a control parameter during the freeze-drying process.

Until vacuum freeze-drying was introduced for the conservation of clinker-built waterlogged shipwrecks, the method for bending conserved planks into ship shape was to completely replace the water in the wood with PEG before subjecting the timbers to high temperatures for several hours until bending was possible. Whereas the full PEG-impregnated archaeological wood becomes flexible and can be bent after steam heating, this method cannot be recommended for vacuum freeze-dried wood. These timbers have been impregnated in 35–40% PEG 2000 and the application of steam on the degraded porous surfaces after freeze-drying may cause collapse or shrinkage of the wood. Most vacuum freeze-dried timbers have a light appearance and the tool marks are well preserved. These features might be lost in a steaming process. Moreover, application of heat in the absence of water degrades the PEG molecules. Oxidative degradation processes are accelerated at elevated temperatures and lead to a decrease in molecular weight. Degrading PEG produces formaldehydes that are a health hazard. Shaping of the timbers while the wood is still in a wet, impregnated and flexible condition eliminates these risks; the 3D puzzle of the conserved timbers is then possible.

Shaping, fixing and adding moulds before each freeze-drying process is time-consuming and requires the final shape of the ship and timbers to be known. Vacuum freeze-drying of ship parts requires drying chambers that are at least 5–7 m long. A critical aspect of the process is the actual shaping of the wet, impregnated timbers when they are taken out of the impregnation bath. It is very important to avoid uncontrolled drying while arranging them in the right shape; thus plastic sheets, cloths soaked in PEG solution and spraying containers with a solution of PEG in water must be at hand while shaping the individual pieces.

Two logboats – Bingen and Ejsbøl

Vacuum freeze-drying has proven to be a good method for the conservation of logboats.

Logboats are cut out of tree trunks, frequently oak, lime, or alder. As most of the core material is removed from the trunk, log boats will often have a relatively large content of sapwood. A typical degradation pattern for logboats is that their sides, ends and surface areas are relatively degraded. Logboats usually of a larger cross-section tend to have some less degraded areas in the centre of the wood, whereas the smaller logboats are often more homogenously degraded throughout the entire object.

The *Bingen logboat* was excavated at Sørum in the southeast part of Norway in 1997. The oak boat was almost 10 m long, 0.7 m wide, and it was dated to 170 BC. The bottom part of the boat was 13–15 cm thick. Original tool marks from the axes and adzes were still evident in the surface. The densities of the wood varied from 365 kg/m^3 in the most degraded areas to 450 kg/m^3 in the better preserved parts. Being the oldest Norwegian boat ever found, successful conservation was high priority. Although the thickness of the boat was very close to the limit of the dimensions where efficient vacuum freeze-drying could be applied, it was assumed that the method would be safer and provide a better result than the full impregnation method. As no large vacuum freeze-drying plant was available in Norway, it was decided to carry out the impregnation in Norway and perform the vacuum freeze-drying in Denmark. An impregnation plan, intended for vacuum freeze-drying, was worked out. From 2001 to 2004 the boat was impregnated with a sequence of aqueous solutions of PEG 200 and PEG 4000. In the first year a 10% solution of PEG 200 was applied. Then solutions of increasing concentrations of PEG 4000 were added, up to 40%. In 2004, the logboat was taken out of the impregnation bath, wrapped in plastic, placed in a freezing container and sent to Denmark. As the logboat was 2 m longer than the freeze-drying tank, it had been decided to cut the boat upon arrival in Denmark. The cut was made by sawing – not as a direct cut, but in steps, in order to enable a better assembly of the two pieces after drying.

The handling of one 10 m long piece of wood weighing 1,500–2,000 kg required a good lifting system, heavy tools, straps, skilled personnel, and a lot of free space in the room where the boat was being handled. The drying process lasted six months. However, during the first couple of months that vacuum freeze-drying was applied, owing to the dimensions of the wood, the exchange of energy and water vapour to and from the ice core stagnated, and the temperature in the drying chamber had to be gradually increased. This method can only be recommended when the drying process has reached a stage where the most degraded parts in the outer area are dry already, and when the degree of degradation of the object is above the collapse limit. Another difference from the usual conservation treatments was the impregnation with both low and high molecular weight PEG. This solution was recommended because impregnation of thick, hardly degraded oak wood objects with high molecular mass PEGs is extremely slow and close to impossible. As the degree of degradation indicated that shrinkage could be expected upon drying, the introduction of a bulking agent, PEG 200, prior to impregnation with PEG 4000 was used. As the concentration of high molecular PEG in the most degraded surface areas was sufficiently high, no collapse in the surface was observed after drying. Some longitudinal cracks occurred during the drying process. However, as the impregnation period was only for three and a half years, the cracking was less than expected for these types of objects. The conservation was still considered successful.

The *Ejsbøl logboat* was excavated from an Iron Age bog in the southern part of Denmark in 1998. The boat was made from oak, the bottom and sides were between 2 and 10 cm thick. The boat, 3.5 m long and 0.75 m wide, was not complete – parts of one side and one end were missing. The logboat was heavily and homogeneously degraded, with an estimated wood density of 200–250 kg/m^3.

A special feature of the boat was that several longitudinal cracks had been repaired by sewing with bast fibres, and the sewing fixed with wooden nails. Cracks developed during the lifting of the logboat from the peat. Thus, a challenge during the impregnation and drying processes was to protect the broken parts to enable a precise fit of the pieces upon assembly.

After documentation, all pieces were wrapped in polyethylene film until immersion in the impregnation tank with PEG 2000. The impregnation, starting with 16% w/w and ending with 44% w/w PEG 2000, lasted for eight years.

After impregnation, the boat was assembled while still wet. This enabled a perfect fit of each piece. Supports for the sides and stem during the drying process were created. After assembly, the wood was wrapped in plastic and frozen. When the structure was totally frozen and the shape fixed, the plastic was removed from the boat and the vacuum freeze-drying process initiated. The freeze-drying was carried out over a period of five months. This process was run at −25°C the whole time.

The wood would probably have collapsed if the freeze-drying temperature had been elevated during the process, but fortunately, this was not necessary. The maximum thickness of the wood was 8–10 cm, and the wood was heavily degraded. More porous wood allows a more efficient diffusion of water vapour from the ice in the wood outwards.

After freeze-drying, the surplus PEG on the surfaces was removed and the pieces glued together with Jet Melt 3792-Q from 3M. Although the boat was conserved for study purposes, supports were made to prevent the ship from falling apart during transportation and storage.

Ropes and lines

Sometimes ropes and lines are found in or with archaeological ships and boats. They are

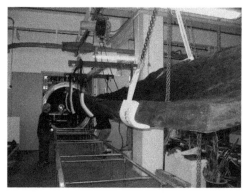

The *logboat from Bingen* after freeze-drying. Photograph: Conservation Department, National Museum of Denmark

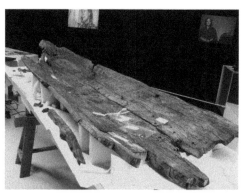

The *logboat from Ejsbøl* after vacuum freeze-drying before final cleaning of the surface. Photograph: Conservation Department, National Museum of Denmark

either integral parts of the ship such as rigging or anchor cables, or associated with the cargo, or they were lines used for the handling of the ship. Waterlogged rope is an extremely delicate material, and freeze-drying is the best method to preserve it.

The fundamental problems concerning archaeological fibre materials are related to the degradation of the fibres, to the open construction of the objects, and to the fact that the materials themselves are so inhomogeneous.

The dominant fibre in the rope is the bast from the bark of the lime tree. The best way to describe bast as an archaeological material is as 'a collection of pieces of fibres arranged in a specific order and position in relation to each other'. Unlike all the other organic archaeological materials such as wood, bone, leather, etc., the bast material in the rope structure is not able to bear its own wet weight – and indeed cannot carry the weight of the water that fills up the open areas in the structure either. When the water surrounding the rope is drained, the original round shape will collapse and the object becomes flat. Fortunately, when replaced in the water, buoyancy enables the rope to regain its original shape. It is remarkable how much 'memory' there can be 'stored' in the material. Another property of ropes is that – unlike objects made of other organic materials – they will disintegrate if they are placed freely in water; even the smallest movement of the water will make them swim apart.

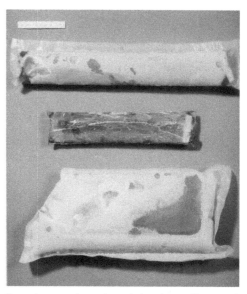

Ropes in water, frozen in sealed packages. Photograph: Conservation Department, National Museum of Denmark

Salvaging rope from excavations

The rope must always be placed on a stable support; bigger objects must be lifted as a block.

Cleaning

The cleaning must be undertaken with a very small and soft jet of water. It is helpful to place the object on a very smooth support e.g. glass, which can be tilted differently to clean different parts of the rope.

Packing

Packing of the object is an absolute prerequisite for successful conservation. As a packing

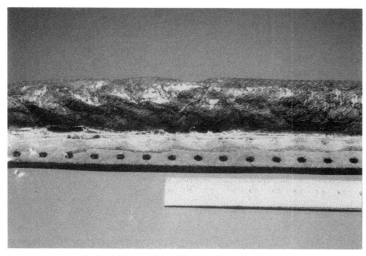

Rope after freeze-drying, still in perforated foil. Photograph: Conservation Department, National Museum of Denmark

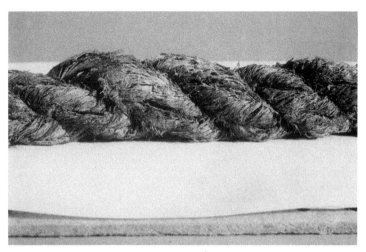

Rope after freeze-drying, placed upon a support and unpacked. Photograph: Conservation Department, National Museum of Denmark

material, perforated PE foil is very suitable: it is light, smooth, transparent, stable, inert, dimensionally stable, allows water and impregnation agents to permeate, and it is quick and easy to form around an individual object. In order to handle the object in a safe manner, it will often be necessary to fasten the package to a support.

Impregnation

A proper mixture of high and low molecular mass PEG in low concentrations ensures a successful vacuum freeze-drying.

Freeze-drying

Because of the above mentioned properties, rope has to be immersed in water and frozen in order to maintain its round shape during the freeze-drying process.

Mounting

Mounting the dry rope on a stable support on which it can be handled, is considered to be an integral part of the conservation of rope.

Notes to Chapter 8

– Detailed studies on various aspects of the freeze-drying of waterlogged wood have been published by Andersen, 1993; Jensen et al., 1993; Jensen et al., 2002; Jensen and Schnell, 2004; Jensen and Jensen, 2006; Schnell and Jensen, 2007.
– Very useful information on examples of equipment for freeze-drying is given by Jensen et al., 2007.
– The practical performance of freeze-drying ships timbers in moulds is described by Straetkvern et al., 2009.
– McCawley et al., 1981, have reported on a practical experiment on outdoor freeze-drying in the Canadian winter climate.
– The Roskilde ships found in the harbour of the Roskilde Viking ship museum are not to be confused with the Skuldelev Viking ships found in the Roskilde fjord in 1961. The documentation of the Roskilde ships has been published by J. Bill et al., 2000.
– The Bingen logboat and its treatment for conservation are described by Arisholm and Nymoen, 2005.
– A more detailed description of the freeze-drying of delicate rope can be read in Bojesen-Koefoed et al., 1993.

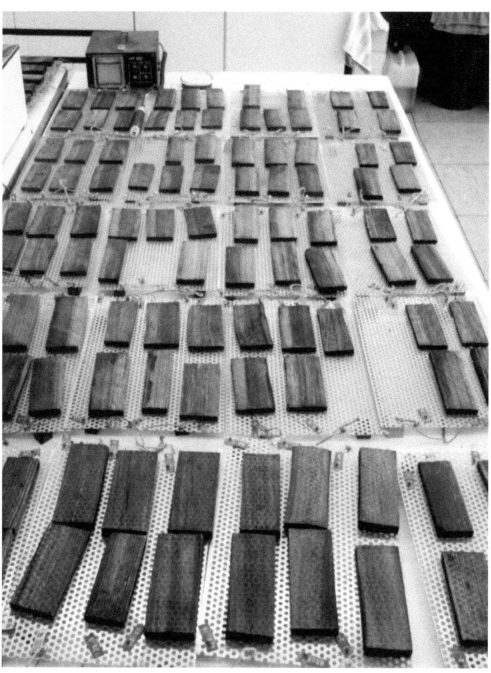

A rare stroke of luck: large amounts of available waterlogged wood made it possible to conduct extensive comparative studies on a homogeneous sample material. Photograph: Per Hoffmann

9 Choosing the 'best' method from PEG, sucrose, Lactitol and Kauramin

9.1 Assessment of the methods taking various factors into account

Although the stabilisation potential is extremely important, it is only one of the factors which need to be taken into account when choosing a conservation method. Other factors include: the reliability of the treatment method, the colour and look of the treated wood, its weight and other physical properties, the rendering of surface detail, the complexity of technical installations, control and maintenance requirements, the type and level of manpower and competence of staff, the duration of the procedure, and its overall costs. Reversibility or retreatability is considered to be indispensable for conservation methods. However, the conservation of a ship or boat is always a very expensive, time consuming and stressful project; the chances of someone wanting to reverse such an effort at some point are minimal, but the possibility of future retreatment must be considered.

Based on my experience in scaling-up laboratory experiments to full-size ship treatments, and in installing large conservation projects in institutions mainly occupied with other sorts of work, the above factors are discussed and assessed below. Comparing the performance of the four methods described in previous chapters – PEG, sucrose, Lactitol and Kauramin – all were tested on samples taken from the same degraded wood pieces. To decide on the method which is most appropriate for a ship or boat depends on its particular circumstances, bearing in mind the possibilities and limitations for each method. The methods are discussed below in the order of their performance.

Stabilisation

It was fortunate that the availability of large quantities of waterlogged archaeological wood from three different species, one softwood and two hardwoods, made it possible for me to carry out an extensive comparative study on the stabilisation efficiency of the different methods on specimens from the same timbers. Specimens could be cut in relatively large sizes, and ten parallel sets of experiments were run.

Rather degraded pine wood logs (u_{max} = 200–315%) came from a Neolithic trackway from the Camper Moor in Lower Saxony (see photograph by Gabriele Hoffmann). Heavily degraded split beech wood planks (u_{max} = 500–800%), and two quality oak wood logs (u_{max} = 100% and 590%) came from a 12th century settlement in Mecklenburg, where the whole fortification, palisades and towers, had tumbled into the water-filled moat. Test specimens were cut as flat boards of about 12 × 6 × 1.5 cm, with radial orientation. Thus, the oak specimens all contained one part non-degraded heartwood, and one part heavily degraded sapwood.

Stabilisation of the specimens was conducted under near-ideal conditions for the different methods, which are described in previous chapters. Assessment of the success of a method of stabilisation is based on

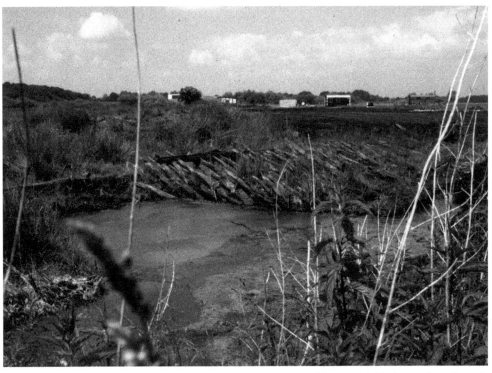

The oak and beech wood fortification of the 12th century settlement at Löddigsee in Mecklenburg collapsed into the water-filled moat 800 years ago. Photograph: Per Hoffmann

measurements of the specimen dimensions before treatment and after drying in ambient conditions. The residual cross-grain shrinkages and the shrinkage of non-stabilised specimens are calculated as mean values from the tangential and radial shrinkages of each specimen. The results are shown in the illustration by Per Hoffmann and Reinhold Breden. Warping, collapse, colour, and surface appearance were assessed by visual inspection.

Shrinkage in both untreated slightly degraded and heavily degraded wood may vary considerably from one specimen to the next, and is strongly determined by the occurrence of collapse of the cellular structure. Collapse is an irregularly occurring phenomenon, both in extent and local distribution. Specimens cut from the same timber may contain degradation of varying extent and thus develop different amounts of collapse. All four stabilisation treatments generally lead

to much more uniform shrinkage behaviour of specimens; the occurrence of collapse is strongly reduced, or even totally suppressed in all woods. There are, however, differences in the efficiency of the stabilisation methods. The various treatments are being assessed against each other based on natural air drying after treatment, not freeze-drying or kiln drying.

The Kauramin method gives the best dimensional stabilisation of all three woods, and perfect shape retention for pine and degraded beech wood. However, non-degraded oak heartwood can suffer some collapse and warping.

The next best dimensional and shape stabilisation is achieved with PEG treatments for all three woods. Even if the mean values for cross-grain shrinkage are higher than for sucrose and Lactitol treated specimens, the variation of the results is smaller. PEG 3000 stabilises highly degraded beech better than either sucrose or Lactitol.

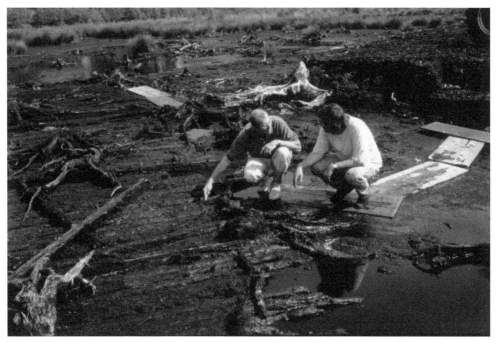

A Neolithic trackway was uncovered in the Camper Moor in Lower Saxony when several metres of peat had been removed for commercial use; it offered a wealth of degraded pine wood. The stumps of pine trees which had overgrown the trackway 5,000 years ago can still be seen. Photograph: Gabriele Hoffmann

Stabilisation of heavily degraded woods is the weak point of sucrose and Lactitol treatments: results can range from good to bad; they are unpredictable. Both sucrose and Lactitol treatments can cause substantial collapse and warping in degraded wood. A Lactitol treatment may even be dangerous to degraded wood as extensive crystal growth in the tissue may rupture the wood. A sucrose treatment, however, also gives unpredictable results in less degraded woods, softwoods and hardwoods.

All methods tested – except Kauramin – give better results for coniferous wood – pine – than for deciduous wood – beech and oak. This is a well-known phenomenon and will be to do with the more uniform structure of softwoods on the cellular level.

Reliability

An important factor when choosing a stabilisation method is the reliability of its performance. This means the probability that an expected result, known from experience or reported in the literature, will be achieved.

The PEG methods are the most robust ones. When the molecular weight of the PEG is adjusted to the wood quality the method is quite reliable; residual shrinkages will stay in the range 1–5%. The only risk in PEG treatments is an insufficient impregnation. But if enough time is allowed for impregnation – and this can be controlled by analysing wood cores taken at time intervals – an acceptable to good stabilisation will very highly probably be achieved.

In applying the Lactitol method, even close adherence to the instructions given by the authors of the improved method will not always prevent crystal growth and rupture in heavily degraded hardwoods. These woods also have a strong tendency to develop warping. At least for heavily degraded deciduous

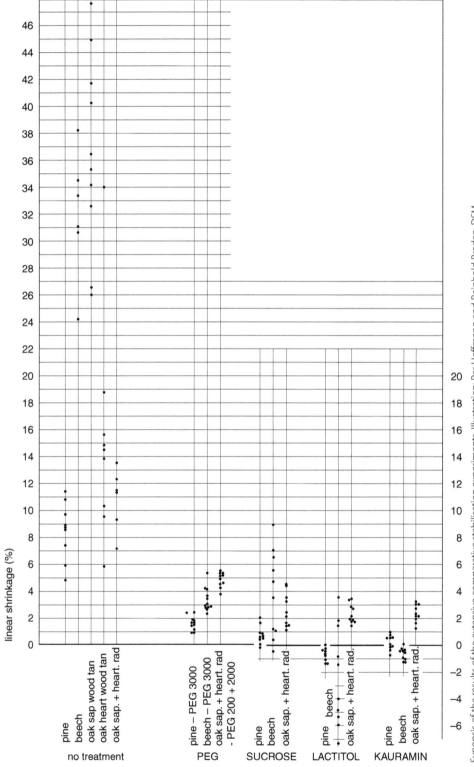

linear shrinkage (%)

pine
beech
oak sap wood tan
oak heart wood tan
oak sap. + heart. rad

no treatment

pine – PEG 3000
beech – PEG 3000
oak sap. + heart. rad
- PEG 200 + 2000

PEG

pine
beech
oak sap. + heart. rad.

SUCROSE

pine   beech
oak sap. + heart. rad.

LACTITOL

pine
beech
oak sap. + heart. rad.

KAURAMIN

Synopsis of the results of the extensive comparative stabilisation experiments. Illustration: Per Hoffmann and Reinhold Breden, DSM

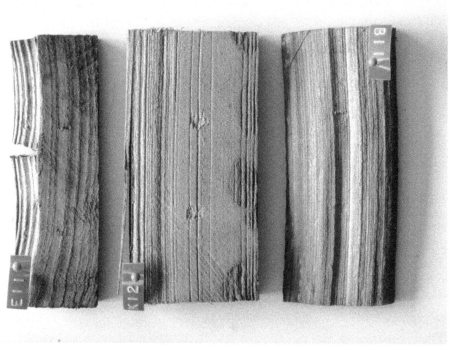

Left to right: waterlogged oak, pine, and beech specimens air dried without stabilisation; shrinkage, collapse, and cracks occur in all woods. Photogrraph: Per Hoffmann

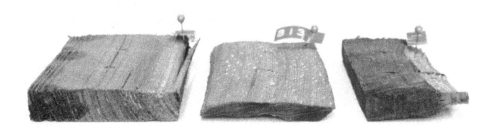

The same samples as above, rearranged. Left to right: pine, beech, oak. Photograph: Per Hoffmann

woods, the Lactitol method does not seem to be a reliable one in the hands of a conservator who does not have intimate experience of it.

The Kauramin method, too, seems to work with varying reliability on degraded and non-degraded wood. While all degraded woods are excellently stabilised, non-degraded oak heartwood is not. In our study, collapse occurred in the heartwood part of all oak specimens, resulting in surface depressions in the boards. It seems to be a consequence of too low a penetration of the amino resin prepolymer. When this effect becomes evident on drying the wood, it is too late for any action – the resin in the outer regions of the wood has polymerised, and no additional impregnation is possible. A premature polymerisation is always a risk with the Kauramin process, even if it is controlled by a careful pH regime.

The sucrose method, applied to ships and boats, is unreliable. It suffers from the incalculable risk of an infection of the treatment solution with air- and soil-borne microbes, which degrade the sucrose and destroy the stabilisation process. Such an infection may happen even when ample biocide has been added to the solution. With insufficient stabilisation, the result is collapse and warping of the timber. Even under sterile conditions in laboratory experiments, stabilisation results with heavily degraded hardwoods can vary considerably, from a slight swelling to about 10% shrinkage.

Surface appearance and colour of treated wood

The surface appearance and colour of treated and air-dried woods should only be compared when all woods have been cleaned properly. In particular, PEG-treated wood is often not cleaned thoroughly enough, and therefore it looks oily, waxy, and dark brown to black. Such an unattractive appearance often occurs on wood containing a high percentage of PEG. In my ranking, however, PEG-treated wood holds third place in terms of appearance behind sucrose and Lactitol-treated wood.

Sucrose and Lactitol impregnated woods look absolutely natural in colour, texture, and surface detail. The appearance of treated wood is an often praised feature of these methods.

Wood treated only with PEG 200–400 needs no cleaning. After drying it looks dry and natural and with fine surface detail, although it may have a soft touch. Wood treated with PEG 2000–4000, and cleaned carefully and thoroughly, preferably with a well-adjusted steam jet as described in Section 10.1, will dry to quite a natural look. With less deep cleaning the colour will stay somewhat darker and more intense, and have

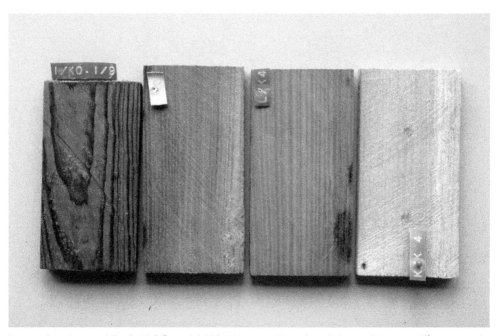

Pine wood specimens stabilised with (left to right): PEG 3000, sucrose, Lactitol + trehalose, and Kauramin; differences in colour and in transparency of the surface are obvious. Please note the specimens are of different sizes. Photographs: Per Hoffmann

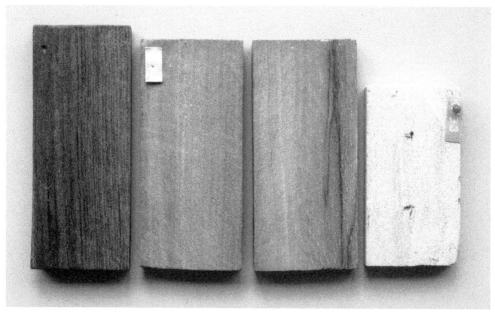

Beech wood specimens stabilised with (left to right): PEG 3000, sucrose, Lactitol + trehalose, and Kauramin. Please note the specimens are of different sizes

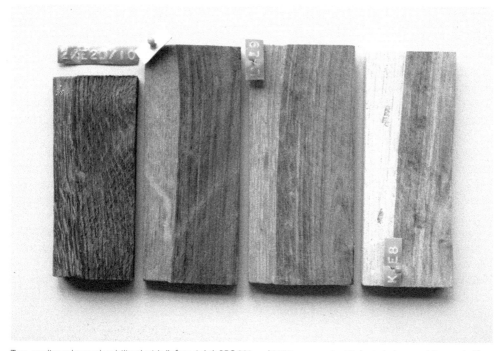

Two-quality oak wood stabilised with (left to right): PEG 200 and 3000, sucrose, Lactitol + trehalose, and Kauramin. Please note the specimens are of different sizes

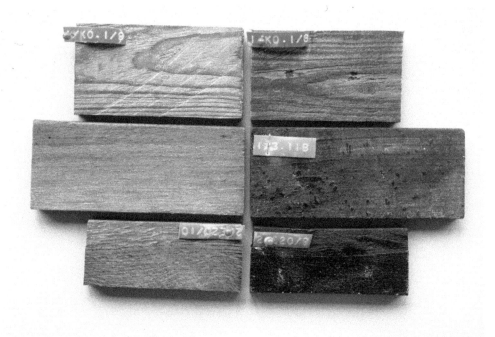

Pine, beech, and oak specimens stabilised with PEG 200 and 3000; surface cleaning (lefthand samples) changes the appearance of the woods

more contrast. The wood can be made to look as if it had been treated with a light oil. Well cleaned, the wood will look dry and all surface details will be visible. The more or less PEG-filled wood will be beneath a very thin layer from which most of the PEG has been extracted.

Kauramin-treated wood looks too dry and bleached to be natural, and may be greyish to cream in colour. An application of brown coloured wax dissolved in petroleum spirits is recommended to improve the colour, but a natural appearance of the wood is not easy to obtain. Kauramin-impregnated wood gives the impression of being light in weight, and that it is. The impregnation loads the wood with only about half the amount of stabilising material compared to PEG, sucrose, or Lactitol treatments. The latter treatments render wood of about the same weight as it had in its waterlogged state. Kauramin-treated wood weighs only one-third to two-thirds of its wet weight.

Technical requirements and difficulties of the treatment processes

The PEG treatments are the simplest in terms of their technical requirements. An unheated tank or container of any sort, lined with heavy-duty plastic sheet is sufficient for treatments with PEG 200 to 2000. No circulation and filtration of the solution is necessary. When solutions of higher molecular weight PEG are used, the treatment tank must be heated to 40–60°C and then the tank needs efficient insulation and a close-fitting cover, and all materials must be heat-resistant. Various heating systems can be used inside the tank or outside on its walls. Convection will lead to an even temperature and concentration distribution, so no circulation pump is needed except when mixing in additions of PEG, biocide, etc. If a spray treatment is chosen in order to save the costs of constructing a large tank and buying the large amount of PEG required for the tank solution, then standard garden equipment can be used: pumps, hoses, nozzles and sprinklers – even commercial greenhouses with waterproof plastic flooring to catch and recirculate the treatment solution – have been very successfully and economically employed for the conservation of ships. Any pump used to handle PEG solutions needs to be robust and made of corrosion-resistant materials. It may have to operate for years, and breakdowns are a nuisance and can be expensive. A standby pump is always a good investment.

For a Lactitol + trehalose treatment, the same sort of impregnation tanks can be used as for PEG treatments: non-heated tanks for softwoods and slightly degraded hardwoods, where a solution of 65% Lactitol + trehalose is sufficient; and heated tanks for solutions of higher concentrations up to 85% for hardwoods, especially for those which are heavily degraded. The main challenge with this method, apart from the difficulty of obtaining Lactitol, seems to be that a practical procedure for monitoring the progress of the impregnation has not yet been published. It is therefore not easy to find the right time to end the impregnation, and failures associated with insufficient impregnation may result. The drying of the impregnated wood and the formation of stabilising crystals within it are very slow processes at room temperature. Therefore it is recommended to dry the treated wood at 50°C which requires the installation and running of a heat chamber of some description big enough to house the ship.

For a Kauramin treatment, a heat chamber is always necessary. After the impregnation with resin and the start of the polymerisation in the wood, the curing needs to be carried out at 40–50°C. The chamber does not have to be very robust – it only needs to work for a few days. The impregnation itself can take place at room temperature, in any tank. The difficulty with this method is to prevent a premature polymerisation during the long time of impregnation. One needs understanding and experience to run the required pH regime which controls the chemical processes in the solution and in the wood. Another problem is the restricted service life of the resin solution.

The measures required to prolong it may totally inhibit the final curing of the resin in the wood.

The difficulties inherent in the sucrose method, especially when applied on a large scale, are so severe that they cancel out the advantage of technical simplicity and bring its ranking down to last place. An infection of the sucrose solution which will start its fermentation cannot always be stopped by the addition of more biocide. Having to purchase more sucrose for a replacement solution will consume whatever costs were hoped to be saved by choosing this method. Another difficulty with the sucrose treatment is the possible growth of sucrose crystals on and in the wood surface. A near-saturated solution gives best stabilisation; but slight evaporation of water or a drop in temperature may trigger an unnoticed crystallisation. The large crystals are very difficult to remove.

Attention, control, and maintenance

PEG treatments in a tank require the least attention due to the simplicity of the process and of the technical installations. Evaporation of water from the solution has to be controlled, and the tank has to be checked for possible leaks now and then. If there is a heating system, this has to be checked regularly. But it is not necessary to keep to a tight schedule for the control. PEG spraying systems need more maintenance and should be checked daily. Cleaning of clogged nozzles, control of pump performance, refitting of leaking hoses, replacing water which has evaporated from the spraying solution, and repair of leaks in the floor or catchment sheeting will be necessary at times. In timbers thicker than about 10 cm the progress of impregnation needs to be monitored. Wood cores should be taken about once or twice a year and analysed for PEG content and distribution. This is the only way the correct time for ending the impregnation can be determined.

A Lactitol impregnation requires about the same attention as a PEG tank treatment.

The level of the solution has to be checked for evaporation. In a heated impregnation, the functioning of the heating system has to be checked daily. Should the temperature drop, Lactitol will start to crystallise and it does not easily dissolve again when the temperature is increased to the previous level. More attention must be devoted to the wood after impregnation: the wet surfaces have to be dusted with Lactitol powder to initiate crystallisation in the impregnation solution inside the wood. When this process has started and is well established, the wood surface needs to be cleaned of Lactitol crystals. As with PEG treatments, the progress and the end-point of the impregnation must be monitored, possibly via core sample analysis.

A Kauramin treatment needs more attention – at least once a week during the impregnation phase. The resin solution must be monitored for changes in pH, and for the start of polymerisation. Should this happen before the impregnation is completed, the solution must be replaced by a fresh one. After impregnation, the wood has to be thoroughly cleaned of adhering resin solution, and then enveloped in foil before curing. The curing process has to be monitored, and after its completion a very slow drying process must be set up and maintained for a long time. This may involve a lot of work.

A large-scale sucrose treatment is a precarious affair. The impregnation which may take several years needs close surveillance. Should the solution start to ferment, immediate action is imperative – either dosing with more or stronger biocide or disposing of the whole solution, washing and disinfecting the wood, and preparing a fresh solution. A sucrose treatment needs to be inspected at least twice a week.

Personnel and competence

To run a PEG treatment needs few personnel and only basic technological competence. It is a process that most of the time can easily be monitored and maintained by one person with other responsibilities. The extraction and analysis of wood cores to monitor the impregnation progress will normally be done by a trained conservator or chemist.

The Lactitol treatment has comparably low requirements of personnel and competence during impregnation. But during the initiation of Lactitol crystallisation and during drying, daily monitoring is necessary. Experience of this method is needed during the crystallisation process in order to be able to recognise potential damage due to excessive crystal growth.

The sucrose treatment needs more man-hours for its control during impregnation. At least twice a week someone has to monitor the state of the sucrose solution, and if any action needs to be taken in case of a failure of the solution, personnel have to be on hand at short notice. It is advisable to establish contact with a microbiological laboratory before starting a sucrose treatment. You may be able to arrange this through the sucrose supplier. Problems can only be adequately solved with the advice and help of these experts.

The Kauramin treatment requires more chemical understanding and laboratory competence than the other methods. Also, more time has to be spent on monitoring and testing in order to control the impregnation, polymerisation, curing, and drying processes involved in the method. A good deal of experience is indispensable for satisfactory stabilisation results on large objects.

Duration of the treatments

The duration of the treatments is determined by the time necessary for impregnation, subsequent drying, and a final surface treatment. The main factor governing the speed of impregnation is the molecular size of the impregnant.

Impregnation with PEG 200 and with Kauramin will take about the same time. The sizes of the molecules which have to diffuse into the wood are comparable molecular weights of 200 and 140 respectively, and so are the concentrations of consolidants which have to be obtained in the water in the wood, 30% and 25–45% respectively. A ship treated with PEG 200 needs no attention during drying, and no cleaning or surface treatment. The duration of the treatment ends with the impregnation. A ship impregnated with Kauramin has to be heat-treated to cure the resin, and then the slow drying has to be set up and laboriously controlled. This could take months or years, depending on the thickness of the timbers.

Impregnations with sucrose and with Lactitol + trehalose will take more time than with PEG 200 or Kauramin. The molecules are of comparable size, molecular weights being: 342 sucrose, 344 Lactitol, 342 trehalose, but the final concentrations required are higher, about 70% for sucrose and 65–85% for Lactitol + trehalose. In both cases the wood needs to be cleaned and in the case of Lactitol, the treatment with crystal powder takes additional time. If controlled heat-drying is applied, this prolongs the process.

Impregnations with high molecular weight PEG 2000 to 4000 will take the longest time. Diffusion of the large molecules into wood is slow, and the required final concentration is high, 75–90%. However, high molecular weight PEG is only applied to degraded wood which has a good permeability, and this reduces the impregnation time. The wood will need a thorough cleaning, but the final air drying requires no special attention.

Impregnation times are governed not only by the method, but also by the thickness of the timbers, the wood species, and the degree of degradation. The more degraded the wood, the easier it can be impregnated. General guidelines on impregnation times are not available, but here are some examples:

– The *ship from Friesland* has oak planking 9 cm thick, which was slightly degraded in the centre (u_{max} = 130%), and moderately degraded in the surface layers (u_{max} = 250%). The impregnation with a 68% sucrose solution took 25 months. We would have liked to extend the impregnation for another 4–6 months, but the solution started to ferment. A two-step PEG

treatment of the ship would have taken three years. The first step – total impregnation with 30–40% PEG 200 – would have taken two years, and the second step with 80% PEG 3000, about one year, as only the thin degraded surface layer of the timbers would have needed to have been stabilised with this PEG.

– The *ship from the Teufelsmoor* near Bremen was sprayed with PEG 200 for 4 years. Its thickest oak timbers measure 12 × 30 cm in cross-section.

– The two *barges from Rohrsen* in Lemgo had very little degraded oak wood. The thickest timbers, the mast steps, measure 30 cm in diameter. The barges were sprayed with PEG 200, and it took three years for them to become sufficiently impregnated.

– The *Bremen Cog* has timbers of up to 50 cm in diameter. The use of PEG of different molecular sizes in two steps would have made it possible to minimise impregnation times. Given enough money to buy PEG, the ship could presumably have been impregnated satisfactorily in about 6–7 years, instead of the 19 years as dictated by a limited budget.

The duration of the drying period is of relevance when planning a Lactitol or a Kauramin treatment as any operations necessary in this time need to be carried out before the object can be shown to the public. On the other hand, drying after a PEG or sucrose treatment can take place in the museum gallery if the relative humidity is kept stable by reliable climate control – it is of no relevance that it takes several years even for a 6 cm thick plank.

The duration of a final surface treatment depends on the nature of the procedure chosen and on the number of staff available.

Costs

The same treatment method will produce different costs when carried out at different locations and in different workshops. Prices for chemicals vary from one country to the next. The cost of construction and installation depend on design and availability of materials and rents, energy costs and wages.

To compare the costs for different treatments it can be helpful to break them down into categories, such as:

– construction or rent of workshop;
– impregnation tank or spraying installation;
– heating system and process heating during impregnation;
– heating chamber for curing and/or drying;
– chemicals for stabilisation, disinfection, process control;
– disposal of spent treatment solution and installation;
– manpower needed during the process and afterwards;
– climate control requirements in store and gallery for the treated object.

The case studies presented in previous chapters all benefitted in various degrees from support given in kind: rent-free workshops and price reductions for materials; manpower and help with cranes, pumps, and construction work; expertise and specialist advice; free water and electricity. A rough order of the conservation methods with regard to their costs, starting with the least expensive, will be as follows:

1 Unheated PEG treatments; tank or spraying treatments are the cheapest methods.
2 A sucrose treatment will be about the same low cost – but only if it goes well at the first attempt.
3 A Kauramin treatment needs a heat chamber for curing the resin in the wood.
4 A Lactitol treatment requires large amounts of expensive consolidant and a heat chamber for drying the impregnated wood.
5 Heated PEG treatments, one-step or two-step, require more expensive tanks, and heating energy for the impregnation. They are the most expensive methods.

Reversibility and retreatability

Impregnations of waterlogged wood with PEG, sucrose, and Lactitol are regarded as being reversible because these consolidants are water-soluble, and they are not supposed to establish chemical bonds with the wood substance. However, an attempt to remove PEG 200 from a 6 cm thick plank after a successful impregnation showed that at the end of more than one year in repeated changes of fresh water, there were still a few percent PEG in the wood. This residual amount would not diffuse out of the wood; it seemed to be held back by physical forces. Similar observations can be expected with wood impregnated with sucrose and Lactitol. The removal of the majority of the consolidant may, however, be sufficient if a re-conservation should become necessary. In any case, the removal of consolidants from wood will take years. Solid PEG, and crystals of sucrose and Lactitol only dissolve reluctantly, even with heating, and dissolved molecules diffuse out of wood as slowly as they diffused into it.

A Kauramin treatment is not reversible. The resin forms a three-dimensional network in the wood cell walls which cannot be dissolved. However, the porosity of the Kauramin-treated wood may allow further treatment in the future.

Interim result

An assessment of the sucrose method reveals several decisive drawbacks in the four most important aspects – stabilisation, reliability, difficulties of the process, and control requirements. It should be rated last in order of choice. However, it ranks first in visual appearance of the treated wood, and second regarding cost, but should the process fail and the sucrose solution needs to be exchanged for a new one, then the costs multiply and one might even lose the object being conserved. The risk of infection cannot be ruled out, because it is neither tolerable nor allowable for health reasons to use the large quantities of strong biocides which would be necessary to lower the risk.

Over the years I have stabilised two ship finds successfully with sucrose, and one

Box 13

Stabilisation results for some ship projects

Ship	Stabilisation treatment	Shrinkage without stabilisation (%)	Shrinkage after stabilisation (%)	Drying time (years)
Barge II from Yverdon-les-Bains	80% PEG 4000	13–48	2–4	0.6
Bremen Cog	40% PEG 200 / 76% PEG 3000	6–29	0–3.1–5.4	6
Karl	40% PEG 200 / 60% PEG 3000		4–6 (planks) 10–15 (ribs)	3
Oberländer	40% PEG 200 / 85% PEG 3000		0–2.9–5	5
Teufelsmoor	40% PEG 200		0.5–1.7	5
Rohrsen	40% PEG 200		0	3
Vasa	45% PEG 1500 + 600		6–8	30
Beck's ship	74% sucrose		0–0.8–2.5	4
Friesland	67% sucrose		1.5–4.9–7.5	2
Oberstimm	25% Kauramin		0.5–1	2

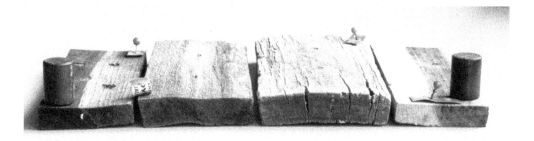

Warping in (left to right): oak, beech, beech, oak specimens stabilised with PEG, sucrose, Lactitol + trehalose, and Kauramin. Crystallising Lactitol has split and cracked the heavily degraded beech specimen (second from right). Photograph: Per Hoffmann

without success – the latter one happened to be the historically most important – and I know of two more unsuccessful sucrose ship projects: one in Konstanz on Lake Constance in southern Germany, and one in Bonn, where the sucrose treatment was getting out of hand and had to be halted. In the latter case, the ship was then successfully stabilised with a PEG treatment. I cannot recommend the sucrose method for large-scale conservation projects, and I will not consider it in the discussion in the next chapter.

For obvious reasons, no representative samples could be cut from most ships to determine the shrinkage of the untreated wood. However, some shrinkage values of untreated archaeological woods, obtained on laboratory specimens, are given in the illustration by Per Hoffmann and Reinhold Breden earlier in this section on page 124, and more can be found in the literature.

9.2 How to select the most appropriate method

The discussions and assessments of the various factors involved with conservation treatments for large waterlogged wooden objects demonstrate that a simple comparison of methods under the headline 'Which method is best?' is not possible. The headline can only be 'Which method is best for me and my object in the given circumstances?' The different factors may not have the same weight for every project. Nevertheless, based on our current knowledge some general recommendations can be given. The following synopsis will not be comprehensive and it may have to be modified in the future. However, it may sharpen the awareness and be helpful for the process of decision-making for the time being.

Regarding the wood

- If your object consists of softwood – coniferous wood – of any degree of degradation, then all methods can be applied with a reasonable certainty of success. As softwoods only need low levels of PEG impregnation for a good stabilisation, even a PEG 2000 treatment at room temperature can be considered.
- If your object consists of hardwood – deciduous wood – which is only slightly degraded throughout its thickness, then a low molecular weight PEG 200 treatment is appropriate, either as a tank treatment or applied as a sprayed solution. A Lactitol stabilisation can also be considered.
- If your object consists of hardwood which in its bulk is heavily degraded, then a Kauramin treatment will give the best stabilisation; second best is a treatment with PEG 3000 or PEG 4000 in a heated tank.
- If your object consists of hardwood which is both slightly and heavily degraded in considerable amounts, then a two-step PEG treatment with PEG 200 and PEG 3000 or 4000 is advisable. A Kauramin treatment can also give good results, but splits may develop at the border between slightly degraded and heavily degraded areas of the wood.

Regarding the delicacy, uniqueness, and general importance of the object

- If your object is coarse and simple, or very numerous – like logs from a ship's cargo, timbers from a raft or a wharf construction, a trackway built from unhewn logs – and not regarded as highly significant, then a cheap method may be chosen even if the expected stabilisation will not be optimum. However it should be noted that significance has to be judged against local and regional criteria. An object type common in Germany might be very scarce elsewhere. Neolithic trackways may be coarse and simple but are very delicate and certainly deserve the best conservation treatment possible if they are to survive in a state worth having. A cold PEG 2000 treatment can be applied. In its most simple form it can be the last resort for someone who has no facilities, and next to no money, but wants to save the object. One will have to accept the risk of second-rate stabilisation in heavily degraded hardwoods, but the timbers will look much better afterwards than without any treatment at all.
- If, on the other hand, your object is of high value, complex in its structure, and/or delicate, then the best possible method has to be chosen. That is the one which will give the best dimensional stabilisation with the highest probability. Depending on the wood species and the state of degradation of the wood, this will be a Kauramin treatment, or a one- or two-step PEG treatment.

Regarding costs, manpower, and competence of staff

- If you have little money and no competent personnel, then PEG methods designed to work without heating can be considered, employing PEG 200 to 2000.
- If you have money but no competent personnel are available, then all PEG methods

should be considered. The PEG methods are simple to install, run, and monitor. You could, however, spend some of the money on getting some competent personnel, even on a consultancy basis.

– If you have little money but competent personnel, then all methods can be considered. The choice will principally have to follow cost calculations.

– If you have money and sufficient and competent personnel, then you are lucky! A Kauramin treatment and all PEG methods

should be considered. The choice can be made according to your preferences and on sound assessment of the various project parameters.

Note to §9.1 Assessment of the methods taking various factors into account

– The experiments summarised here are described *in extenso* in P. Hoffmann, 2007.

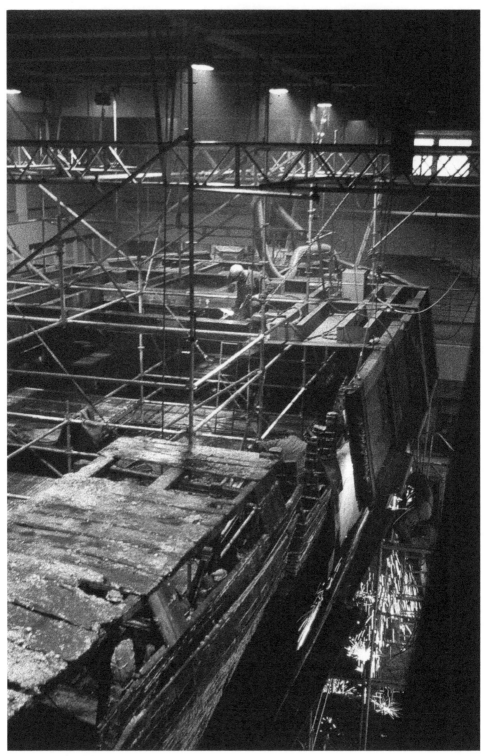

The route from conservation to presentation begins with the removal of the treatment tank. For the *Bremen Cog* this was a job for steel workers from a nearby shipyard. No steel parts or droplets of molten steel from their plasma torches were allowed to fall onto the wood. Photograph: Per Hoffmann

10   From conservation to presentation

10.1   Cleaning and surface treatment

At the end of an impregnation treatment the ship or boat is lifted out of the treatment tank, or more often, the treatment solution is pumped out of the tank and the tank is then dismantled. In both cases, some solution containing consolidant, and probably dirt, slime, and fungal films that had been floating on the surface of the bath, will settle on the wood. It will look dirty, and fine surface details, tool marks, remnants of tar or paint, traces of typical wear and tear will be obscured. The wood has to be cleaned.

Cleaning

When the ship has emerged from the impregnation bath, it should be cleaned as soon as possible, before the adherent solution dries and the dirt and consolidant solidify – otherwise they become difficult and time-consuming to dissolve and remove. In the course of a Kauramin treatment the cleaning must always take place before the curing of the resin. Once cured, Kauramin is not soluble at all. Wood which is going to be freeze-dried also has to be cleaned before it is frozen and freeze-dried. If freeze-dried wood is wetted again, the anti-collapse effect of the treatment is spoiled: water is soaked into cell lumina and cell walls, and capillary forces arise resulting in collapse and warping.

The techniques applied in cleaning should avoid any wiping and rubbing. The surfaces of the still wet, or damp archaeological wood are the most degraded parts of the timbers, they are soft and most vulnerable. Edges, corners, fine details are easily rubbed off or blurred. However, it is the surface of the timbers that often tell a lot about the life of the ship – a sort of record. The surface should be conserved as well as possible. A carefully handled steam jet is the best tool for the cleaning of a boat or ship. Steam washing is at the right

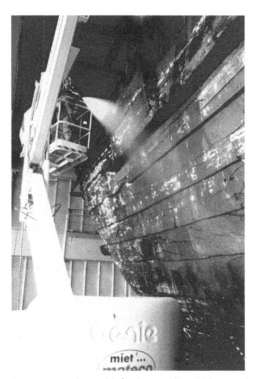

A steam jet is indispensible for cleaning a large PEG-covered ship. Photograph: Per Hoffmann

intensity when the surface is just cleared without removing too much consolidant from too deep in the surface layer. This takes a little experimentation and practice.

After steam cleaning, consolidant may collect at edges, cracks, bore holes, joints and seams, etc. It may take several days before it becomes visible, or before it effloresces on the wood. If it is sucrose or Lactitol, it must be dabbed off with a sponge and a little hot water; if it is high molecular weight PEG, a hot-air blower can assist in melting/dissolving the deposit which is then dabbed off, if it is not absorbed by the wood.

With PEG-treated wood, the cleaning can be controlled to give, or enhance, a certain desired visual appearance to the wood: a natural dry look, as if it contained no consolidant at all, or an oiled or waxed look, to deepen the colour and sheen of the material. If the surface of PEG-treated wood has been washed too intensively and on drying has attained an unpleasant dry appearance, it is possible to heat it with a hot-air blower just enough to melt some PEG in subsurface wood layers, which will then be absorbed by the overdried surface. The surface will then lose some of its chalky appearance and look much better.

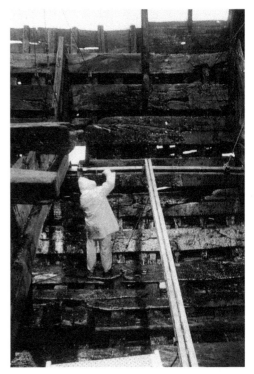

There is no way around sponges. Photograph: Per Hoffmann

Surface treatment

A final surface treatment can be considered with various intentions: to strengthen and protect the surface, to smooth it and thus make routine dusting easier, or to enhance the visual appearance. In an archaeological ship or even boat the combination of its heavy weight and delicate surface is an inherent problem. Not only are the surfaces of the timbers easily damaged or abraded during the lifting, transportation, and handling in conservation, but also during the years of exhibition in a museum. The ship may be moved around in the gallery due to new exhibition concepts or building maintenance requirements. Also, as a ship is seldom enclosed in a showcase, visitors love to go and touch it, incise their names in it, or even break off splinters for souvenirs. It can

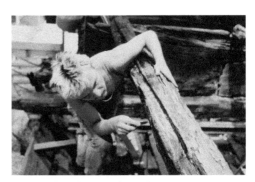

White PEG in deep cracks is the worst case scenario. Photograph: Per Hoffmann

be an option to try and strengthen the surface of the stabilised ship in order to protect it as far as possible, while keeping it aesthetically acceptable.

In selecting a strengthening medium, its long-term performance, chemical stability, and light-fastness are important. Also, the aspect of reversibility of the planned surface

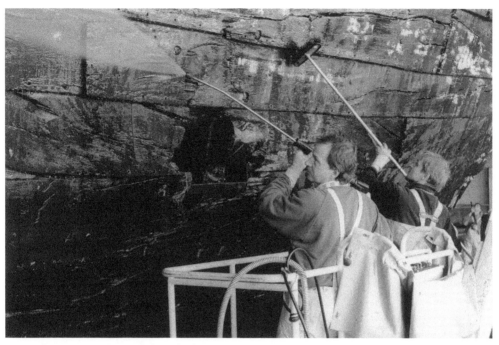

Two weeks were required to wash down the *Bremen Cog*. Photograph: Egbert Laska, DSM

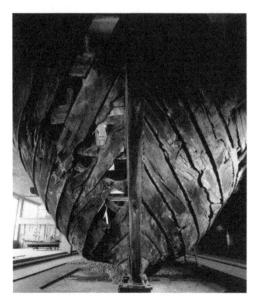

PEG efflorescence grew along cracks and edges while the timbers dried. Photograph: Clariant AG

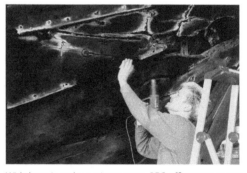

With hot air and a moist sponge, PEG efflorescence can be melted/dissolved and removed. Photograph: Per Hoffmann

treatment must be considered. Acrylic solutions, high molecular weight PEG solutions, hardening oils, or wax dispersions can serve the purpose. A free-standing ship in any gallery collects dust within a remarkably short time. A greyish tint will disfigure the wood which already has lost most of its original brown colour during the ages of submersion. The wood will look dull, and the ship neglected and not particularly interesting. Perhaps once a year, the dust has to be removed. This action, repeated endless times over the years, inadvertently exerts some wear and abrasion on the wood. Depending on the state of the wood surface, it can be a good idea to give it some

139

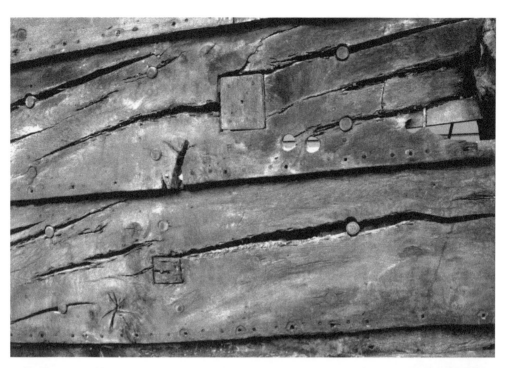

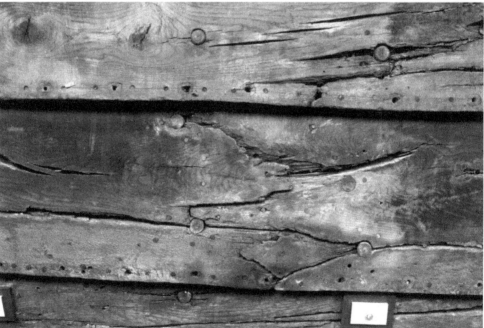

After the final air drying the surface of the *Bremen Cog* looks perfect: dry, and its natural colour, every detail standing out clearly. Photograph: Per Hoffmann

protective strengthening, and at the same time a smoother surface, which will facilitate dust removal.

The surface treatment for purely aesthetic reasons is a question of taste, and of personal and subjective preferences. Some museums have a purist point of view and leave the cleaned wood untreated. Others want to have the look of the stabilised and cleaned wood enhanced towards a more brownish and deeper sheen. Oils and waxes, and high molecular weight PEG can produce this effect, with pigments added, if so desired. Some museums want the wood to be surface coated, like the outside of the hull of the *Vasa* in Stockholm. Here, a paste of dissolved PEG 6000 was brushed onto the wood, left to dry, and then the PEG was melted down to a glossy coating with a hot-air blower.

Any surface treatment must be tried out on a hidden area to see how the wood reacts, and whether the treatment needs to be adjusted. When working with hot-air blowers, there is the risk of scorching the wood, or of overheating the PEG, producing dark degradation products. Industrial hot-air blowers must be used with great care.

A surface treatment will normally be discussed with the future exhibition of the ship or boat in mind: how should it look when it is finally presented to the public?

10.2   Restoration and presentation

Restoration is an indispensable part of the conservation project. It comprises all the necessary measures to secure and safeguard the structural integrity of the ship far into the future. Typical measures in restoration include: mending cracks and splits in timbers; assembling broken pieces; replacing loose or lost treenails and dowels; substituting corroded nails and rivets; reshaping warped and distorted timbers; fastening and supporting loose ends; and repositioning displaced timbers, and timbers that have lost their connection with the rest of the ship. The idea of restoration is to relieve the ship of as many mechanical stresses

as possible – in the individual timbers and in the whole structure – in order to minimise any future deformation or damage that may occur due to gravity, and thus to secure a long life for the find as an exhibit.

Restoration work is best done before the wood is dry throughout, when the timbers are still flexible. They will become more brittle on drying. Shipwright tools can be used on archaeological wood stabilised by all methods. However, working sucrose-filled wood requires the tools to be washed frequently. The sucrose in the interior of the wood takes years to solidify completely, and until then it will stick to anything or anyone in contact with it.

The reshaping of warped or buckled timbers to their original shape can be part of the restoration. PEG-treated timbers become quite pliable on heating and can be reshaped in the hot state. However, reshaping freeze-dried or Kauramin-treated timbers is very limited. Both stabilisation methods render the wood rather brittle. The better option is to bring distorted timbers to their correct shape before they are treated, or at least before they are dried after impregnation, and keep them fixed in this shape while drying.

Restoration is a prerequisite for good presentation. They belong together, they depend on each other, and they influence each other. They are the final steps in the conservation project, and the conservator has to be involved in their planning and execution. He may work together with a shipwright, an engineer, an exhibition designer, the archaeologist, or the museum director, but he is the one who knows the object best, the archaeological wood and its properties, and what it can and cannot tolerate in terms of loads, climate conditions, vibrations, and the effect of impacts during moving, etc. The conservator can decide about working materials, their compatibility, service life, possible side-effects, and removability. He will know which measures are necessary to safeguard the wood and the ship, and how much interference its materials can stand. The conservator has to take part in the discussion and planning where additions are to be made during restoration, and where loads are to be put on the ship and the support structures. A successful restoration and presentation is the result of an agreement between conservator and exhibition designer.

Presentation concepts span from the purist, more academic reconstruction of the ship find as discovered in the excavation situation, to the fully reconstructed ship with the original find supplemented and completed with modern material, set in an installation giving an impression of when the ship was afloat and in service. The intention pursued with the presentation could be to show the archaeological find as an extraordinary water craft, as representative of a certain type of craft, or of a certain time period. This would be an historical engineering approach. Alternatively the intention could be to show the context of which the ship was once a part, how it was used, and by whom – in other words, a cultural history approach.

Whatever the presentation concept may be, the professional imperative for the conservator and exhibition designer is that all measures taken must be reversible, and must not violate the integrity of the archaeological object.

Fulfilling the demand

The following case studies give some examples of how the demand for reversibility can be met, regardless of the presentation concept adopted for the ship.

While the *Nydam boat* in Schleswig, Germany a large seaworthy rowing boat from the 4th century AD and the *Oseberg* and *Gokstad* Viking ships in Oslo, Norway, were restored in the early 20th century using modern timbers painted with creosote to resemble the original wood, most scholars and museum directors today prefer concepts in which the original find is not supplemented with new material. Should it be necessary, however, for mechanical, safety or interpretational reasons, then the additions should be restricted to a minimum, and they must be clearly discernible as being new. The wreck

of the Carolingian river craft from the Rhine, the *barge from Niedermörmter*, was about two thirds of the original ship. The Rheinisches Landesmuseum in Bonn wanted to demonstrate the full length of this long and slender type of transport vessel from the days when it was poled along the river, carrying everything from sandstone building blocks to wine barrels, from cattle to crops, from pedestrians and ox carts to knights and their ladies on horseback. So conservator Axel Peiss completed the ship with visibly new, easily detachable, timbers.

Pioneering the modern concept was naval architect Ole Crumlin Pedersen with his work on the interpretation and presentation of the wrecks of the five *Skuldelev Viking ships* from Roskilde fjord in Denmark. From the analysis of the wreck timbers he reconstructed the ships' original lines, and had these lines set up in fine brass strips. He positioned the original timbers, held and supported by the cradle, into these light and elegant indicators of the original ships' lines. The museum visitors see five beautiful ships, despite only between one-fifth and three-quarters of their timbers having survived. It is an astounding aesthetic experience, evoking the characteristics of this type of ship.

The restoration of the original material was minimal. It was restricted to a puzzle of sticking together hundreds of pieces of broken planks and ribs with molten PEG, using toothpicks as dowels and retouching the glue lines before the mended planks could be laid into the support cradle. The overlapping clinker planks are not fastened to each other, but rest individually on the flanges of the L-shaped brass strip which indicates its run from bow to stern. The cradle stands on the ground, held by props along its sides, in the same way as boats are propped up on the beach. Information on the construction of the ships, sailing performance, historical and sociological background is given in unobtrusive text and graphic presentations.

The unfortunate stabilisation treatment of the Carolingian river barge *Karl* in Bremerhaven has already been described in

Section 4.3. The inadequate PEG impregnation resulted in heavy shrinkage of the wooden dowels holding the clinker planks and half-ribs together – they all fell out, and the ship disintegrated into its constituent timbers. The director of our museum, however, wanted to exhibit the ship as a very rare example of an early medieval large watercraft, so we set out to restore it.

On drying, the heavy bottom and side planks, about 10 m long, 30 cm wide, and 4–5 cm thick, not only shrank in width, but also buckled and warped. They had to be flattened before they could be reassembled. Wrapped in electric heating mats as used in underfloor heating, and warmed overnight to about 80°C to melt the PEG in the wood and soften the lignin, the timbers became pliable and were laid out on the floor and weighted down flat with piles of sand bags while they cooled. The PEG solidified again, the lignin stiffened, and the planks stayed flat. Splits in some planks were mended with long dowels of 10–12 mm diameter and a flexible polyurethane sealant was used as a strong glue on the PEG-impregnated wood. Once the side planks had been attached to each other and to the bottom planks using new oak dowels in the original holes, the sides of the ship took on a nice curvature.

Most of the surviving half-ribs were broken at the angle, and steel ribs had to be inserted into the ship to hold the bottom and the only preserved side together. The two surviving half-ribs had quite different angles, obviously the result of shrinkage. For the reconstruction I decided to adopt the angle between side and bottom which was least stressful to the dowelled seams. This position would be close to the original shape of the hull. As only one side was completely preserved up to the gunwale and most of the other side was gone, we tried to reconstruct the missing starboard side with just a few steel ribs and a thin metal strip connecting them to indicate the line of the gunwale. This changed the impression of the ship dramatically, now it became a heavy-duty carrier with a large volume, where it was previously a wreck.

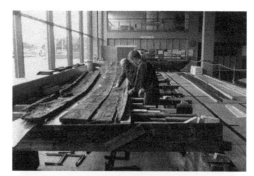
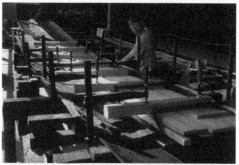
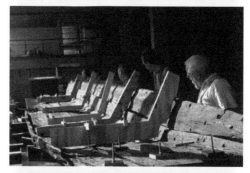
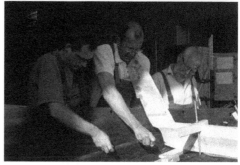

The bottom planks of *Karl* rest on a heavy plywood baseplate with their original curvature. The warped planks were heated and pressed flat again. The side planks were held in place, and fastened with new dowels put into the original holes. Photographs: Egbert Laska, DSM and Per Hoffmann

The bottom planks rest on a strong plywood base plate, so that they will not sag between individual supports over time; the steel ribs are bolted to this base plate, which in turn stands on a steel frame on the floor. All bolts pass through original dowel holes from floor timbers and half-ribs, no new holes were bored in the bottom or side planks. The fragments of the original ribs are laid along the steel ribs which are positioned in the original places to take advantage of the dowel holes. A cushioning of felt has been placed wherever steel comes into contact with original wood. Felt is a superior material with well-known properties and proven durability over many centuries. The service-life of modern polymer materials is not comparable. The whole 12 m exhibit is self-supporting and can be moved around in the gallery – which it is, every now and again.

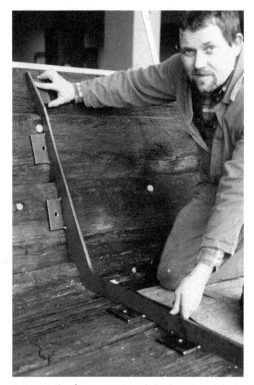
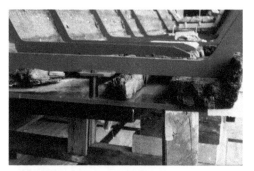
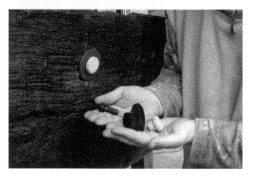

Exact wooden frame templates held the sides while steel frames were made and fastened to the baseplate without pressing on the bottom planks. The side planks were then fastened to the steel frames through the original dowel holes. Photographs: Per Hoffmann and Egbert Laska, DSM

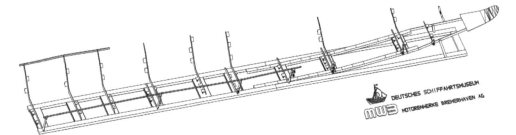

The self-supporting steel skeleton holds the ship from within. Drawing courtesy of Motorenwerke Bremerhaven

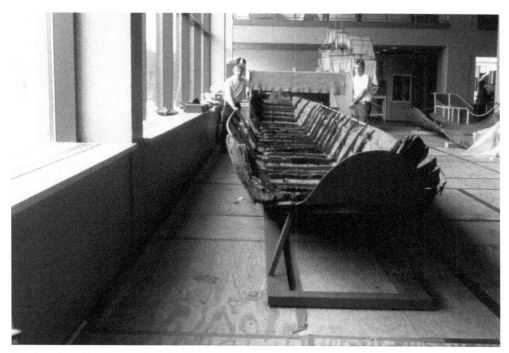

Experimenting with a mirror to show the ship at its original full length. Photograph: Per Hoffmann

Reshaping distorted timbers is feasible even in thicker and wider dimensions. The heavy timbers of a strange small river craft from the Rhine, an *Oberländer* from the 10th century AD, were about 8 cm thick, and up to 60 cm wide. They were stabilised with PEG 200 and PEG 3000 in our museum, and when we tried to reassemble them, a colleague and I found that the two wide hollow side planks, carved from the two halves of the same oak trunk about 100 cm in diameter, had warped and twisted considerably during the 13 months in the hot PEG 3000 bath. The distortion was presumably due to the relaxation of growth stresses that had built up in the spiral-grown stem. We heated the timbers repeatedly and applied great bending forces on them, until the hollowed-out inner surfaces showed the same profile from one end to the other, and then the parts fitted together again. The direction of bending can be governed by the way supports are positioned under the timber while pressure is exerted between the supports from above. Heavy-duty jacks, braced against the ceiling of the hall, produced great forces. The

ship's timbers are now mounted on the outside of a steel skeleton of ribs and stringers using only original dowel holes, and this composite is set on a base plate resting on a steel frame. Taking into account the need for mobility of exhibits in our museum, we have even put rollers under the steel frame.

The ship's timbers had been extracted one by one from a former backwater of the Rhine. However, to help with the reconstruction of the hull we had a number of pointers: the timbers themselves; the report of the diver who fastened the lifting ropes to the submerged timbers; and the drawings for the archaeological documentation by Werner Lahn, shipwright at our museum and head of the reconstruction of the *Bremen Cog*, and Detlev Ellmers ship archaeologist and museum director. We also had one rib which gave us the interior curve of the side from bottom to gunwale. In addition, an archaeological report about a ship find from *Meinerswijk* on the river Waal had dealt with a ship resembling the *Oberländer* in every detail. From contemporary sources – a panorama woodcut of the Rhine at Cologne

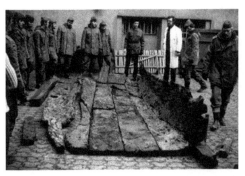

The first arrangement of the timbers of the *Oberländer*, the suggestion of a diver who had helped to salvage them from a water-filled sand extraction pit. Photograph: DSM

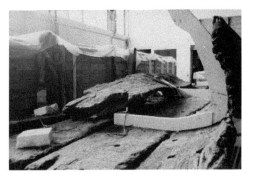

During a hot impregnation, one side of the shell of the *Oberländer* had warped considerably, probably due to the release of growth stresses in the wood. Photograph: Per Hoffmann

from 1531, a relief in a vault in Saint Kastor's church in Koblenz from 1499, and a Flemish painting from the early 19th century – the type of ship is well known. The shape we have given to the reconstructed ship will be very close to the original.

In the case of a large and almost complete Carolingian (9th century) dug-out canoe of 12 m length, called the *barge from Noyen-sur-Seine*, the bottom had buckled during a hot PEG treatment, which caused the sides of the boat to fall outwards, and the whole shape of the craft changed its character. Following discussions of our experiences in Bremerhaven, Quoc Khôi Tran and his colleagues at the Atelier Régional de Conservation in Grenoble reheated the boat in a hot PEG bath, then placed it on a steel base plate and pressed the bottom flat with a series of jacks. With this, the sides came up and the boat once again became a slender canoe.

The limits of theory

The concept for the *Bremen Cog* was to reconstruct the huge ship from its individually salvaged waterlogged timbers, have it PEG-stabilised, and then present it free-standing in the Cog Hall. No outer props or supports were to interfere with the view of the unique ship. It was planned to hang the

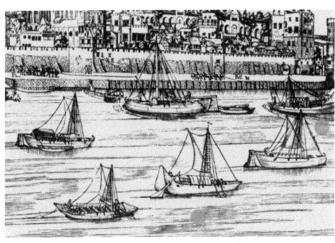

Two medium sized *Oberländer* on the Rhine. Detail of the great prospect of Cologne by Anton Woensam, 1531, Stadtmuseum, Köln. Image: Stadtmuseum, Koln

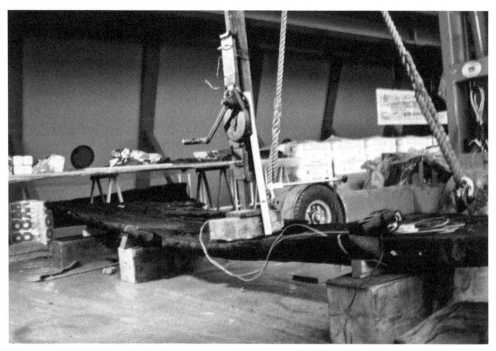

The heated side shell of the *Oberländer* was pressed back into shape with the help of a heavy-duty jack. Photograph: Per Hoffmann

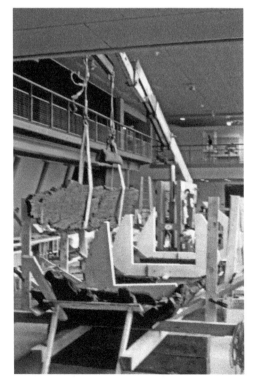

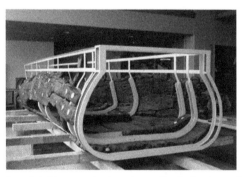

A steel skeleton was developed according to the shape of surviving frame timbers. Photograph: Per Hoffmann

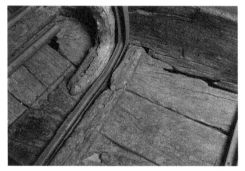

A mobile crane was necessary to mount the heavy timbers onto provisional templates. Photograph: Per Hoffmann

Detail of the arrangement of wood and steel frames in the ship. Photograph: Per Hoffmann

147

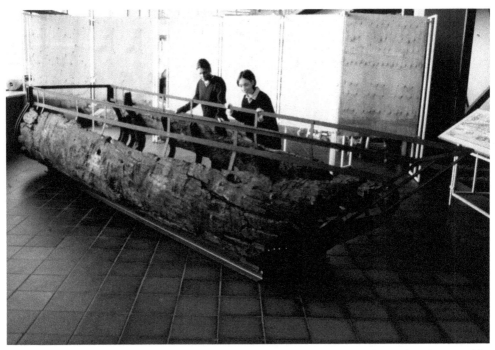

The *Oberländer* ready for exhibition. The steel skeleton is rather heavy in its design to match the robust character of the ship; it is painted the colour of the wood, but slightly darker to make it stand back a little. If visitors were allowed to get close, they would probably like to lean on the gunwale! Photograph: Egbert Laska, DSM

ship from the roof on steel rods, but to let the keel stand on the ground. Two-thirds of the ship's weight would be borne by the ceiling; one-third would rest on the ground.

With the decision to put it on exhibition, the *Bremen Cog* changed from being simply an object of science and scholarly documentation to also being a museum object, an exhibit. With this, the rules that were to be applied to it changed: an exhibit must be mechanically stable, must emphasise its characteristics, and express what is intended with its presentation. It must also be safe to museum visitors. The theory of no interference with original material came to its limits. The preparation of the *Cog* for presentation was not possible without a certain amount of slight interference with the archaeological wood.

Reassembling 40 tonnes of wet timbers meant not only solving a puzzle with 2,000 pieces, but also finding methods to mend wet broken planks and timbers, and fastening the timbers to each other. The shipwrights in the museum developed a method to join broken planks by gluing strips of fresh wood into recesses cut across the fracture on the back of the timber. The wood surface in the recesses was dried using infrared heaters just enough to let a phenol resin glue establish a strong and water-resistant bond between the wet wood and the insert. Waterlogged wood is heavy; many planks and timbers weighed several hundred kilograms and could only be handled with a mobile crane. Strong connections were needed. Various screws and steel bolt systems were tested, but finally wooden dowels as used by the medieval shipwrights proved to be the best choice.

The original facetted oak wood dowels fastening the planking to floor timbers, ribs, and knees, and connecting other heavy timbers, were replaced by slightly tapered turned oak wood dowels up to 100 cm long. The original dowel holes were bored to the same conical shape, so the long dowels could be driven

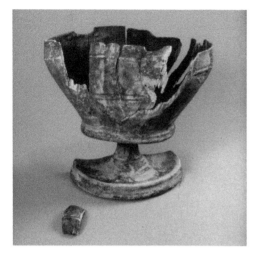
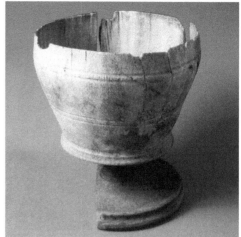
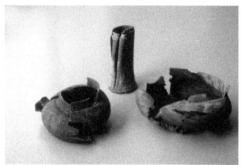
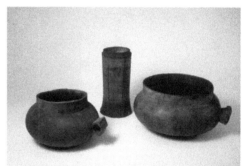

A dried-up late medieval wooden goblet and crushed, turned bowls could be brought back to their original delicate forms by boiling, reshaping, and stabilising the resulting waterlogged wood. Photographs: Per Hoffmann and Egbert Laska, DSM

home without getting stuck prematurely. Once the dry dowels sat tight in the wet wood, they started to swell, and could never be removed again. In place of the clinker nails that had rusted away, thousands of small beech wood treenails in new holes were used to assemble the clinker-laid planks of the hull. They all survived more than twenty years immersion, first under sprayed water while the ship was reconstructed, and then in PEG solutions during stabilisation.

A few years after the ship came out of the conservation tank, the hanging concept proved to be inadequate. It would have worked only with a stiff and strong ship. However, the *Cog* is a clinker-built vessel, flexible by construction and intention. Furthermore, it has survived non-symmetrically: the port side is partly

missing and the cross-beams are no longer holding both sides. As a result, the hull began to sag, and a new support had to be installed. I called in a group of experts –Detlev Ellmers, director of our museum, Ole Crumlin-Pedersen, and Thorkild Thomasen, shipwright and specialist in exhibition design for archaeological ships – and we discussed possible ways to stabilise the ship's structure. In the end we developed a design for an internal self-supporting steel construction consisting of floors, ribs, cross-beams, and stringers. It will be installed discreetly between the outer and inner planking, the steel ribs running alongside the original wooden ones. This steel cradle will stand on short legs, some protruding through the bottom of the ship, and some positioned to prop up the bow and stern. The

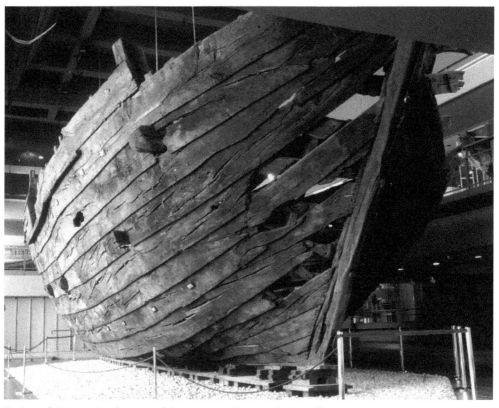

The beautiful *Bremen Cog* after successful conservation. Photograph: Per Hoffmann

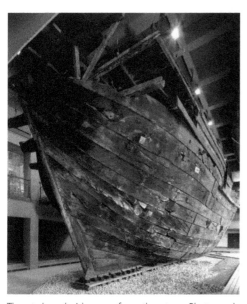

The starboard side seen from the stern. Photograph: Clariant AG

timbers of the ship will be fastened to the inflexible cradle with bolts passing through the original nail holes and with heads resembling the original wrought iron nail heads. The keel will stand on the ground, and the *Cog* will be presented as if it were sitting high and dry on a tidal flat, as was the custom for loading and unloading ships in medieval times.

To achieve a certain presentation concept may demand some interference with the original wood substance, going beyond the minimal measures to stabilise the structure of the archaeological ship find. The question is: what is and is not acceptable? For the new support for the *Bremen Cog*, up to twenty holes about 10 × 10 cm were to be cut into the hull in order that the legs of the steel cradle could pass through. The alternative, with no holes, would be an external support system, which would then interfere heavily with the best possible view of the hull and its beautiful lines accentuated by

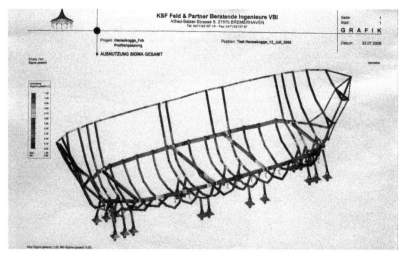

Engineer Hans-Jürgen Meyer designed this self-supporting steel skeleton to be built into the *Bremen Cog*. It would stand on 20 short legs under the hull. © KSF Feld & Partner, Bremerhaven

the clinker seams. The argument for the holes is that to achieve certain intentions of display and installation, it may sometimes be necessary to interfere slightly with the original material.

The technique to fashion complicated and individually fitted steel ribs was developed in collaboration with an engineering firm, and has been tried out successfully on a prototype. However, at the time of writing, work on the project has come to a halt. The three decisive people who had worked with dedication on the *Bremen Cog* for years – the director of the museum, the conservator, and the head of the technical workshops – have retired. Hopefully, successors will be nominated who will carry on with the project.

Ships in installations

The short bow section of the *Beck's ship* in Bremen, a medium-sized flat-bottomed ship from about 1489, did not invite any reconstruction as nothing more of the ship remained. All that had to be done after the sucrose treatment was to secure the loose ends of the bottom and side planks, and to strengthen the weak and disjointed construction. Metal bands were screwed on, holes were drilled for dowels and bolts, and broken-off ends of planks were trimmed with saws, knives, and planes. There were no details and no other finds that could

help to interpret the ship. The bow now stands on exhibition in the Bremer Landesmuseum, alongside a Borgward *Isabella* car from the 1950s: both examples of industrial products designed and built in Bremen. The ship is completely detached from any historical, sociological, or technological context. It has been chosen purely for aesthetic and symbolic reasons.

The *ship from the Teufelsmoor* from the end of the 19th century had lost its rudder, and the half-decks and gunwales had rotted away when it was found. Old people in the area, however, still remembered the big peat carriers on the waterways, and knew how they looked. So the local museum had boat builders reconstruct and attach what they thought were the missing parts to one half of the ship. The ship now combines the archaeological evidence with a full reconstruction of its possible original state. People wanted to see the ship as their grandparents had known and worked on them. They donated old pictures, texts and personal belongings to the exhibition. They were proud of their local history.

When the wreck of a 30 m long barge was found in the Havel near Berlin, it was identified as a *Kaffenkahn*, the only surviving representative of a once countless fleet of barges, sailing on the waterways in the 19th and well into the 20th century. These barges carried building materials, commodities, and food

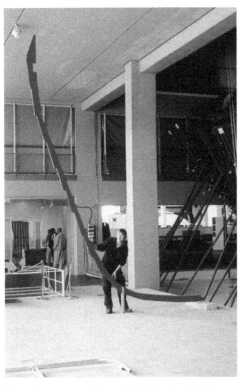

A wooden prototype demonstrates the size of the frames for the proposed steel construction. Photograph: Per Hoffmann

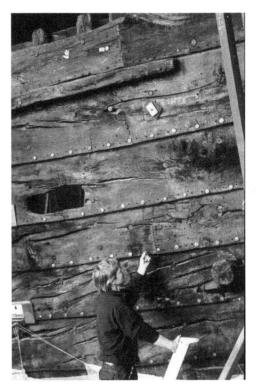

Forged iron replica nails in the original holes give back the characteristic look to the hull, as emphasised in contemporary illustrations of cogs. Photograph: Per Hoffmann

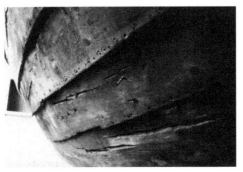

After conservation, the overlapping clinker seams show the original nail holes with the circular imprints from the wide nail heads, and the small wooden pegs used as nails in the re-assembly of the planks. Photograph: Per Hoffmann

for the fast-growing town. The wreck was spray-treated with PEG 600 and PEG 1450 in the hold of a modern barge by conservator Volker Koesling, and brought to the Deutsches Technikmuseum, Berlin. It was decided to reconstruct the missing parts which were

characteristic of this type of ship: the long rising bow which could be seen by the helmsman above the high load of sand, bricks, or other cargo, and which served as a sighter for steering; the pointed stern; the large rudder; and the high mast bearing a spritsail. These sails were a typical feature of the flat and open landscape and could be seen from far away. A thin lath was mounted to indicate the line of the missing top strake. With these additions, the fragmentary wreck attains an aesthetic completeness, and displays its impressive size, volume, and cargo capacity. The additions, however, are not attached to the wreck – they are deliberately and visibly kept at a distance. It is left to the eye of the beholder to join them to the ship.

The mast is fitted with an original sail, and a good portion of the original cargo of about 40,000 tiles is piled into the hold of the ship. Information on the goods which were transported in barges with open decks is provided

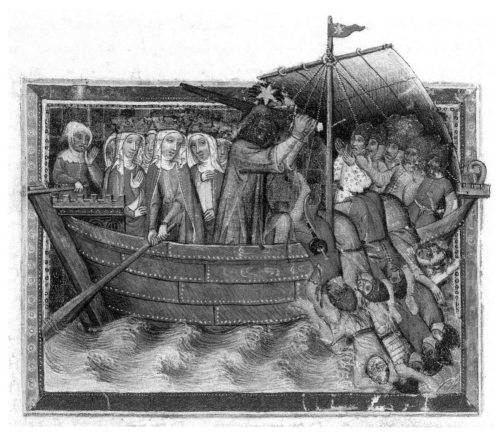

Willehalm takes command of the ship. Ulrich von dem Türlin, Wolfram von Eschenbach, Ulrich von Türheim. 1334. Universitätsbibliothek, Landesbibliothek und Murhardsche Bibliothek der Stadt Kassel: 2° Ms. poet. et. roman. 1, fol. 32 rb

in a group of showcases. Based on old pictures and descriptions, even the small cabin of the ship has been reconstructed and furnished with original and reproduction equipment of the time. It was decided not to construct the cabin actually on the wreck, but to place it alongside, so that visitors can now creep into it and experience how cramped and difficult life once was aboard this ship. Detailed information about life on a barge, and about the barge itself, is offered via headphones.

This type of presentation takes advantage of as much of the archaeological find as possible. It shows the wreck, and how the ship once looked, but also informs about the economic context of the ship in its time. In addition to the physical object itself, the people who worked and lived with it are placed at the centre of the installation.

10.3   Foreseeing the future

Opening the ship gallery to the public and presenting the stabilised and reconstructed ship in an exhibition is not the end of the conservation project, as much as everyone involved may wish! It is a fantasy to think that a conservation project for an archaeological ship can ever come to an end. The museum housing the ship is not a stable system. Several parameters change with time, and changing conditions can have detrimental effects on the ship. Archaeological wood itself is not a stable material.

Gravity is a constant burden to the ship, and the viscoelastic property of PEG-treated archaeological wood – its ability to 'creep' i.e. to yield to a permanent load – results in the deformation of individual timbers, and of the whole structure.

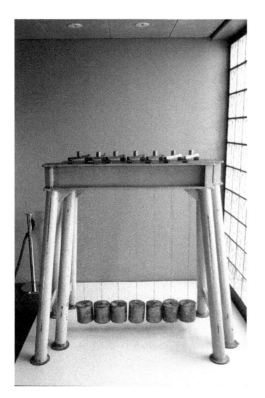

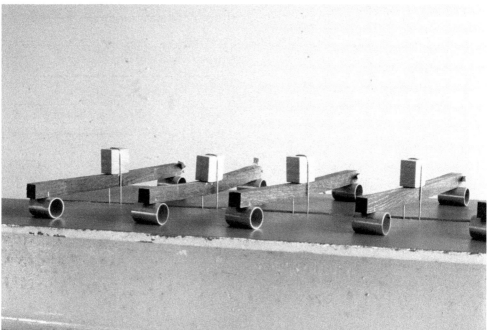

Arrangement of 2 × 2 cm staves cut from PEG-treated plank fragments from the *Bremen Cog* for a long-term bending test. The weight on each stave is 30 kg. Photographs: Per Hoffmann

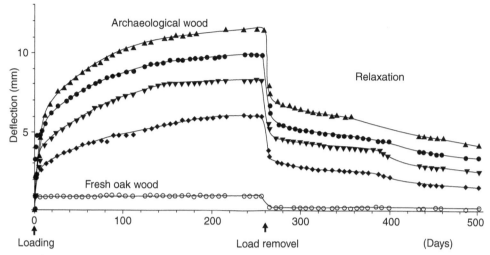

Result of the bending test in four staves of PEG-treated archaeological oak wood, and one stave of fresh oak wood. Loading results in an instant elastic deflection, followed by a slow further deflection caused by so-called 'creep'. On removal of the load the elastic deflection is released instantly, whereas the creep deflection is only reduced slowly. A certain permanent deformation is expected to remain even after a long period of recuperation. Illustration: Silvia Weidner, DSM

Materials used in the restoration and in supporting the ship may turn out to be inadequate. Modern materials may have convincing properties, but not much is necessarily known about their service life. Experience is mostly restricted to a few years, but a museum life is expected to be for longer.

Daylight, especially the UV component of its radiation, provides a constant flux of energy impinging on the wood. Energy-induced reactions take place, lignin and brown extractives in the surface are slowly degraded, and the wood is bleached.

Visitors themselves affect objects on exhibition in several ways. They bring in dust, or produce it by grinding the floor with their shoes. The dust will then settle on the ship. Visitors bring humidity into the museum – they breathe out damp air and their clothes may be wet. Not every climate control unit can cope with several bus loads of visitors on a rainy day. Visitors will even touch and scratch and incise their names into a ship, and with time their touches will polish the accessible parts of it.

Fluctuations in the relative humidity of the air influence the equilibrium in the wood between water vapour, bound water in the

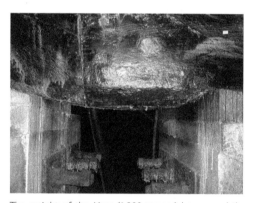

The weight of the *Vasa* (1,300 tonnes) has caused the keel blocks on which she rests (shown left and right) to make impressions in the wood of the keel, resulting from a reduced compression strength of the wood. Photograph: Swedish National Maritime Museums

wood substance, and liquid water in the capillaries in the cell walls. Changing amounts of liquid water change the equilibrium of dissolved and crystallised minerals in the wood. For example, if iron sulphate crystals are present, they may recrystallise repeatedly, grow, and finally disrupt the wood tissue. This phenomenon can often be seen around the holes of iron nails or rivets where the archaeological wood is full of iron salts. The changing water

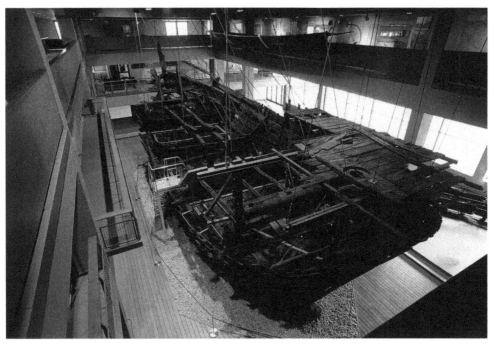

Vacuum cleaning is not so easy on the *Bremen Cog*. Photograph: Hans-Jürgen Darlison

content, and the associated changing concentrations of dissolved minerals and other chemicals in the wood promote reactions with the chemical constituents of the wood. Some of these reactions can lead to the degradation of cellulose molecules, and after a long time perhaps to a reduction of the mechanical strength of the wood. Fluctuations of temperature in the gallery influence the relative humidity of the air, and affect the kinetics of chemical reactions taking place in the wood: higher temperatures promote chemical reactions. Museum curators can also be dangerous. With time they will want to set up a new exhibition and also, where possible, move the ship around. Mechanical damage is unavoidable.

Air drying wood following a stabilisation treatment may take many years. Heavy timbers impregnated with high molecular PEG may take more than five years to reach equilibrium with the museum climate. During this time shrinkage may still occur in the treated wood, with unpleasant consequences: flat surfaces may 'dish' and warp, cracks may open, and dowels loosen. The ship will look a little shabby, and the coherence of the ship's structure may weaken.

As a result of all these processes, the ship will be affected not only in surface appearance, but also in its shape and mechanical stability, and in the integrity of the stabilised archaeological wood. An indispensible part of the conservation project is to foresee these future threats to the ship and take measures to avoid them, or at least reduce them as far as possible.

A thorough consideration of the distribution of weight, load, and mechanical forces within the ship is necessary in order to design a support system which will prevent future deformations due to gravity. To begin with, the keel of a boat or ship needs to rest on one continuous base. Setting the ship on keel blocks, as is the custom in a ship yard or dry dock, will lead to the blocks impressing themselves into the keel timber, and the ship will sag between them. Even a small boat set on two supports will either sag in the middle, if the supports are positioned too far apart, or its ends will hang down if they are too close together. One full-length keel support is the only safe setup. A support system should be constructed in such a way that it can be easily dismantled, in case one day it should need to be modified or replaced. Using screws and bolts is better than welding.

When we planned a new support system for the *Bremen Cog*, we investigated a series of materials: aluminium and high-strength aluminium, mild and stainless steels, glass fibre and carbon fibre reinforced resins, even heavy glass sheets. In the end we decided on materials with well known properties, established workability, proven longevity, chemical stability and low reactivity: stainless steel in prefabricated parts bolted together in the ship, wool felt as cushioning between wood and steel, and epoxy paint on the steel to render it unobtrusive.

In the exhibition gallery, the ship and its support must be accessible from all sides. It needs to be cleaned regularly to get rid of dust, sweet wrappings and chewing gum, and access is required in case one needs to work on the ship or on the support. When the support is fixed to the floor enough space must be planned for adequate access. It is questionable whether it is advisable to put a boat on a cradle and place this on rollers. The boat can then be moved without much stress, shock, and with minimum vibrations. On the other hand, the arrangement may just invite personnel to take advantage of the possibility, and then become careless in handling the boat.

Filters in the air circulating system can reduce dust efficiently only in combination with a flooring which does not permanently produce new dust through abrasion by visitors' feet. Textile floorings are quite bad in this respect. Of course, visitors must be kept from touching the ship. Noisy coarse gravel on the forbidden area and trip wires can be helpful to avoid high fences around the ship. The wreck of a boat or ship may seem to be a rather crude and robust exhibit compared to many works of art. But the organic nature of its material, the archaeological wood, makes it sensitive and vulnerable. The physical and chemical processes in the wood described above can be retarded to some

degree with a strict regime of the climatic conditions in the gallery: direct sunshine and UV radiation must be excluded to prohibit bleaching of the wood; the relative humidity of the air should be as low as possible – less than 65% RH – to minimise the amount of water in the wood – the medium where chemical reactions will occur; the temperature, too, should be low to slow down chemical reactions – fluctuations of temperature, and of relative humidity, must be suppressed to avoid changes of the physical and chemical equilibria in the wood, since such changes act as motors for chemical reactions. A climate control system which can maintain a tight range of conditions, even with visitors entering the gallery in irregular numbers at irregular times, is expensive to install and run, but without it damage to the ship's timbers is certain to occur. Conditions which are good for the wood – cold and dry – are not appreciated by the visitors. This is a dilemma. A compromise must be found for each case and balanced against the financial status of the museum. Nevertheless, the ship cannot be put at risk.

Foreseeing the future also means organising regular checks of the ship, its shape, and the condition of its wood, by an expert in archaeological wood conservation. If the museum does not have such a person on its permanent staff, then a long-term agreement with an appropriate institution is strongly advised.

In whatever conditions the ship is presented, a second round of restoration and surface treatment will become necessary five to eight years after the first presentation. It will work wonders on the appearance of the ship. However, it will not be the last time the ship needs a careful brush-up. The conservation of an archaeological boat or ship is a never-ending project.

10.4 Long-term care plans

by James A. Spriggs, Conservation Consultant, York, UK

The word 'conservation' has often been identified with the process of managing change. Even after a lengthy conservation treatment, organic

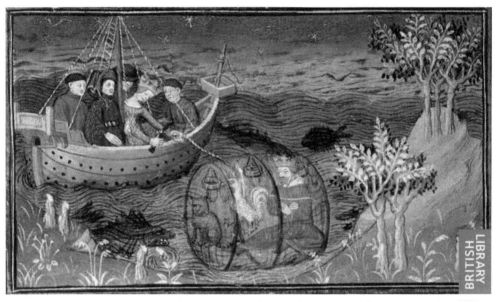

Risk assessment omitted: The Good King Alexander tests how long he, the animals, and the oil lamps can breathe in the glass diving bell; meanwhile, his wife and her lover cut the rope holding the bell, *La Vraye Histoire du Bon Roy Alexandre.* British Library, Royal 20 B. XX. fol. 77 v. With permission of The British Library

materials such as wood are usually still reactive both to their environment and to the components of their physical makeup. The changes involved may be short term, others longer term, and many of the effects of these changes are likely to be harmful. Preventive conservation is an essential element of the long-term protection and survival of the artefact, and a well-designed and properly executed care plan represents a commitment to 'best practice' by those responsible for the collection's curation. Such care plans are important for artefacts and assemblages that are in storage, but are even more important when they are on public display as this is likely to present a greater range of factors and risks that may adversely affect the object. A care plan should be drafted for any collection or major artefact once its future is established with any certainty.

The ideal care plan will be composed of several principal elements, as follows.

Assessment of artefact condition

A description of the physical state of the artefact – strength, fragility, surface condition, chemical stability regarding changes in temperature and relative humidity (RH), pH, and its possible iron and sulphur content – provides basic information on the object. The assessment will also list the contents of the archive relating to the object, including previous assessments, analyses and conservation reports.

Assessment of likely risks and threats

The risk assessment will be based on the artefact's physical and chemical state, and on the environment in which it is planned to display or store the artefact. The effects of dirt, pollution and human contact – accidental or intentional – should be included here, as well as an evaluation of potential threats posed by display options.

Criteria for safe storage and display

Based on the assessment and evaluation of risk (above), criteria are established as to what the required minimum practically achievable conditions are, including temperature, RH, light levels, protection against physical damage and effects of dirt and pollution. Guidelines will need to be set for safe access to the object for inspection and cleaning.

Programme for monitoring change

This identifies how and at what time intervals the object will be inspected and the various risk factors to be checked and monitored; also, what resources – staff time, equipment, external specialist contractors, etc. – are required for this. Details of inspection protocols and reporting procedures are also laid down in the programme.

Actions for reducing the effects of change

Actions are suggested as to how any damage or deterioration is going to be halted or reduced to an acceptable level – for example by tighter environmental control, better physical protection, specialist intervention. Procedures are established for cleaning and other necessary maintenance. Remedial treatments are listed which might be appropriate if certain likely problems arise, and at what point external specialist advice must be sought.

Emergency procedures

Every museum should have a disaster management plan, detailing procedures to be followed in the events of fire, flood, power failure, etc. One aspect which must be decided in advance and laid down in the care plan is whether it is possible to remove the collection or special artefact if the museum building needs to be evacuated – and if so, how best to do it. Contact with outside specialist contractors to assist in case of an emergency must be established and written down.

Staff training needs

Any special training the staff may need to carry out the requirements of the care plan must be established and laid down.

Updating the assessment and care plan

The assessment of the state and the risks of the artefact, and the storage or exhibition conditions, will need updating and the care plan revised as time goes by and as experience dictates. Major changes in the display or storage facility will obviously trigger such a review, as will staff changes and other resourcing factors.

The active application of a care plan represents best practice, but its successful delivery can easily be affected by external factors such as availability of resources: human as well as financial; timetabling; work prioritisation; major changes within the museum, etc. The likelihood of any of these factors coming into play should be identified and, if possible, listed in the *Assessment of likely risks and threats*. The maintenance of the care plan and associated records – the archive – helps to build up a conservation history for the artefact, against which the success of the original conservation treatment and of the care plan may be measured. The effective delivery of care plans must become a primary responsibility of museum staff, and a care plan that is not changed and rewritten as time goes by is one that is not being operated properly.

Notes to §10.2 Restoration and presentation

- A method for bending freeze-dried planks during the restoration of a 16th century whaling boat is described by C. Moore, 2002.
- The alternative approach, to reshape distorted planks and timbers before they are freeze-dried, has been developed by K. Straetkvern and co-workers, 2009.
- The technique behind the presentation of the *Skuldelev Viking ships* and many photographs of the restored ships are published by O. Crumlin-Pedersen, 2002.
- A full report on the reconstruction technique of the *Karl* can be found in Hoffmann, 2005.
- The elaborate technique of the successful reshaping of the large monoxyle from Noyen-sur-Seine has been described by Q.-K. Tran *et al.*, 1998.
- A report on, and a convincing discussion of, the concept for the presentation of the *Kaffenkahn* in an installation of its context is given by V. Koesling, 2011.

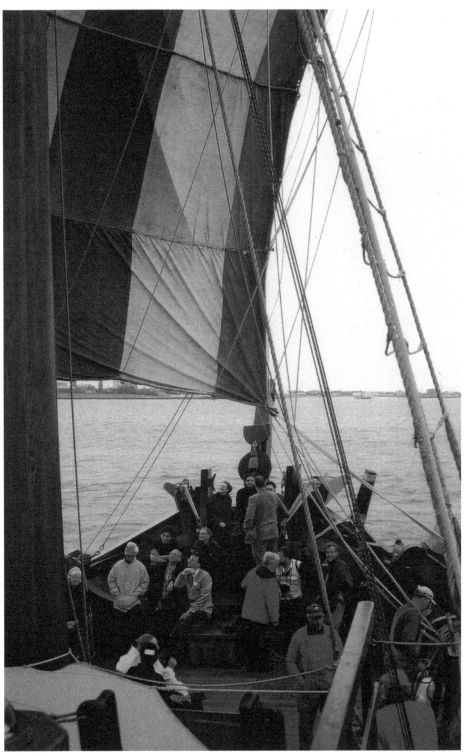

Waterlogged wood conservators and ship archaeologists sailing on a replica of the *Bremen Cog*, the *Ubena*. Photograph: Gabriele Hoffmann

11   Do effort and funds pay off in the end?

An archaeological ship or boat is a rare find. The desire and intention to conserve it are most often expressed immediately after its discovery – by the finders and the public, and before the consequences in effort and cost are fully understood. A ship, and even a boat, fascinates archaeologists and laymen alike.

Looking at an archaeological ship produces thoughts and imaginings about the people who sailed it – who were they, and how did they build and use it? What did they transport, and from where to where? How did they live on board? A ship find asks for interpretation. It will initiate scientific and scholarly investigations and studies into the complex questions that arise from it. A ship find will induce the study of similar finds and of all sorts of documents. These studies may combine to produce a picture of the geographical occurrence of this type of vessel, the time period in which it sailed, and its significance.

The huge hull which emerged in the river Weser in Bremen verified for the first time the reality of the type of medieval ship called a 'cog'. The *Bremen Cog* project produced a well-conserved authentic example of the legendary *Hanseatic Cog*, on exhibition in a new national maritime museum, and it triggered research into the origin and development of this type of ship. Based on the meticulous investigation and documentation of the hull, not only was the medieval building process of the ship reconstructed, but about twenty other less preserved ship finds from the Netherlands to Sweden and Estonia

could be identified as being cogs. Many years of sailing with exact replicas proved the seaworthiness of the cog, but also showed how difficult it is to handle a huge single square sail in a strong wind, and how many hands are necessary. Summer cruises, very popular with the public on board the ship and in the ports of call, established the time it must have taken for voyages between the medieval ports of trade. This helps to estimate trade volumes and values. Studies of miniatures in illuminated manuscripts and of wall paintings in churches showed us that cogs were the most

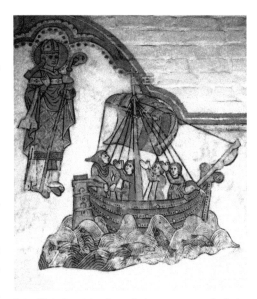

Saint Nicholas giving benediction to a party of pilgrims setting out on a cog. Mural in the cathedral of Mölln, Holstein. Photograph: Hermann Handler

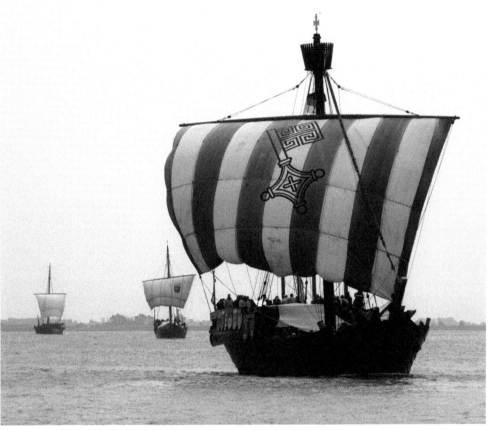

Three cogs in a slight breeze on the river Weser. From left: the *Hansekogge*, the *Roland von Bremen*, the *Ubena*. Photograph: Wolfhard Scheer

prestigious ships of their time: kings, queens and warriors, noblemen and bishops, pilgrims and merchants all sailed in them.

The conservation and exhibition of the reconstructed *Skuldelev Viking ships* from the Roskilde fjord in a purpose-built museum was accompanied by the beginning of extensive research into many aspects of Viking ship-building, seafaring, colonisation and warfare, social and military organisation of society, and everyday life. The visual evidence of the ships in the museum, and the continuously communicated research results together with reports and media coverage of ongoing replica projects, created a public awareness of the reality of a period in Danish and Scandinavian history which until then had been greatly disguised in the clouds of myth and saga.

The *Bremen Cog* and the *Skuldelev Viking ships* are two extreme examples of the impact a ship find can have on scholars and on public awareness. However, the principle holds true down to the small village where a logboat is found in the mill pond. The local people will want to know all about the boat: how old it is, how it came to be in the pond, for what purpose it was built, etc. And they will want to keep the boat and show it in their museum, or in the town hall lobby.

An archaeological boat or ship is the ideal centrepiece in a museum. Its size makes it the visual draw, and it can be the focus of an exhibition addressing quite different aspects and themes: technical knowledge and under-standing, skills and problem-solving con-cepts, aesthetics, trade and transport, and the organisation of society. A ship is a technical monument, but it can tell a lot about the people of its time.

The conservation of an archaeological boat or ship will never be financially viable. No entrance fees can ever cover the costs. Nevertheless, should the opportunity arise to start a conservation project for a ship find, I can only recommend to the conservator to take hold of this exciting opportunity. It is worth all the effort.

References

Agyropoulos, V., J.-J. Rameau, F. Dalard, and C. Degrigny, 1999: Testing Hostacor IT as a corrosion inhibitor for iron in polyethylene glycol solutions. Studies in Conservation **44**, 40–57.

Almkvist, G. and I. Persson, 2006: Extraction of iron compounds from wood from the VASA, Holzforschung **60**, 678–684.

Almkvist, G. and I. Persson, 2009: Iron catalysed degradation processes in the VASA. In: Proc. 10ᵗʰ ICOM Group on Wet Organic Archaeological Materials Conference, K. Straetkvern and D. J. Huisman (eds.), Amersfoort, 499–506.

Andersen, L. M., 1993: Frysetørring af arkæologisk træ. Konservatorskolen, Det Kongelige Danske Kunstakademi.

Arisholm, T. and Nymoen, P., 2005: Stokkebåter. Skrift nr. 49. Norsk sjøfartsmuseum, Oslo.

Bill, J., Gøthche, M. and Myrhøj, H. M., 2000: Roskildeskibene. In: Civitas Roscald, Andersen, M., Christensen, T. (eds.), Roskilde, 211–260.

Björdahl, C. G., 2000: Waterlogged archaeological wood – biodegradation and its implications for conservation. Acta Universitatis Agriculturae Sueciae, Silvestria 142. Swedish University of Agricultural Sciences, Uppsala.

Bockius, R. and Böhler, W., 2002: Die römerzeitlichen Schiffsfunde von Oberstimm in Bayern. Monographien des Römisch-Germanischen Zentral Museums 50, Mainz, 160 p.

Bojesen-Koefoed, I. M., Meyer, I, Strætkvern, K., and Jensen, P., 1993: Conservation of wet archaeological rope. In: Preprints of the 10ᵗʰ ICOM Committee for Conservation Triennial Meeting Washington, DC, USA, Volume I, J. Bridgeland et al.(eds.), 262–265.

Bouix, D., H. Bernard-Maugiron, G. Chaumat, and A. Gelas, 2005: Conclusion and definition of the 'Atomisation' treatment by PEG saturation used for a 12 metre long Greek shipwreck found in Marseilles. In: Proc. 9ᵗʰ ICOM Group on Wet Organic Archaeological Material Conference, P. Hoffmann, K. Straetkvern, J. A. Spriggs, and D. Gregory (eds.), Bremerhaven, 355–364.

Brorson Christensen, B., 1970: The conservation of waterlogged wood in the National Museum of Denmark. Studies in museum technology no.1, The National Museum of Denmark, Copenhagen, 118 p.

Centerwall, B. and R. Morén, 1960: The Use of Polyglycols in the Stabilisation and Preservation of Wood. Meddelanden från Lunds Universitets Historiska Museum, Lund.

Cohen, O., 1990: The recovery of the Kinneret Boat. In: Proc, 4ᵗʰ ICOM Group on Wet Organic Archaeological Materials Conference, P. Hoffmann (ed.), Bremerhaven, 9–16.

Crawshaw, A., 1994: A simple method for PEG analysis. In: Proc. 5ᵗʰ ICOM Group on Wet Organic Archaeological Materials Conference, P. Hoffmann, T. Daley, and T. Grant (eds.), Bremerhaven, 143–166.

Crumlin-Pedersen, O., 2002: The Skuldelev Ships I. Topography, Archaeology, History, Conservation and Display. Ships of the North Vol. 4.1, O. Crumlin-Pedersen and O. Olsen (eds.), Roskilde, 360p.

Fox, L. A., 1989: The acetone/rosin method for treating waterlogged hardwoods at the Historic Resource Conservation Branch, Ottawa. In: Proc of the ICOM Groups on Wet Organic Archaeological Materials and Metals Conference, I. D. MacLeod (ed.), Fremantle, 73–94.

Ginier-Gillet, A., M.-D. Parchas, R. Ramière, Q.-K. Tran, 1984: Méthodes de conservation développées au Centre d'Etude et de Traitement des Bois Gorgés d'Eau (Grenoble – France): impregnation par une résine radio-durcissable et lyophilisation. In: Waterlogged Wood – Study and Conservation. Proc 2nd ICOM Waterlogged Wood Working Group Conference, CETBGE (ed.), Grenoble, 125–138.

Gregory, D., Jensen, P., Matthiesen, H. and Straetkvern, K., 2007: The correlation between bulk density and shock resistance of waterlogged archaeological wood using the Pilodyn. Studies in Conservation, 52, 289–298.

Hoffmann, G., 2001: Schätze unter Wasser. Abenteuer Archäologie. Hamburg-Wien, 382 p.

Hoffmann, G., 2005: Kostbare Koggen: Seltene Bilder aus illuminierten Manuskripten und gotischen Kirchen. Deutsches Schiffahrtsarchiv 27, 2004, Convent Verlag, Hamburg, 7 – 33.

Hoffmann, G. and Hoffmann, P., 2009: Sailing the Bremen Cog. International Journal of Nautical Archaeology, 38.2, 281–296.

Hoffmann, G. and U. Schnall (eds.), 2003: Die Kogge – Sternstunde der deutschen Schiffsarchäologie. Schriften des Deutschen Schiffahrtsmuseums Bd. 60 (Die Kogge von Bremen Bd. 2), Hamburg, 287 p.

Hoffmann, P., 1983: A rapid method for the detection of polyethylene glycols in wood. Studies in Conservation 28, 189–193.

Hoffmann, P., 1984: On the stabilisation of waterlogged oak wood with PEG. Molecular size versus degree of degradation. In: Waterlogged wood – Study and Conservation. Proc. 2nd ICOM Waterlogged Wood Working Group Conference, CETBGE (ed.), Grenoble, 95–115.

Hoffmann, P., 1986: On the stabilisation of waterlogged oak wood with PEG. II. Designing a two-step treatment for multi-quality timbers. Studies in Conservation 31, 103–113.

Hoffmann, P., 1988: On the stabilisation of waterlogged oak wood with PEG. III. Testing the oligomers. Holzforschung 42, 5, 289–294.

Hoffmann, P., 1989: HPLC for the analysis of polyethylene glycols (PEG) in wood. In: Proc. of the ICOM Groups on Wet Organic Archaeological Materials and Metals Conference, I. D. MacLeod (ed.), Fremantle, 41–60.

Hoffmann, P., 1990: On the stabilisation of waterlogged softwoods with polyethylene glycol (PEG). Four species from China and Korea. Holzforschung 44, 87–93.

Hoffmann, P., 1998: Das Frachtschiff aus dem Teufelsmoor. Arbeitsblätter für Restauratoren 31, 2, 270–276.

Hoffmann, P., 2005: Conservation and reconstruction of the Carolingian river barge KARL von Bremen of 808 AD. In: Proc. 9th ICOM Group on Wet Organic Archaeological Materials Conference, P. Hoffmann, K. Straetkvern, J. A. Spriggs, D. Gregory (eds.), Bremerhaven, 377–388.

Hoffmann, P., K.-N. Choi, and Y.-H. Kim, 1991: The 14th century Shinan Ship – Progress i n conservation. IJNA 20, 1, 59–64.

Hoffmann, P. and H. J. Kühn, 1999: The Candy Ship from Friesland. In: Proc. 7th ICOM Group on Wet Organic Archaeological Materials Conference, C. Bonnot-Diconne, X. Hiron, Q.-K. Tran, and P. Hoffmann (eds.), Grenoble, 196–202.

Hoffmann, P. and J. Pätzold, 2002: The stabilisation of wet sediment cores by means of a polyethylene glycol freeze-drying treatment for display and permanent storage. Geo-Mar Lett 21, 4, 245–252.

Hoffmann, P., C. Pérez de Andrés, J. L. Sierra Mendez, R. Ramière, Q.-K. Tran, and U. Weber, 1994: European inter-laboratory study on the conservation of waterlogged wood with sucrose. In: Proc. 5th ICOM Group on Wet Organic Archaeological Materials Conference, P. Hoffmann, T. Daley, and T. Grant (eds.), Bremerhaven, 309–338.

Håfors, B., 2001: Conservation of the Swedish warship Vasa from 1628. The Vasa Museum, Stockholm, 185 p.

Imazu, S. and A. Morgos, 1997: Conservation of waterlogged wood using sugar alcohol and comparison of the effectiveness of lactitol, sucrose, and PEG 4000 treatment. In: Proc. 6th ICOM Group on Wet Organic Archaeological Materials Conference, P. Hoffmann, T. Grant, J. A. Spriggs, and T. Daley (eds.), Bremerhaven, 235–255.

Imazu, S. and A. Morgos, 1999: Lactitol conservation of a 6 m long waterlogged timber coffin. In: Proc. 7th ICOM Group on Wet Organic Archaeological Materials Conference, C. Bonnot-Diconne, X. Hiron, Q.-K. Tran, P. Hoffmann (eds.), Grenoble, 210–216.

Imazu, S. and A. Morgos, 1999: Lactitol conservation in an open-air environment of large wood elements of a 6gh century AD. dugout pipeline. In: Preprints 12th triennial meeting of the ICOM Committee for Conservation, Lyon, Vol. II, London, 614–618.

Imazu, S. and A. Morgos, 2001: An improvement on the lactitol conservation method used for the conservation of archaeological water-logged wood (The conservation method using a lactitol and trehalose mixture). In: Proc. 8th ICOM Group on Wet Organic Archaeological Materials Conference, P. Hoffmann, J. A. Spriggs, T. Grant, C. Cook, and A. Recht (eds.), Bremerhaven, 413–428.

Iversen, T., E. L. Lindfors, and M. Lindström, 2000: Polysaccharide degradation in Vasa oak wood. In: Proc. 10th ICOM Group on Wet Organic Archaeological Materials Conference, K. Straetkvern and D. J. Huisman (eds.), Amersfoort, 493–498.

Jensen, P., Bojesen-Koefoed, I., Meyer, I., and Strætkvern, K., 1993: Freeze-drying from water. In: Proc. of the 5th ICOM Group on Wet Organic Archeaological Conference. P. Hoffmann, T. Daley, and T. Grant (eds.), Bremerhaven, 253–285.

Jensen, P., Salomonsen, E. and Straetkvern, K., 1996: From a waterlogged site to the archaeologist's desk – new packing methods with minimum handling. Preprints of Contributions to the Copenhagen Congress, 26–30 August 1996, Archaeological Conservation and its Consequences. Ashok Roy and Perry Smith (eds.), London, 89–93.

Jensen, P., Jørgensen, G., and Schnell, U., 2002: Dynamic LV-SEM analysis of freeze drying processes for waterlogged wood. In: Proc. of the 8th ICOM Group on Wet Organic Archaeological Materials Conference. P. Hoffmann, J. A. Spriggs, T. Grant, C. Cook, and A. Recht (eds.), Bremerhaven, 319–331.

Jensen, P. and Schnell, U., 2004: The implication of using low molecular weight PEG in impregnation of waterlogged archaeological wood prior to freeze-drying. In: Proc. of the 9th ICOM Group on Wet Organic Archaeological Materials Conference. P. Hoffmann, K. Straetkvern, J. A. Spriggs, and D. Gregory (eds.),Bremerhaven, 279–307.

Jensen, P. and Gregory, D. J., 2006: Selected physical parameters to characterize the state of preservation of waterlogged archaeological wood: A practical guide for their determination. Journal of Archaeological Science, 33, 551–559.

Jensen, P. and Jensen, J. B., 2006: Dynamic model for vacuum freeze-drying of waterlogged archaeological wooden artefacts. Journal of Cultural Heritage 7, 156–165.

Jensen, P., Strætkvern, K., Schnell, U., and Jensen, J. B., 2007: Technical specifications for equipment for vacuum freeze-drying of PEG impregnated waterlogged organic materials. In : Proc. of the 10th ICOM Group on Wet Organic Archaeological Materials Conference. K. Straetkvern and D. J. Huisman (eds.), Amersfoort, 417–437.

Jensen, L. R., J. van Lanschot, K. Botfeldt, and J. B. Jensen, 2009: On treatments for swelling dried-up waterlogged archaeological wood. In: Proc. 10th ICOM Group on Wet Organic Archaeological Materials Conference, K. Straetkvern and D. J. Huisman (eds.), Amersfoort, 639–652.

Jensen, P., Helms, A. C. and Christensen, M., 2010: Evaluating long-term stability of waterlogged archaeological wooden objects through determination of moisture sorption isotherms and conductance in conserved objects and impregnation agents. In: Proceedings of the 11th ICOM-CC Working Group Wet Organic Archaeological Materials Conference 2010. Greenville, USA.

Jones, M. (ed.), 2003: For future generations – Conservation of a Tudor Maritime Collection. The archaeology of the MARY ROSE Vol. 5, Portsmouth, 145 p.

Kaenel, G., 1994: PEG conservation of a gallo-roman barge from Yverdon-les-Bains (Canton of Vaud, Switzerland). In: Proc. 5th ICOM Group on Wet Organic Archaeological Materials Conference, P. Hoffmann, T. Daley, and T. Grant (eds.), Bremerhaven, 143–166.

Kataoka, T., Y. Kurimoto, T. Koezuka, and Y. Kohdzuma, 2009: Conservation of archaeological waterlogged wood by lignophenol. In: Proc. 10th ICOM Group on Wet Organic Archaeological Materials Conference, K. Straetkvern and D. J. Huisman (eds.), Amersfoort, 315–322.

Koesling, V., 2011: Komplettieren, inszenieren oder was? Ein Kaffenkahn in Berlin. Deutsches Technikmuseum Berlin, no.2, 20–23, ISSN: 1869–1358.

Kollmann, F. F. P. and W. A. Côté, 1968: Principles of wood science and technology I. Solid wood. Berlin – Heidelberg – New York, 592 p.

Lide, D. R., 1995: CRC Handbook of Chemistry and Physics, CRC Press Inc., New York.

Lüpkes, V.(ed.), 2001: Im Fluss, Bergung, Konservierung und Präsentation der historischen Weserschiffe, Tübingen/Berlin, 72 p.

McCawley, J. C., Grattan, D.W. and Cook, C., 1981: Some experiments in freeze drying and testing non-vacuum freeze dryers. In: D. W. Grattan (Ed.). Proc. of the ICOM waterlogged wood working group conference. Ottawa, 253–262.

Mikolaychuk, E., 1996: Some Physical Properties for Archaeological Woods from Novgorod. In Proceedings of the 6th ICOM Group on Wet Organic Archaeological Materials Conference. P. Hoffmann, T. Grant, J. A. Spriggs and T. Daley (eds.), York, 583–586.

Moore, C., 2002: Reassembly of the 16th century Basque Chalupa recovered from Red Bay, Canada. In: Proc. 8th ICOM Group on Wet Organic Archaeological Materials Conference, P. Hoffmann, J. A. Spriggs, T. Grant, C. Cook, and A. Recht (eds.), Bremerhaven, 117–135.

Morgos, A., 1994: A bibliography on the conservation of waterlogged wood using sugars. In: Proc, 5th ICOM Group on Wet Organic Archaeological Materials Conference, P. Hoffmann, T. Daley, and T. Grant (eds.), Bremerhaven, 301–308.

Obladen-Kauder, J., 2008: Spuren römischer Lastschiffahrt am unteren Niederrhein. In: M.Müller, H.-J. Schalles, N. Zieling (eds.), Colonia Ulpia Traiana. Xanten und sein Umland in römischer Zeit. Darmstadt, 507–523.

Parrent, J., 1985: The conservation of waterlogged wood using sucrose. Studies in Conservation 30, 63–72.

Schaudy, R., E. Slais, and H. Knoll, 1988: Conservation of archaeological finds consisting of organic fibrous material using radiation-curable impregnants. Bericht des Österreichischen Forschungszentrums Seibersdorf, Seibersdorf, Austria, 13 p.

Schnell, U. and Jensen, P., 2007: Determination of maximum freeze drying temperature for PEG-impregnated archaeological wood. Studies in Conservation, 50–58.

Strætkvern, K., Petersen, A. H., Sørensen, J. N., and Jørgensen, E., 2009: Succesful shaping or destructive devices? Freeze-drying of ship timbers in moulds and frames. In: Proc. 10th ICOM Group on Wet Organic Archaeological Materials Conference. K. Strætkvern and D. J. Huisman (eds.), Amersfoort, 439–453.

Tjelldén, A. K., K. B. Botfeldt, and K. P. Simonsen, 2009: Impregnation depth of PEG in wood from the Roskilde ships, Denmark. In: Proc. 10th ICOM Group on Wet Organic Archaeological Materials Conference, K. Straetkvern and D. J. Huisman (eds.), Amersfoort, 301–314.

Tran, Q.-K., A. Gelas, D. Mordant, 1998: Remise en forme de la pirogue Carolingienne de Noyen-sur- Seine après son traitement au PEG à saturation. In: Proc 7th ICOM Group on Wet Organic Archaeological Materials Conference, ARC-Nucléart (ed.), Grenoble, 188–195.

de Wiltte, E., A. Terfve, and J. Vynkier, 1984: La consolidation du bois gorge d'eau des bateaux gallo-romains de Pommeroeul. In:Waterlogged Wood – Study and Conservation. Proc. 2nd ICOM Waterlogged Wood Working Group Conference, CETBGE (ed.), Grenoble, 339–346.

Wittköpper, M., Current development in the conservation of archaeological wet wood with melamine amino resins at the Römisch-Germanisches Zentralmuseum. www2.rgzm.de/Navis/Home/NoFrames.htm ; last reviewed 5.5.2011. Under Navis I search the Navis HTLM Navigator under conservation, melamine.

Zwick, D., 2010: Neues vom ‚Beluga-Schiff‘. Ein Bremer Klinkerwrack aus dem 15. Jahrhundert. NAU 16, 62–71.

Index

Page numbers in italics refer to images.

Lightning Source UK Ltd.
Milton Keynes UK
UKHW020839271121
394646UK00002B/53